MW01628105

THE WOMAN, THE ICON

Melania Trump's story is one of a tough, stylish woman's rise to the top. She was born Melania Knauss, in the Eastern European country of Slovenia in 1970 at a time when it was a part of the Soviet bloc country of Yugoslavia. Melania's father was a car salesman, and her mother was a designer of children's clothing. Knauss got her start in modeling at a very young age, wearing her mother's designs for Slovenian clothing catalogs. At the age of sixteen, she began modeling professionally. She briefly attended the University of Ljubljana where she studied architecture for a year, but opted out when she signed with an agency in Milan to model full-time. She worked primarily in Italy before moving to the United States in 1996, where her career took off. Her initial runway success caught the attention of famous photographers and landed her the covers of many well-known magazines, including the vaunted *Sports Illustrated* Swimsuit Issue.

Melania Knauss met Donald Trump in 1998 at a Fashion Week party at the Kit Kat Club in Manhattan. Knauss was, by this time, a powerhouse in the modeling world, gracing the covers of the biggest fashion magazines. Trump pursued her and the couple began dating shortly thereafter. They were engaged in 2004 and, the following year, had the wedding of a lifetime in Palm Beach, Florida. On the star-studded guest list was future nemesis Hillary Clinton and her husband and former president, Bill Clinton. 2006 was an amazing year for Mrs. Trump; her son, Barron, was born, and she became an American citizen. Ten years later, when Donald Trump became the 45th President of the United States, Melania Trump became only the second First Lady born outside the United States. (The first was British-born Louisa Adams, spouse of John Quincy Adams.)

Melania Trump's journey from a communist upbringing in Slovenia to becoming First Lady of the United States gives her a perspective on true freedom that most people from western Europe and the United States take for granted. This book details in photographs and words the spectacular journey of a woman who brings a distinctive elegance to the White House.

THE EARLY YEARS

Melania Trump was born Melania Knavs on April 26, 1970,[1] in Novo Mesto, Slovenia. Knavs spent her childhood years in apartment housing in Sevnica, Slovenia, on a bend of the Sava river, the country's longest flowing waterway. Modern photographs reveal a beautiful and picturesque postcard view. However, in the '70s and '80s, during Knavs' childhood and adolescence, pollution from factory chimneys clouded the air, and waste runoff spilled into the Sava.[2] Sevnica castle dominates the small city skyline and likely inspired daydreams of knights and princesses in the imaginations of Knavs, her friends, and her siblings.[3] Melania would eventually make her fairy tale daydreams into a reality.

1 Melania Trump (@MelaniaTrump). "About." Facebook. Accessed April, 13, 2019. https://www.facebook.com/pg/MelaniaTrump/about/.

2 Andrea Park. "Inside the Small Slovenian Town Where Melania Trump Grew Up Under the Communist Regime." *People.* February 25, 2016. https://people.com/politics/melania-trumps-childhood-in-communist-slovenia-in-poverty/.

3 "Sevnica—the town where the First Lady of the United States grew up." I Feel Slovenia. Accessed April 12, 2019. https://www.slovenia.info/en/stories/sevnica-the-town-where-the-first-lady-of-the-united-states-grew-up.

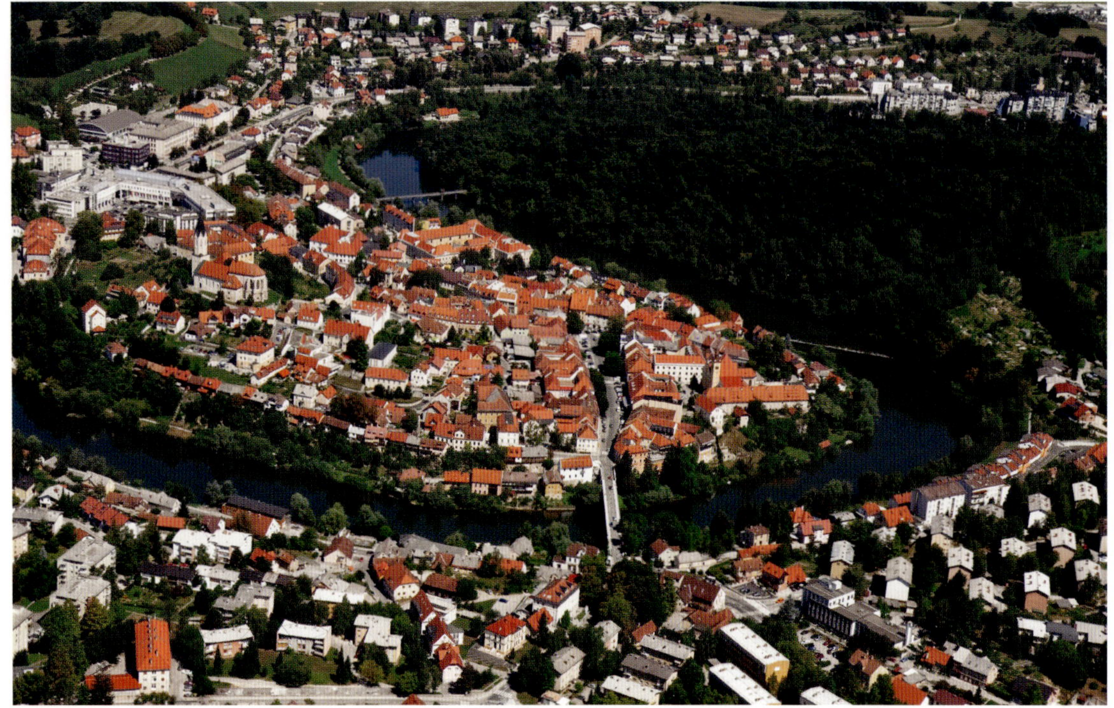

Novo Mesto, Slovenia[25]

Melania Knavs's father, Viktor, drove cars for the mayor of Sevnica, as well as other local dignitaries. Knavs later sold car parts and became a member of the communist party, which bumped the family up a notch on the local social ladder. As a result of this elevated social status, Knavs was able to move his family from their Communist apartment block to a modest home on the Sava River, where Melania spent the rest of her childhood.

UP-AND-COMER

It was Melania's mother, Amalija, who introduced Melania to the fashion business. Amalija designed apparel for a local clothing manufacturer, and Melania modeled her mother's designs for photographs in the company's catalog. Amalija also exposed her daughter to the fashion world by showing her fashion magazines from Europe and the United States, fostering a love of American fashion early in Melania's life.[4] This exposure enabled Melania to dream of a world outside her small Eastern European hamlet. Soon, she began to see a way out of her rural area and the small-town blues that enveloped so many of its inhabitants.

Thanks to Viktor Knavs's position as a communist party member, he was able to move his family to Ljubljana, the capital of Slovenia, where Melania and her sister, Ines, could attend a bigger high school than Sevnica had to offer. The relocation also offered Melania the opportunity to study architecture at the University of Ljubljana. Additionally, she found time to participate in increasingly-bigger fashion shows, still nurturing her dreams of becoming a model. This, in turn, enabled her to meet more influential photographers like Stane Jerko, who takes credit for "discovering" Melania in 1987.[5] After arranging several photo shoots, Jerko believed he'd

4 Matej Klaric. 2019. "Melania Trump: From a small white house in Sovenia to the big one in DC." ABC News (Australian Broadcasting Corporation). Last modified January 26, 2019. https://www.abc.net.au/news/2016-11-17/melania-trumps-journey-from-slovenia-to-the-white-house/8028340.

5 Amanda Harding. "This Is Everything We Know About Melania's Modeling Career." Culture Cheat Sheet. June 15, 2018. https://www.cheatsheet.com/culture/this-is-everything-we-know-about-melanias-modeling-career.html/.

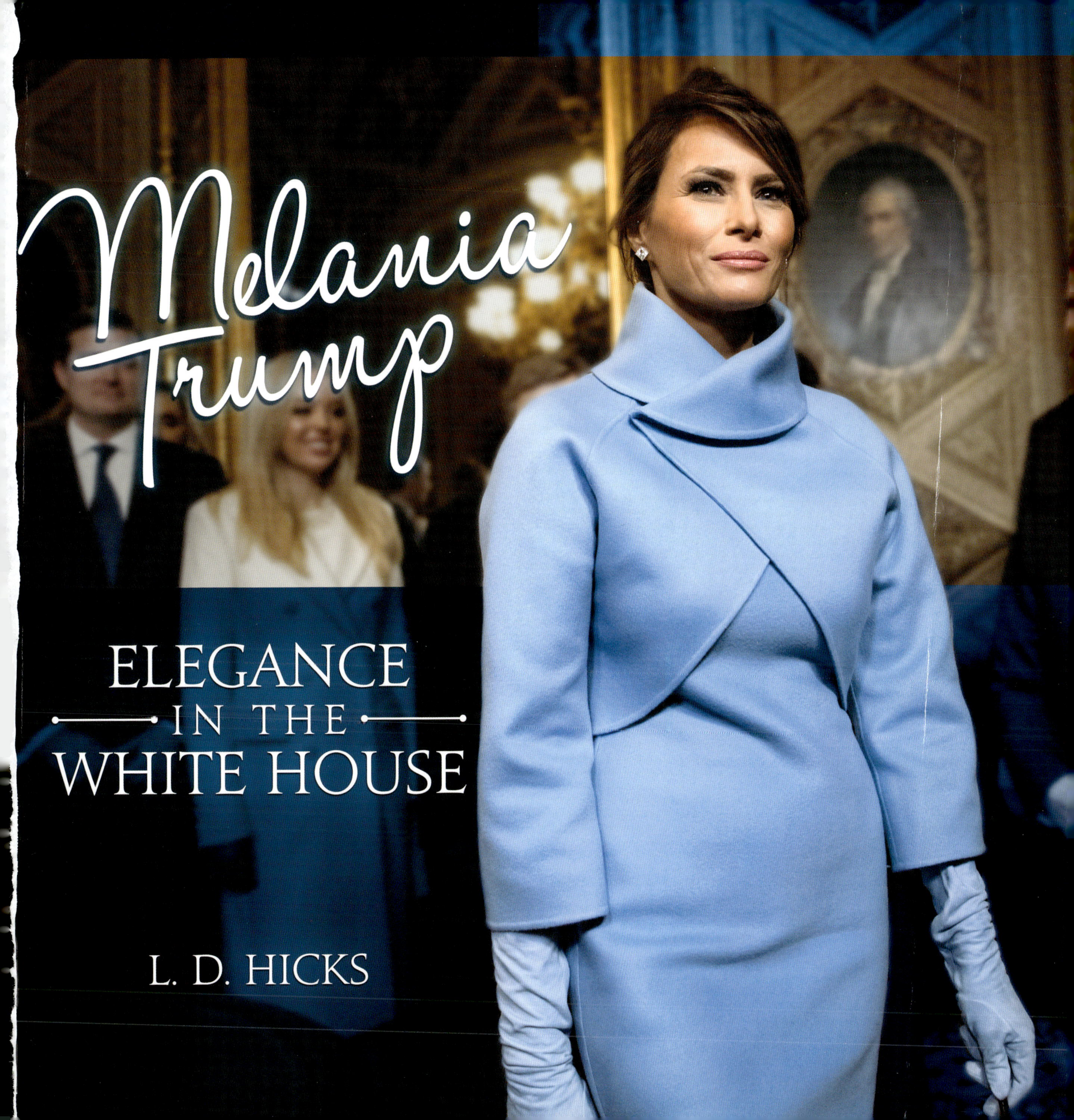
Melania Trump
ELEGANCE
IN THE
WHITE HOUSE
L. D. HICKS

A POST HILL PRESS BOOK
ISBN: 978-1-64293-326-0

Melania Trump:
Elegance in the White House

Cover art by Cody Corcoran
Author photo by Theresa Tellez, Venusian Photography

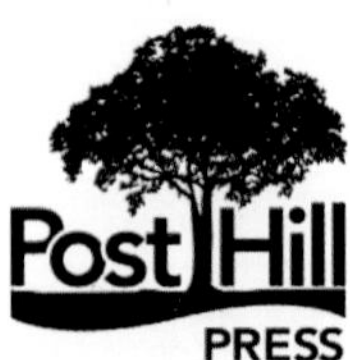

Post Hill Press
New York • Nashville
posthillpress.com

Published in the United States of America
Printed in China

discovered a new sensation, and Melania Knavs began to rise from obscurity. Like many performers, musicians, and actors, Melania changed her last name from "Knavs" to the Germanized version "Knauss," and dropped out of her architecture program to focus on modeling full-time. She signed with a modeling agency in Milan at the age of eighteen. Her big break came when she nearly won the Slovenian women's magazine *Jana's* "Look of the Year" contest in 1992.[6] Though she was the runner-up, the young star did not go unnoticed by scouts and photographers, and Melania was more determined than ever.

A CELEBRATED STAR

Melania Knauss's modeling career exploded. According to Melania Trump's Facebook page, during the early years of her career, "Melania was jet setting between photo shoots in Paris and Milan." Knauss's roommate in the '90s, Victoria Silvstedt, described Melania as "very determined, very ambitious, so strong-minded, very Slovenian, and such a good person." At the time, Melania was modeling for Marilyn Gauthier.[7] Gauthier is a French-Parisian modeling agent who is widely acclaimed as the "top model maker." In the early 1990s, Gauthier founded Marilyn Agency, which would ultimately become one of the most successful international modeling agencies in the world.[8]

Knauss would attend up to twelve casting calls a day in Paris, competing with hundreds of other models. Victoria Silvstedt is quoted as saying that Melania was a fighter who was motivated by a desire to take care of her family. Modeling was her platform to success and, no matter what happened, she would never surrender or give up.[9] That headstrong attitude led Melania Knauss to New York in 1996. There, she began appearing in high-profile ad campaigns. Knauss worked with a number of photographers who were widely considered at the top of their game: Patrick Demarchelier, Helmut Newton, Arthur Elgort, Ellen VonUnwerth, Peter Arnell, Antoine Verglas, and Mario Testino, to name a few.[10]

She finally had the opportunity to see the world she'd always dreamed about beyond the Sava and Mirna rivers of her hometown. It's even possible that she began to experience a life more glamorous than that of the royalty that had once lived in Sevnica castle, which dominated her childhood landscape. The once-gawky, long-limbed teen had evolved into a sleek runway model and fashion beauty who glared elegance into the camera. Melania graced the covers of top fashion magazines such as *Vogue*, *Harper's Bazaar*, *British GQ*, *Ocean Drive*, *Avenue*, *In Style*, and *New York Magazine*. She will probably be the only First Lady to have ever appeared in the *Sports Illustrated* Swimsuit Issue, or to have had a brain transplant with the AFLAC duck. Only drive, elegance, and a determined work ethic could elevate Melania Knauss to this level of success.

---

6 Francesca Specter. "Melania Trump: What is Donald Trump wife's CV? First Lady's modelling history revealed." Express.co.uk. Last modified February 16, 2018. https://www.express.co.uk/life-style/life/919981/melania-trump-donald-news-model.

7 Rosemary Feitelberg. "Melania Trump's Modeling Days in Paris: Lessons in Determination." *Women's Wear Daily*. November 11, 2016. https://wwd.com/eye/people/melania-trumps-mode-paris-donald-trump-10704025/.

8 "Biography." MarilynGauthier.com. 2016. http://www.marilyngauthier.com/biography/.

9 Rosemary Feitelberg. "Melania Trump's Modeling Days in Paris: Lessons in Determination." *Women's Wear Daily.* November 11, 2016. https://wwd.com/eye/people/melania-trumps-mode-paris-donald-trump-10704025/.

10 Melania Trump (@MelaniaTrump). "About." Facebook. Accessed April, 13, 2019. https://www.facebook.com/pg/MelaniaTrump/about/.

FAIRY TALE ROMANCE

Donald Trump, the future President of the United States, met Melania at a party during New York Fashion Week in 1998. Because Trump was at the party with another date, she refused to give Trump her number, but instead asked for his. Melania said that Trump gave her every number he had. She blew him off for a week. However, after their first date in Greenwich Village at the nightclub Moomba, romance began to bloom. Suddenly, the typically-quiet Melania Knauss was thrust into the super-spotlight life of "The Donald."[11]

The future president and First Lady were on-again, off-again during that first year, but eventually Melania moved into the penthouse of Trump Tower.[12] Gradually, Melania's tough, elegant side began to shine next to Trump's brash, combative style, and they began to complement each other. In 1999, when accused of being a gold digger after Trump's millions, she replied, "The press could be sometimes very mean. They love to make a joke, that's how they're selling the newspapers. But I think you can't be with the person if it's not love, if they don't satisfy you. You can't hug a beautiful apartment, you can't hug an airplane, you can't talk to them."[13]

Early on, the stage was set for Melania's ascent to elegant First Lady. When asked in a 1999 interview what her role would be if she and Mr. Trump ever ended up in the White House, she said, "I would be very traditional. Like Betty Ford or Jackie Kennedy. I would support him."[14]

On April 26, 2004, Donald Trump proposed to Melania Knauss at the Costume Institute Gala in New York with an engagement ring worth almost two million dollars.[15] The ring held a flawless, emerald-cut, twelve carat diamond, and featured tapered diamond baguettes set in platinum. Melania immediately said yes.[16] When interviewed by the *New York Post* the following day, Melania said, "It was a great surprise. We are very happy together."[17]

It was surely a fabulous moment that again evoked memories of Sevnica castle and fairy tale knights and princesses. But Melania was no princess in need of saving. She speaks four languages fluently and had, by this time, made a name for herself in the competitive world of modeling, making her a complementary force beside her future husband.

---

11 Biography.com Editors. "Melania Trump Biography." The Biography.com website. Last modified April 17, 2019. https://www.biography.com/people/melania-trump.

12 Ibid

13 Joyce Wadler. "PUBLIC LIVES; A Model as First Lady? Think Traditional." *The New York Times*. December 1, 1999. https://www.nytimes.com/1999/12/01/nyregion/public-lives-a-model-as-first-lady-think-traditional.html.

14 Ibid

15 Helin Jung. "A Definitive Timeline of Donald and Melania Trump's Relationship." *Cosmopolitan*. January 27, 2017. https://www.cosmopolitan.com/politics/a8646265/donald-trump-melania-trump-relationship-timeline/.

16 Richard Johnson. "How Trump 'Iced' The Deal—$2 Mil Sparkler For His Fiancée." *New York Post*. April 30, 2004. https://nypost.com/2004/04/30/how-trump-iced-the-deal-2-mil-sparkler-for-his-fiancee/.

17 Ibid

WEDDING BELLS

Melania Knauss became Melania Trump on January 22, 2005, in Palm Beach, Florida. Melania wore a custom-made $100,000 couture gown that weighed sixty pounds. Billy Joel and Tony Bennett sang at the reception, and guests dined on a fabulous menu prepared by French chef Jean-Georges Vongerichten. Martha Stewart, the maven of the modern class, said it was one of the most talked-about weddings of 2015. It still ranks as one of the world's top ten most extravagant weddings.[18]

Melania had a hand in planning the entire wedding from start to finish. She wanted Louis XIV glamour and elegance: gold, glitter, jewelry, and class.[19] She walked down the aisle at Bethesda-by-the-Sea, an Episcopal church in Palm Beach. The reception was held at Trump's reinvented Versailles-inspired ballroom at Mar-a-Lago. Even heads of state don't often dance in ballrooms with marble floors, real gold moldings, and custom-made crystal chandeliers.[20].

The guest list was a who's who of celebrities, artists, and irony: Bill and Hillary Clinton, Simon Cowell, P. Diddy, Katie Couric, Heidi Klum, Gayle King, Rudy Giuliani, Anna Wintour, Don King, Russell Simmons, Shaquille O'Neal, Matt Lauer, Star Jones, Barbara Walters, Mort Zuckerman, Kathie Lee Gifford, Les Moonves, Julie Chen, Jeff Zucker, Kelly Ripa, Chris Christie, Paul Anka, Steve Wynn, Chris Matthews, George Pataki.... The list goes on and on.[21] The irony is that after Melania Trump became First Lady of the United States, many of the same guests who gladly accepted Tiffany gift bags, sipped on Cristal, and dined on fine caviar will now have nothing to do with the Trumps and do their best to denigrate them to the press. Many are even reluctant to admit they were at the wedding.

Melania's maid of honor and sister, Ines Knauss, wore a magnificent Vera Wang gown. Donald Trump's sons, Donald Jr. and Eric, were their father's best men. As part of the ceremony, Donald and Melania lit her baptismal candle that had been brought by her mother from Slovenia. (The same candle was later used in their son, Barron's, baptism to maintain the tradition.) Instead of rice, guests tossed rose petals as the couple left the church and headed to the reception hall at Mar-a-Lago.

The couple was serenaded by Paul Anka, Elton John, Billy Joel, and Tony Bennet. The first dance was played by the Michael Rose Orchestra of Palm Beach: the Puccini aria "Nessun Dorma."[22] Almost every bride-to-be longs for a fairy tale wedding, and Melania Trump was certainly blessed in that regard. One could hardly imagine a more amazing or splendid event than Melania and Donald Trump's wedding. In an interview with *Parenting* magazine, Melania Trump shared her perspective on her marriage:

---

18 Lisa Gutierrez. "A 13th anniversary look back on Melania and Donald Trump's extravagant wedding." *The Kansas City Star*. January 22, 2018. https://www.kansascity.com/news/nation-world/article195959754.html.

19 Ibid

20 Ibid

21 Kelsey Borreson. "These Are The Famous People Who Attended Donald Trump's Wedding To Melania—You know, in case you were curious." *Huff Post*. August 3, 2016. https://www.huffpost.com/entry/famous-people-who-attended-donald-trumps-wedding-to-melania_n_579fc3d-ce4b08a8e8b5f1d09.

22 Lisa Gutierrez. "A 13th anniversary look back on Melania and Donald Trump's extravagant wedding." *The Kansas City Star*. January 22, 2018. https://www.kansascity.com/news/nation-world/article195959754.html.

> It's a lot of responsibility for a woman to be married to a man like my husband. I need to be quick, smart, and intelligent. My life is very normal—for me. Maybe for some people, they would not think that. But for me it is. I know my husband. We have a great relationship. We are both very independent. We know what our roles are and we are happy with them. I think the mistake some people make is they try to change the man they love after they get married. You cannot change a person. You accept the person. He loves business—he breathes business. I love that about him, I love that. Doesn't bother me. I am very independent. It is important to understand each other. If you need to change someone it will never work. You will try your whole life and never succeed.[23]

FAMILY LIFE AND POLITICS

A year after their wedding, on March 20, 2006, Melania Trump gave birth to her son, Barron William Trump. He was Melania Trump's first child and Donald Trump's fifth. Melania describes her parenting style as protective but pragmatic. When asked about her time with her son, Barron, Trump explained:

> I am a full-time mom; that is my first job. The most important job ever. I started my business when he started school. When he is in school I do my meetings, my sketches, and everything else. I cook him breakfast. Bring him to school. Pick him up. Prepare his lunch. I spend the afternoon with him. Sometimes I have obligations, but I also think children need to see a parent do what her passion is. It is a good example for a child. So the child can find passion as well and follow that passion in the future.[24]

When Melania Trump claims in interviews that she keeps busy, it is not an exaggeration. In addition to her full-time job as a mother and wife, Melania is also well-known for her impressive work as a philanthropist. In 2005, she was an honorary chairperson for Martha Graham Dance Company. She was named a Goodwill Ambassador by the American Red Cross, where she served for four years. Melania was also an honorary chairwoman for the Boys Club of New York and was named Woman of the Year by the New York City Police Athletic League. She participates often in National Love Our Children Day and National Child Abuse Prevention Month, and she was allowed the honor of ringing the closing bell at NASDAQ. In 2010, she was the Chairwoman for the American Heart Association and helped raise almost two million dollars for research.[25] Many would consider these to be a lifetime of accomplishments; she married the man of her dreams, had a successful career as a fashion model, made a name for herself by her philanthropic works, and raised a beautiful son. However, more was to follow as Donald Trump became President of the United States, and Melania became the elegant First Lady we know today.

On October 27, 2016, just days before the election that would make Melania Trump the second foreign-born First Lady of the United States, Donald and Melania sat down for an interview with *Good Morning America* co-anchor, George Stephanopoulos. Stephanopoulos asked:

---

23 Sabrina James. "Melania Trump Juggles Motherhood, Marriage, and a Career Just Like Us." *Parenting*. Accessed April 13, 2019. https://www.parenting.com/blogs/hip-mama/melania-trump-shares-her-1-parenting-tip-and-secrets-lasting-marriage.

24 Ibid

25 "Melania Trump: First Lady of the United States." Whithouse.gov. Accessed April 11, 2019. https://www.whitehouse.gov/people/melania-trump/.

"You said at the beginning if you run, you'll win. Do you still feel that?"

Melania Trump was the first to answer: "I feel that. I feel that. I see the connection with the American people and my husband, and—he created a movement. It was nothing like that ever. And the crowd and the people that are behind him, it's unbelievable to see."[26]

In the same interview, Stephanopoulos asked about how the election was affecting Barron. According to Melania, Barron was handling it well, thanks to Melania's willingness to explain to him, honestly, what is being said about his father, and what his father is saying in return.[27] Still, Melania expressed her desire to keep Barron out of the spotlight without sheltering him from the world. Despite all the pressure of the election that was two weeks away, Melania's focus was on her son and family first, then her husband. She knew Donald could handle the pressure. In fact, based on previous interviews, she knew he loved and thrived in the crucible.

Two weeks later, on November 8, 2016, Donald Trump became the 45th President of the United States, and Melania became the second foreign-born First Lady in the history of the United States. "While Melania Trump became a household name in modeling and a contributing member of her community, she is first and foremost a mother and wife, and in 2017, Melania Trump made the White House and Washington home for her family," states the White House website.[28]

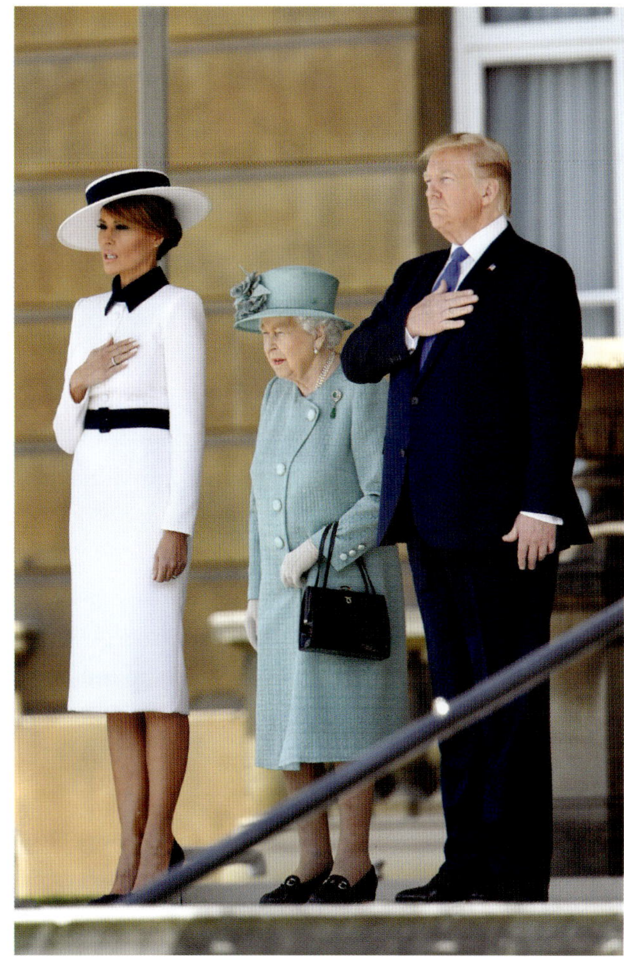

MELANIA THE PHILANTHROPIST

Issues impacting children are the primary focus of her role as First Lady. Meeting with children in national and international hospitals and care centers is one of her numerous personal passions and diplomatic pursuits. Her list of volunteer and philanthropic engagements is extensive, including: bringing valentines to the Children's Inn at the National Institutes of Health and Cincinnati Children's Hospital in 2018; gifting Easter baskets to the children of St. Mary's Medical Center in Palm Beach, Florida; meeting and supporting families impacted by Hurricane Harvey; and offering support in the aftermath of appalling mass shootings in Las Vegas and Parkland. Her time in the White House has so far been marked by these demonstrations of strength and resilience.

26 Melania and Donald Trump. "Transcript." Interview by George Stephanopoulos. ABC News. October 27, 2016. https://abcnews.go.com/Politics/transcript-george-stephanopoulos-interviews-donald-melania-trump/story?id=43104094.

27 Ibid

28 "Melania Trump: First Lady of the United States." Whithouse.gov. Accessed April 11, 2019. https://www.whitehouse.gov/people/melania-trump/.

With her inspiring good works and uplifting attitude, it's an undeniable fact that "an unwavering characteristic of the First Lady is her aptitude for showing love and compassion in all that she does."[29]

THE FOUNDATION OF BE BEST

Melania Trump said it best when she stated: "It remains our generation's moral imperative to take responsibility and help our children manage the many issues they are facing today, including encouraging positive social, emotional, and physical habits…"[30] These principles are the foundation of her public awareness campaign, BE BEST, which advocates for the overall well-being of our country's youth.

According to the official White House website:
The mission of BE BEST is to focus on some of the major issues facing children today, with the goal of encouraging kids to BE BEST in their individual paths, while also teaching them the importance of social, emotional, and physical health. BE BEST will concentrate on three main pillars: well-being, social media use, and opioid abuse.

BE BEST will champion the many successful well-being programs that provide children with the tools and skills required for emotional, social, and physical health. The campaign will also promote established organizations, programs, and people who are helping children overcome some of the issues they face growing up in the modern world.[31]

The BE BEST campaign has three pillars, the first of which is well-being. This pillar promotes healthy living, respect towards others, and an understanding that all adults can take part in preparing children for their futures. With these values laid down as a solid foundation, children will be better prepared to cope with the negative effects of social media and the threat of a nation-wide opioid crisis.

The second pillar is centered solely on social media. The aim is to teach children how to use social media as a tool for positivity and productive social change. Mrs. Trump believes children should be seen and heard and, it is our job as adults to foster and encourage these younger voices to be used wisely, with both respect and compassion.

The third and final pillar of the BE BEST program is opioid abuse prevention. The First Lady describes her plan like this: "Opioid dependence, addiction, and abuse are an epidemic in this country. BE BEST will support the families and children affected by this crisis, bring attention to neonatal abstinence syndrome, and help educate parents on the importance of healthy pregnancies."[32]

BE BEST is only one of Melania Trump's attempts to protect others from abuse and bullying, which she has dealt with firsthand…

29 Ibid

30 Ibid

31 Ibid

32 Ibid

COMPOSURE IN THE FACE OF ADVERSITY

In the last week of January 2019, Britain's *Daily Telegraph* published a court-ordered apology and retraction for claiming that Melania Trump's father had been abusive and controlling. That same article had suggested that Melania's success as a model was due to Donald Trump's influence, despite the fact that she was already successful when they first met. There were numerous other items that were clarified and cleaned up in the article along with the apology:

> "We apologize unreservedly to the First Lady and her family for any embarrassment caused by our publication of these allegations," reads the statement. It also noted that the paper has "agreed to pay Mrs. Trump substantial damages as well as her legal costs."[33] Mrs. Trump's communications director, Stephanie Grisham, stated: "Mrs. Trump often refers to opportunists out to advance themselves by disparaging her name and image. She will not sit by as people and media outlets make up lies and false assertions in a race for ratings or to sell tabloid headlines."[34]

In her trademark elegant fashion, without a Twitter war or verbal threats, Mrs. Trump filed suit, cleared up the false allegations in court, and received financial compensation. In 2017, she also won a nearly three-million-dollar settlement against the *Daily Mail*. However, in that case, the writer adamantly refused to retract their false allegations.

A FIRST LADY TO REMEMBER

In all her endeavors, Melania Trump's toughness shines through. One could assume it was born of her upbringing in a small, tough little communist town, finding success in a tough modeling industry with stiff competition, and holding her own with her brash, hot-headed, outspoken husband. Melania Trump is no pushover. She understands her rights as an American citizen, and she will go to the mattresses to protect her son, her family, and her country. We are fortunate to have a First Lady who understands what it is like to endure trials and to have to earn her success through hard work and determination. Though she's learned to play hardball along the way to protect herself and her loved ones, she still manages to do so with the elegance and class that will become her legacy as First Lady.

33 Caroline Halleman. "British Paper Agrees to Pay Melania Trump 'Substantial Damages' Over 'False Statements.'" *Town and Country*. January 28, 2019. https://www.townandcountrymag.com/society/politics/a26065753/melania-trump-telegraph-apology-damages-false-statements/.

34 Ibid

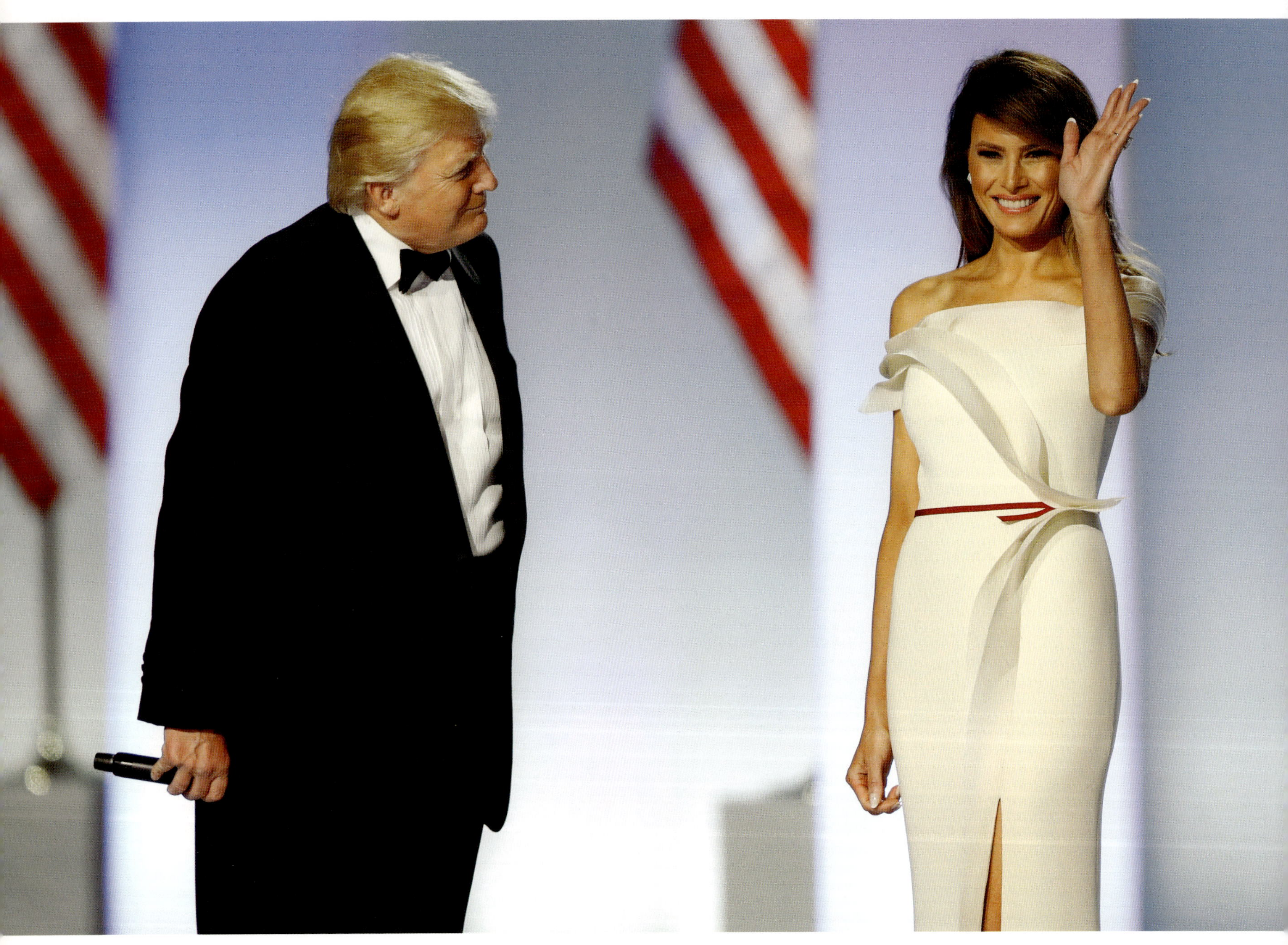

President Donald Trump has first lady Melania Trump take a bow at the Freedom Inaugural Ball at the Washington Convention Center January 20, 2017, in Washington, D.C. The day Trump was sworn in as the 45th U.S. President.[1]

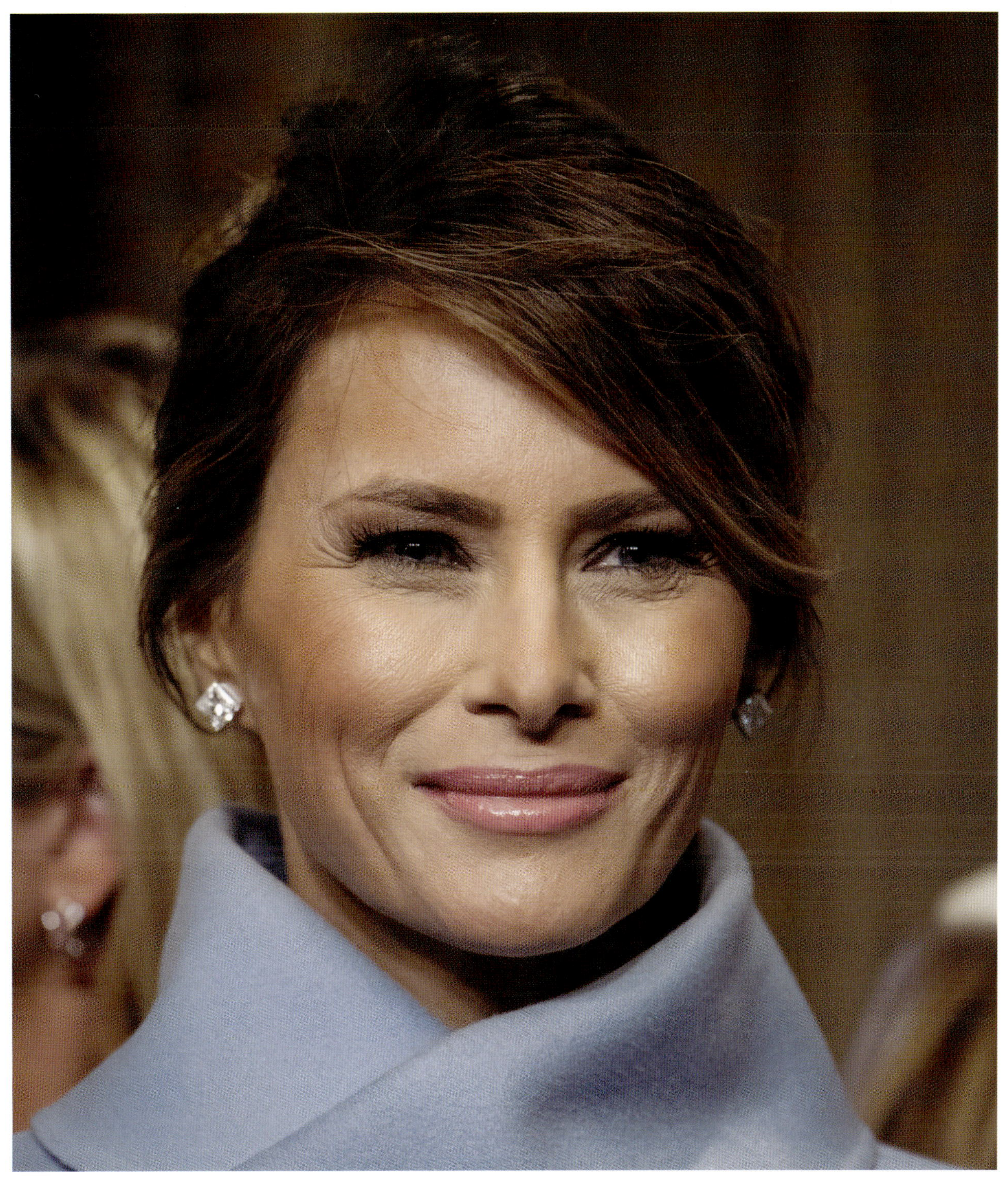

Melania Trump, elegance in motion, leaves the President's room of the United States Senate during the 58th U.S. Presidential Inauguration, January 20, 2017.[2]

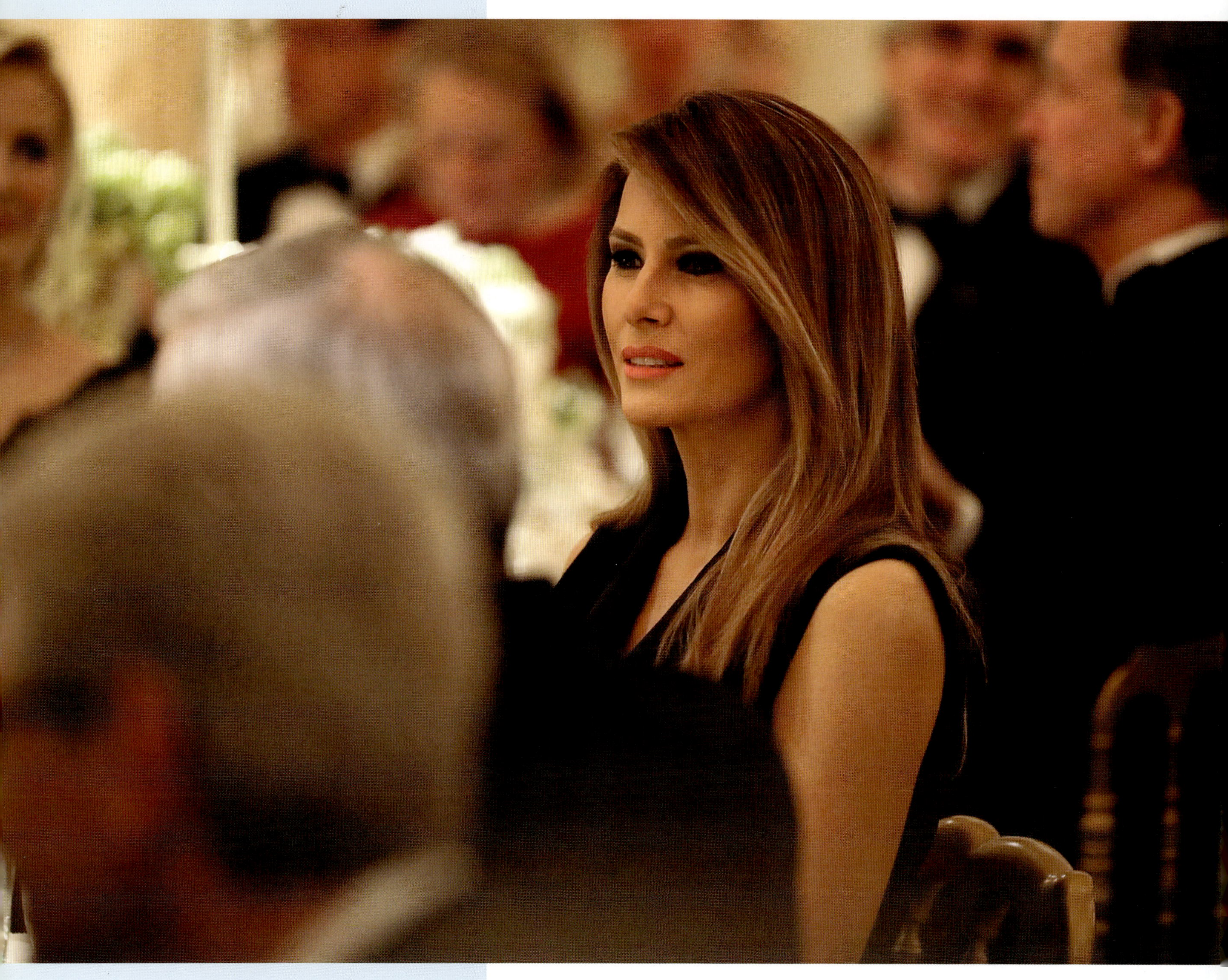

Melania Trump lights up the room while hosting the President's first black-tie event of Trump's new administration, the Governor's Ball, February 26, 2017.[3]

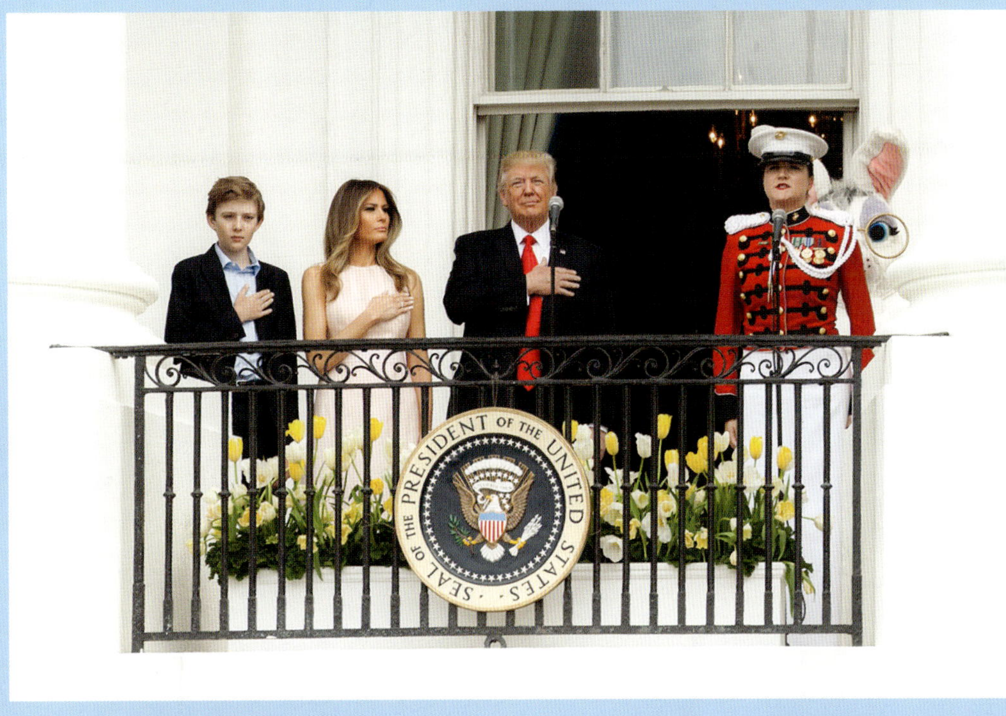

Melania Trump, her son Barron, and President Donald Trump stand at attention as the National Anthem is played at the first annual White House Easter Egg Roll of the new occupants of the White House. April 17, 2017.[4]

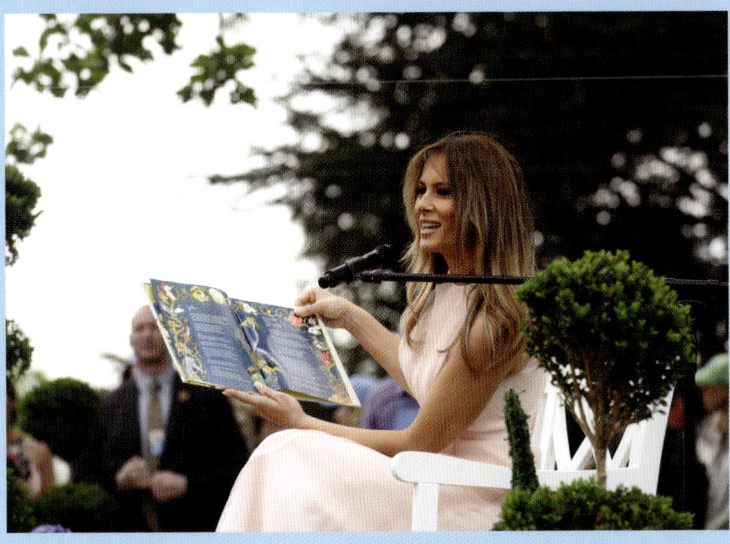

First Lady Melania Trump enjoys reading to children at the White House Easter Egg Roll, Monday, April 17, 2017.[4]

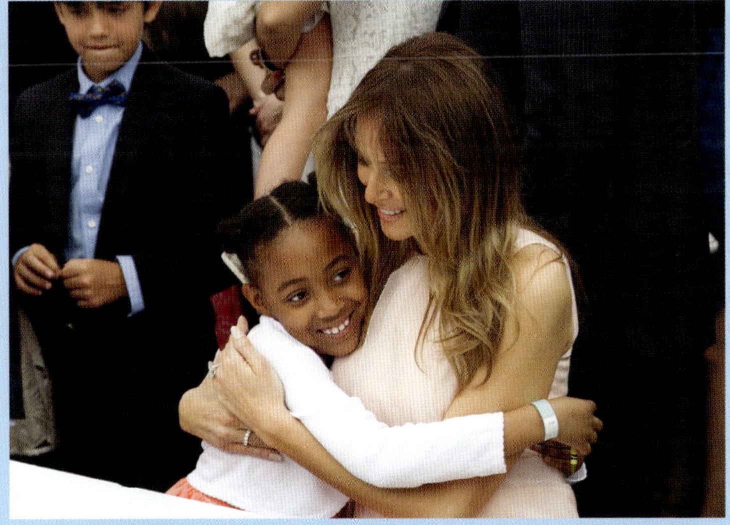

Melania Trump hugging a child while doing arts and crafts at the first Easter Egg Roll of the Trump Administration.[5]

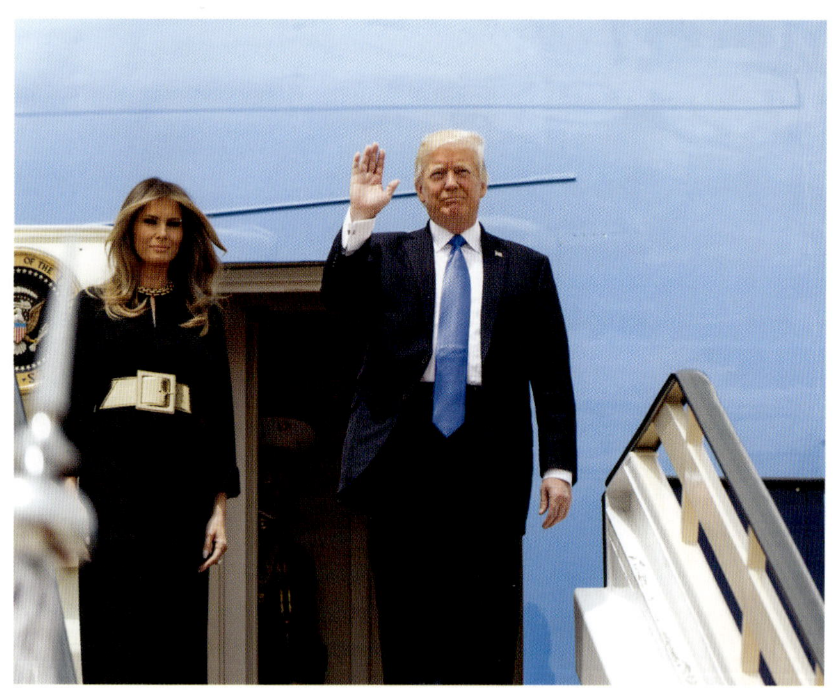

President Donald Trump and First Lady Melania Trump arrive on the tarmac, Saturday, May 20, 2017, to King Khalid International Airport in Riyadh, Saudi Arabia. Mrs. Trump is dressed conservatively to match Saudi Arabia's strict dress code for women.[5]

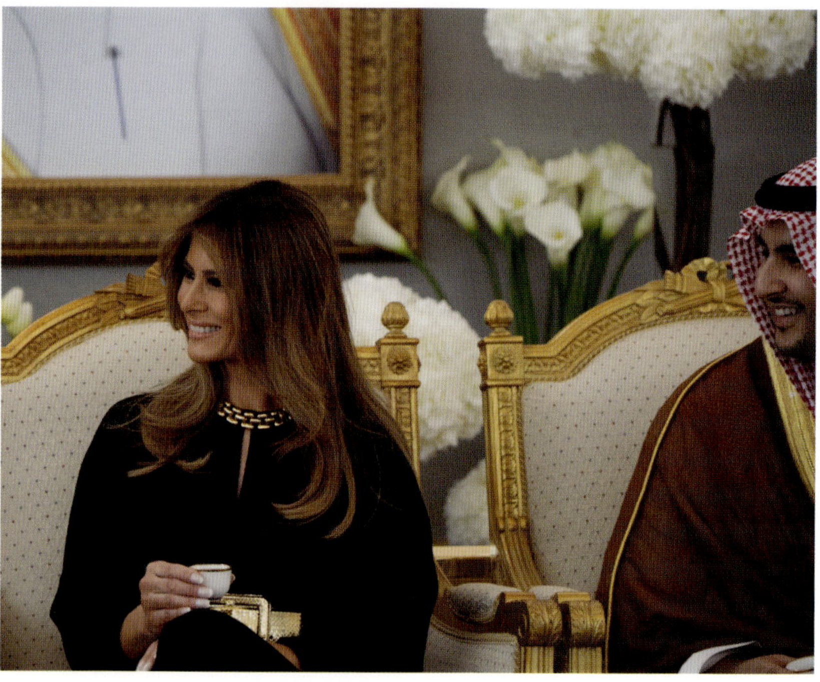

The First Lady is allowed a moment to relax and smile at a Saudi ceremonial welcoming tea, after exiting Air Force One.[6]

Right: Melania Trump exhibits elegance and style for her official White House Residency Photograph.[7]

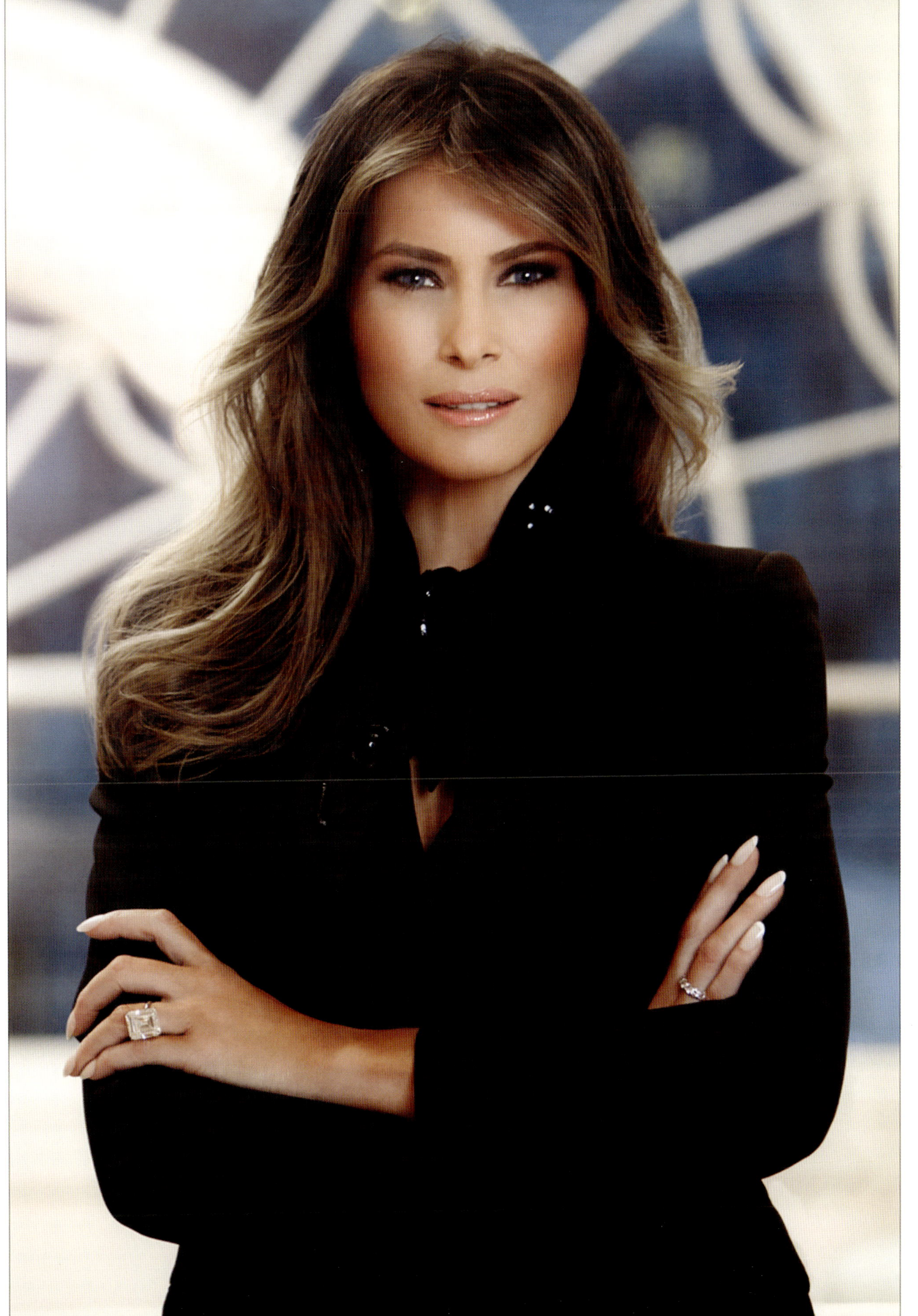

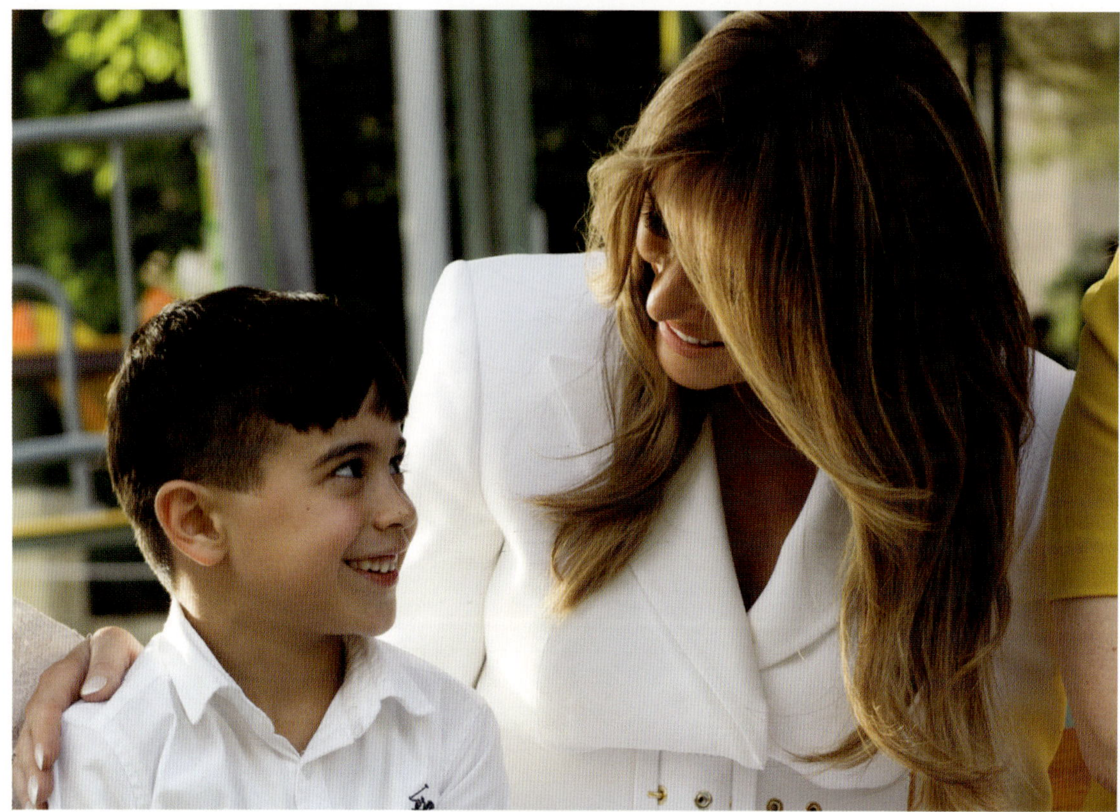

The First Lady makes new friends while visiting the Hadassah Medical Organization facility in Jerusalem. Mrs. Trump often visits medical facilities for children.[6]

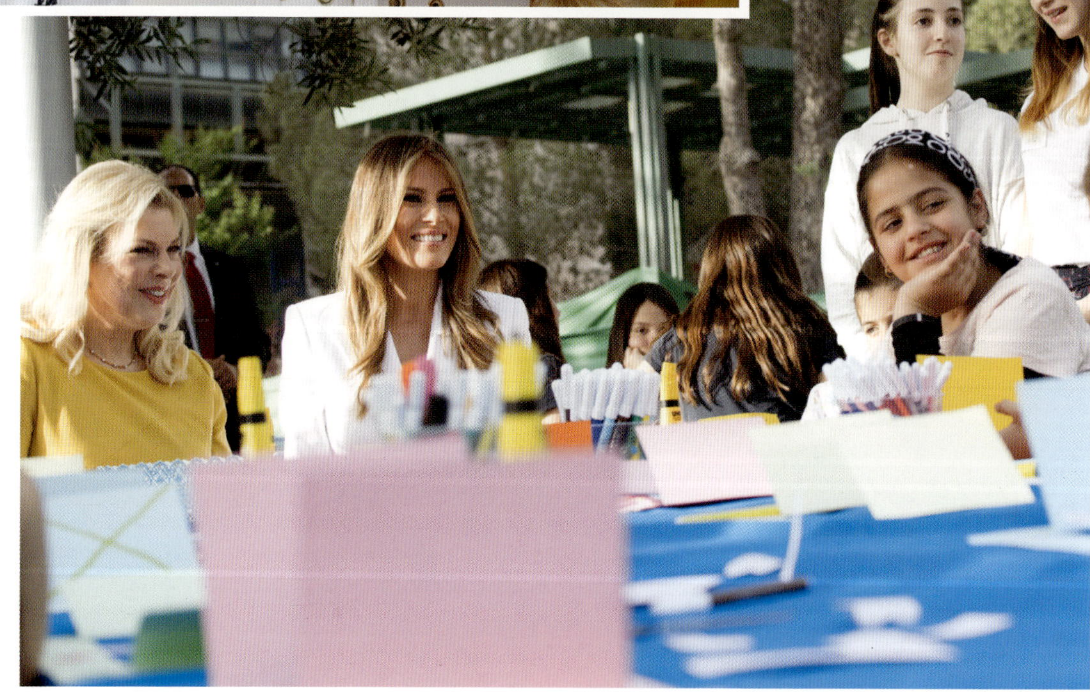

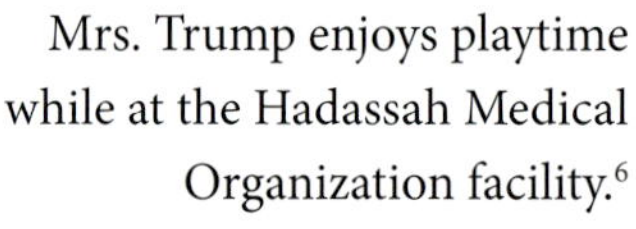

Mrs. Trump enjoys playtime while at the Hadassah Medical Organization facility.[6]

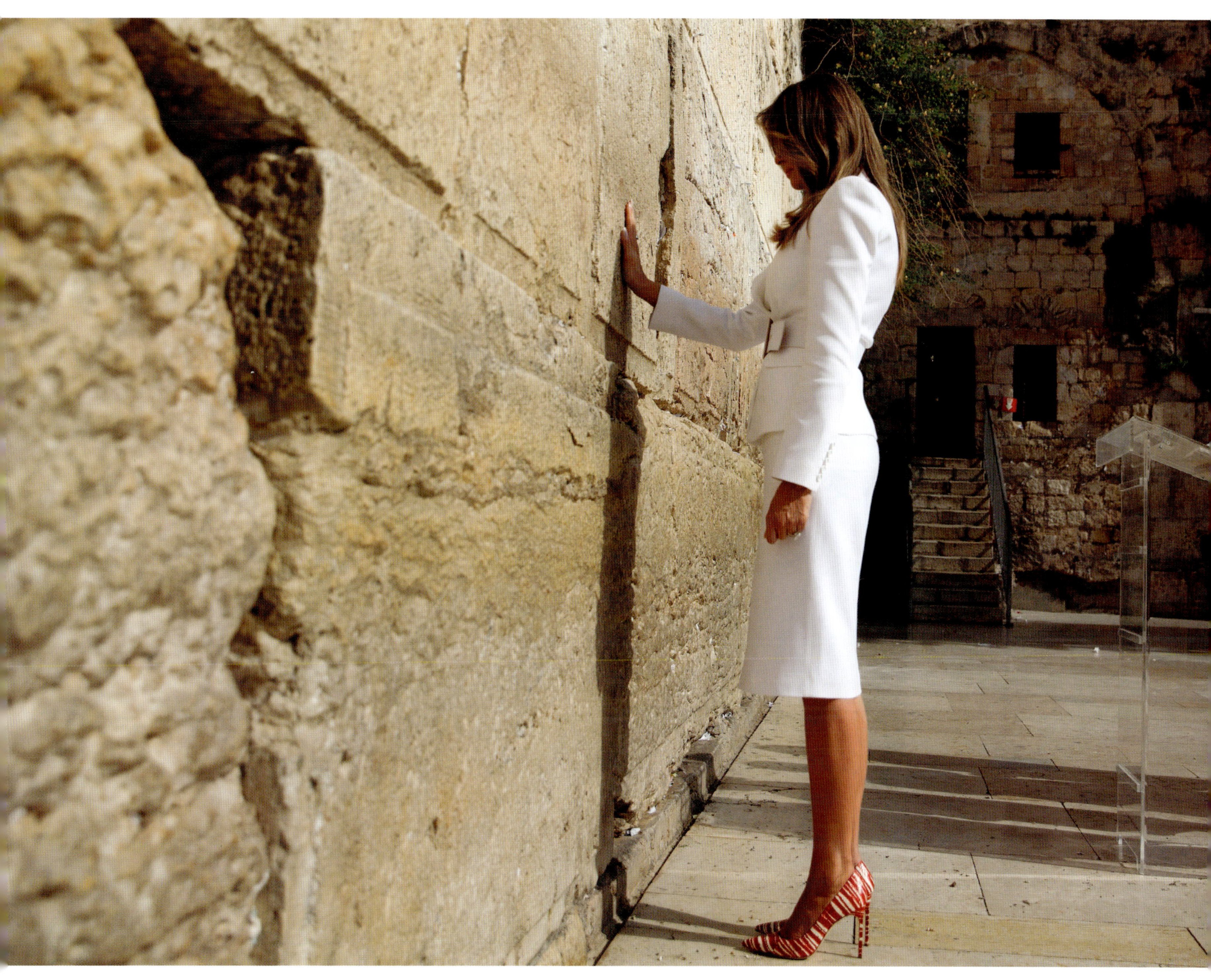

While visiting Jerusalem, the First Lady reverently prays at the Western Wall, the holiest site in Judaism. Rabbi Shmuel Rabinowitz, the rabbi of the Western Wall said that the Trump's visit "showed respect for the Jewish people and for tradition."[8]

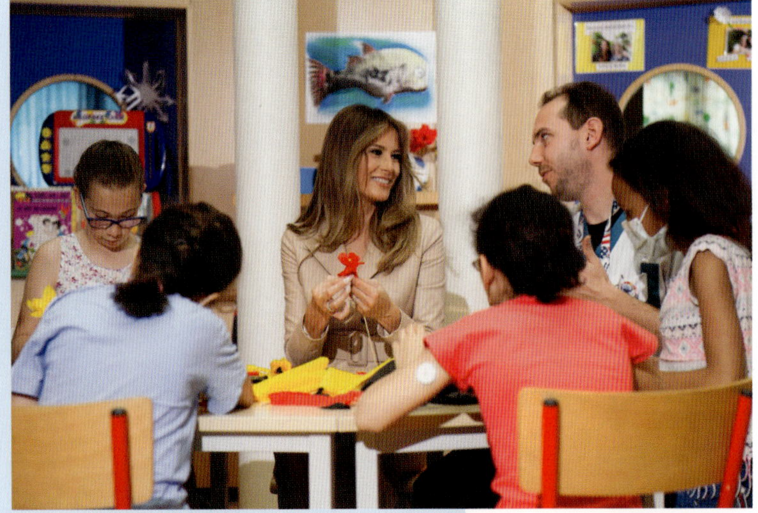

Here the First Lady visits the Queen Fabiola Children's University Hospital in Brussels, Belgium. The only university hospital in Belgium reserved for children's medicine.[6]

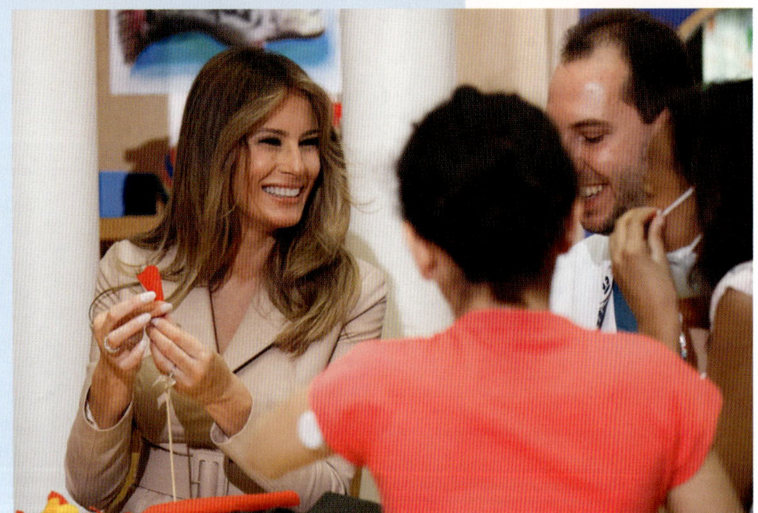

Making tulips at the children's hospital.[6]

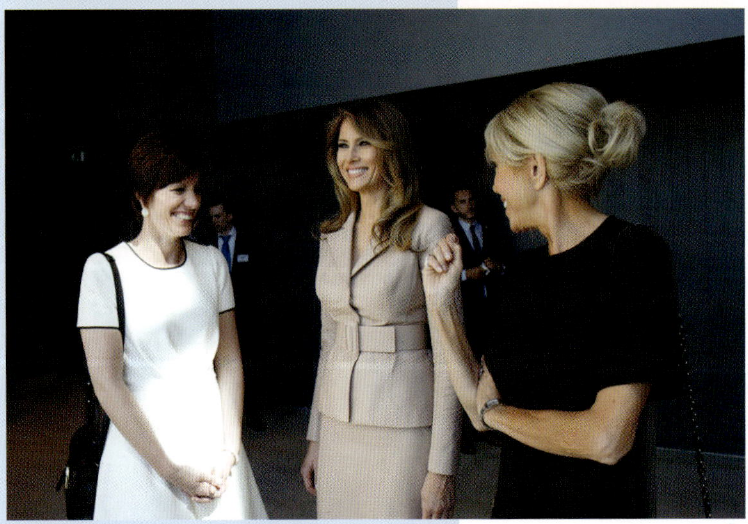

Mrs. Trump, the First Lady of France, Brigitte Trogneux, and Belgium's Amélie Derbaudrenghien, enjoy a visit to the Magritte Museum in Brussels, The Royal Museum of Fine Arts of Belgium.[6]

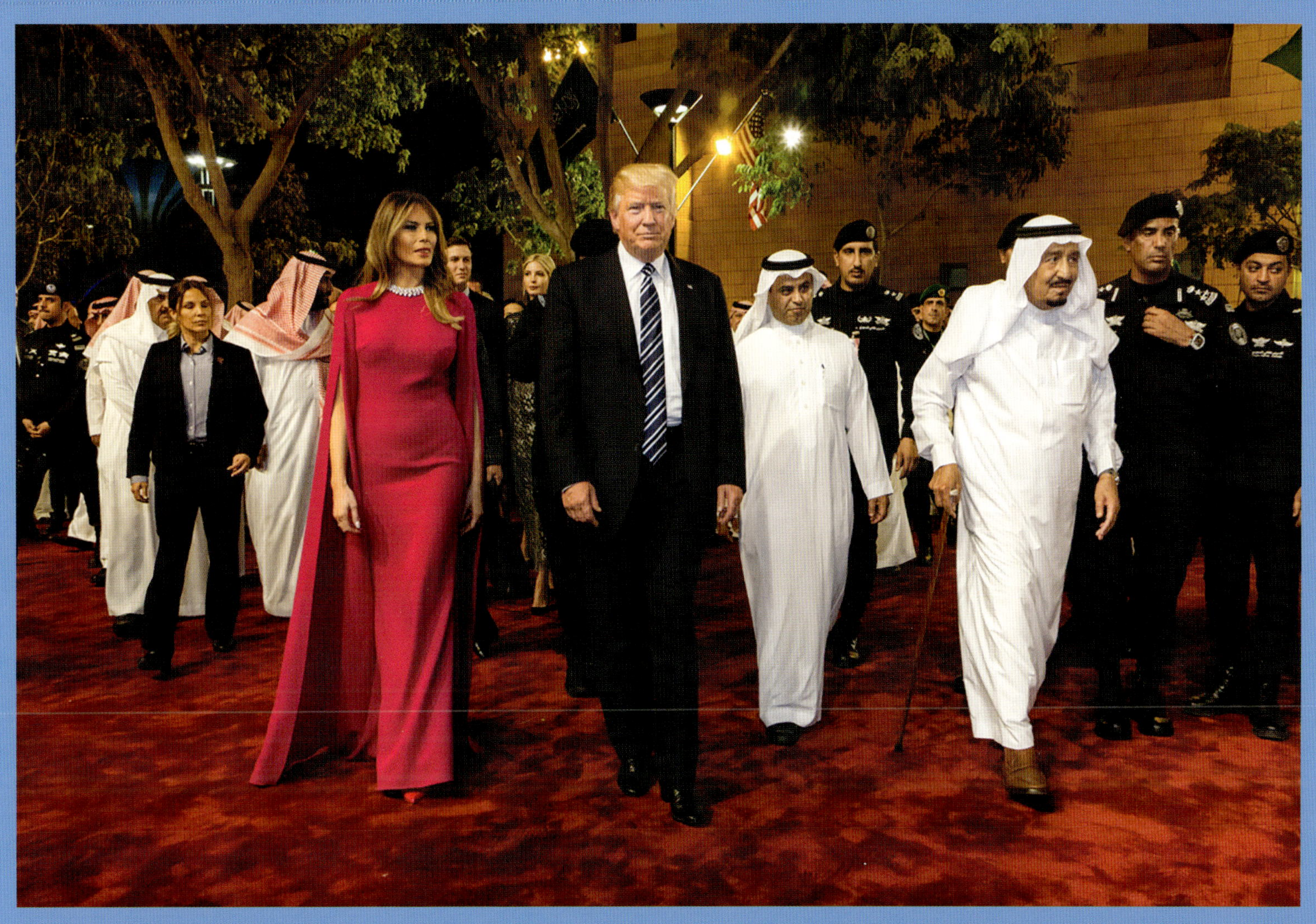

King Salman bin Abdulaziz Al Saud escorts the President and his wife to a banquet in the Murabba Palace, in Saudi Arabia.[5]

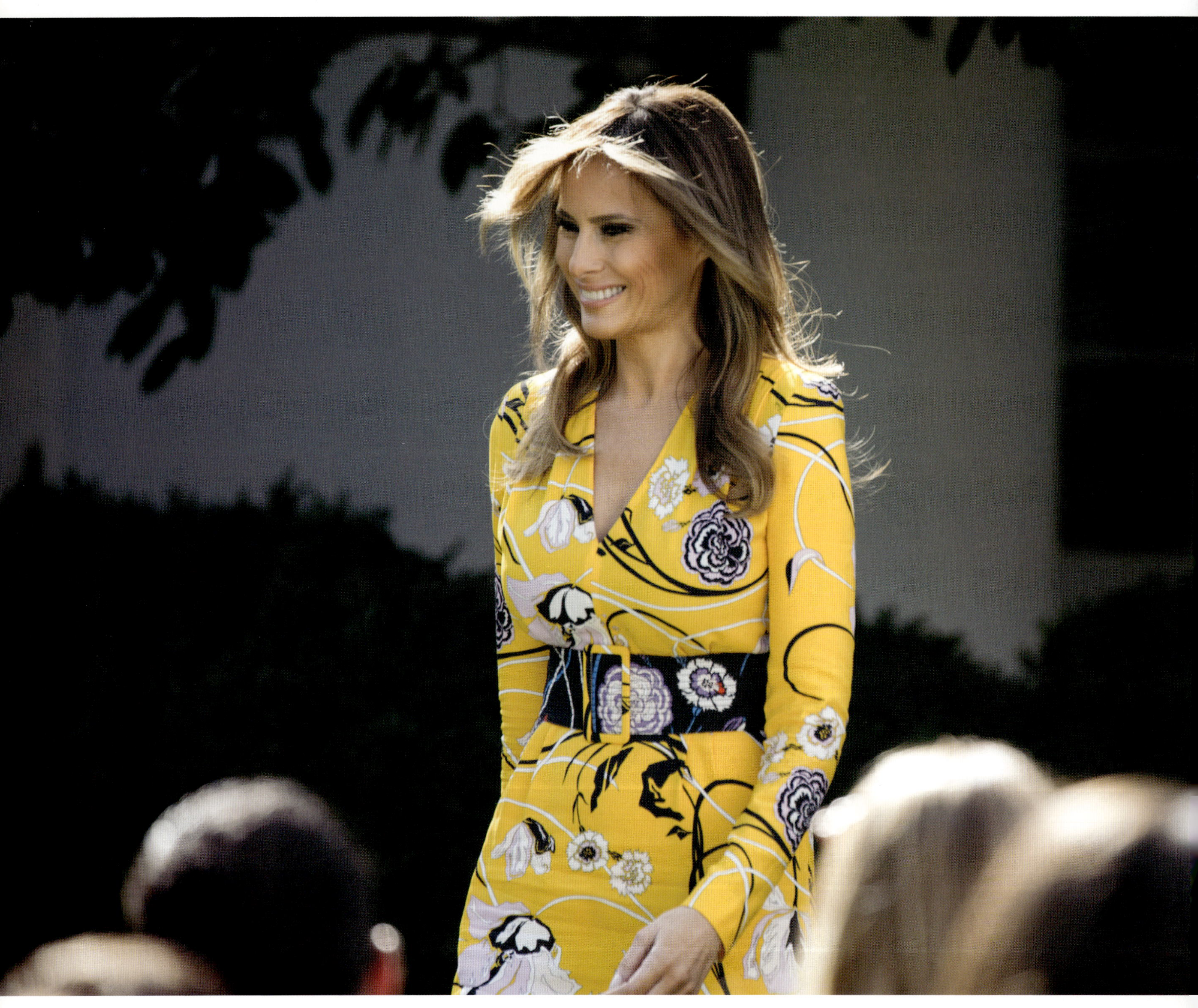

Melania Trump stuns with elegance at a press conference given by her husband in the Rose Garden of the White House.[9]

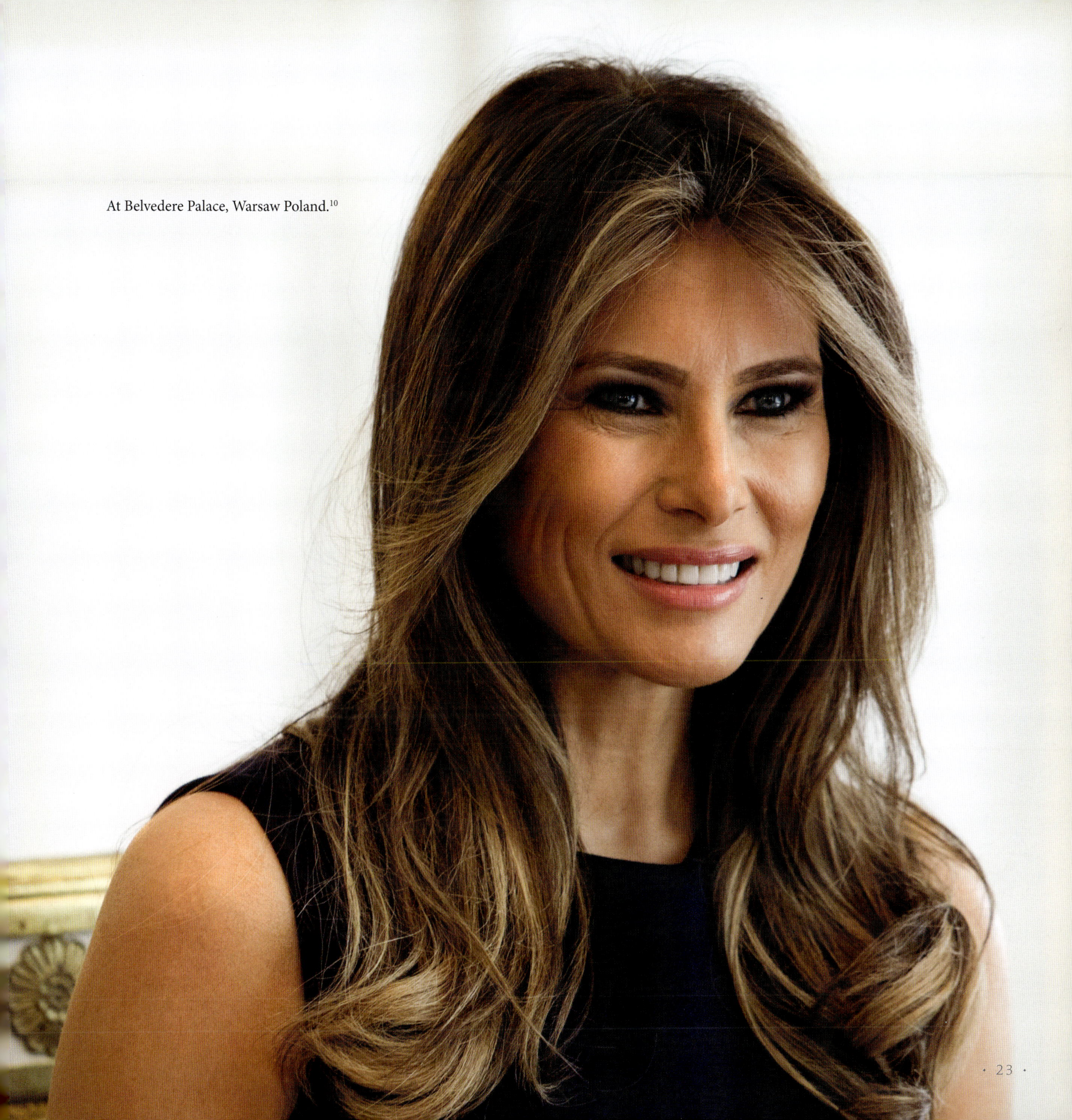

At Belvedere Palace, Warsaw Poland.[10]

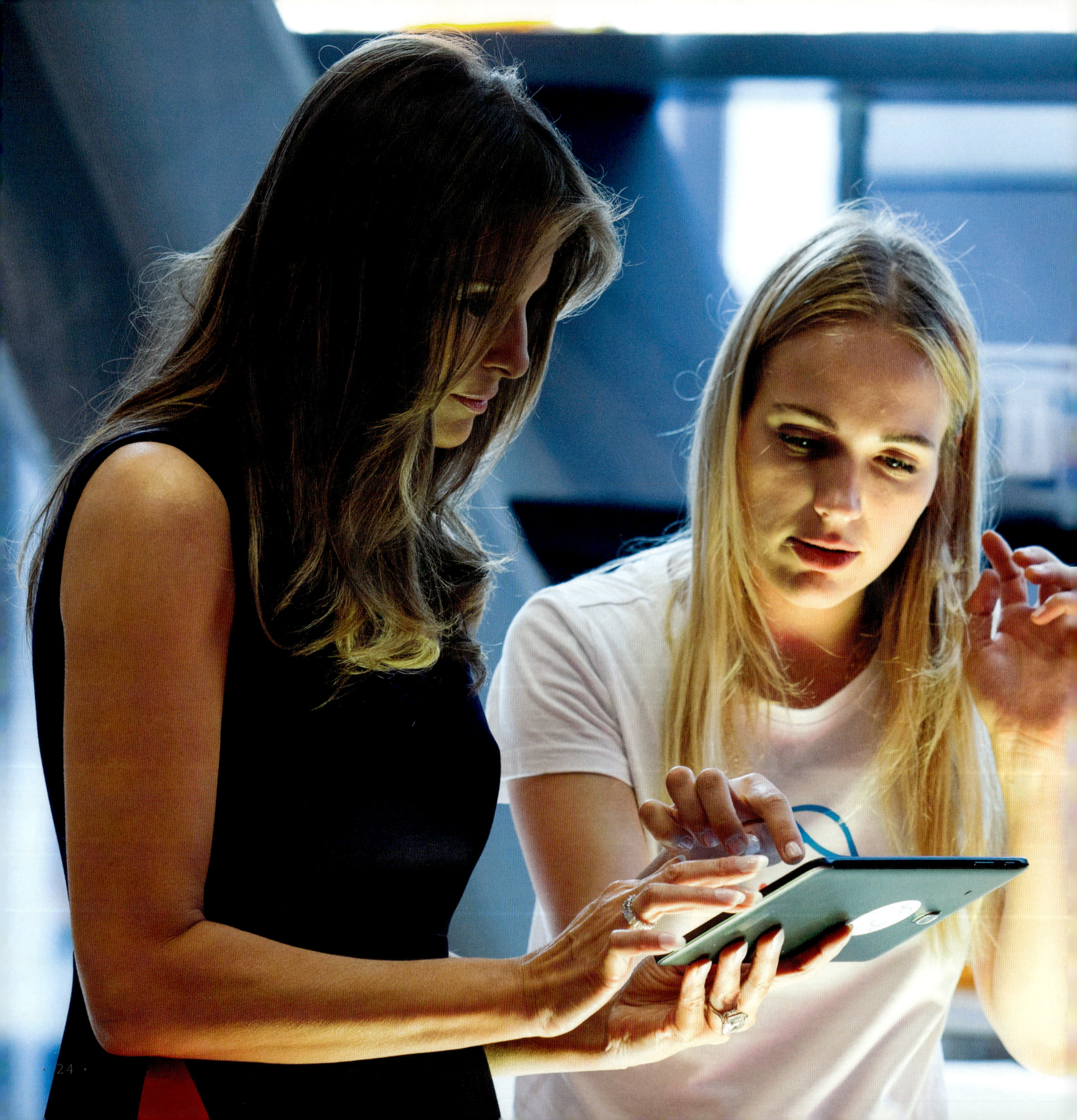

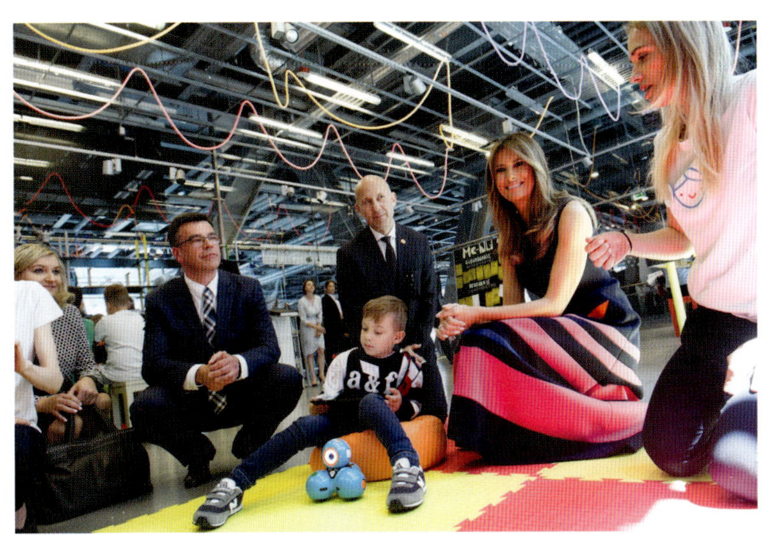

Robots in action and big smiles![6]

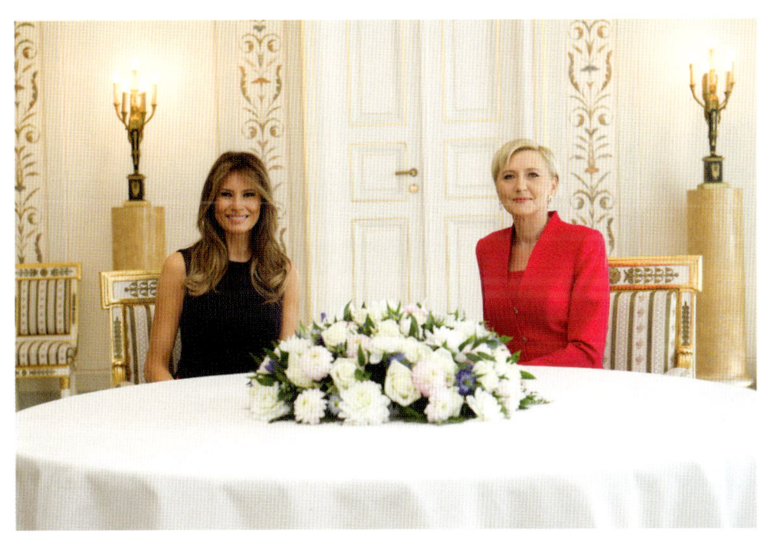

First Lady Melania Trump and First Lady of Poland Agata Kornhauser-Duda, July 6, 2017.[6]

Left: Learning about electro-fashion accessories at the Copernicus Science Centre in Warsaw, Poland. Mrs. Trump was hosted by the First Lady of Poland.[10]

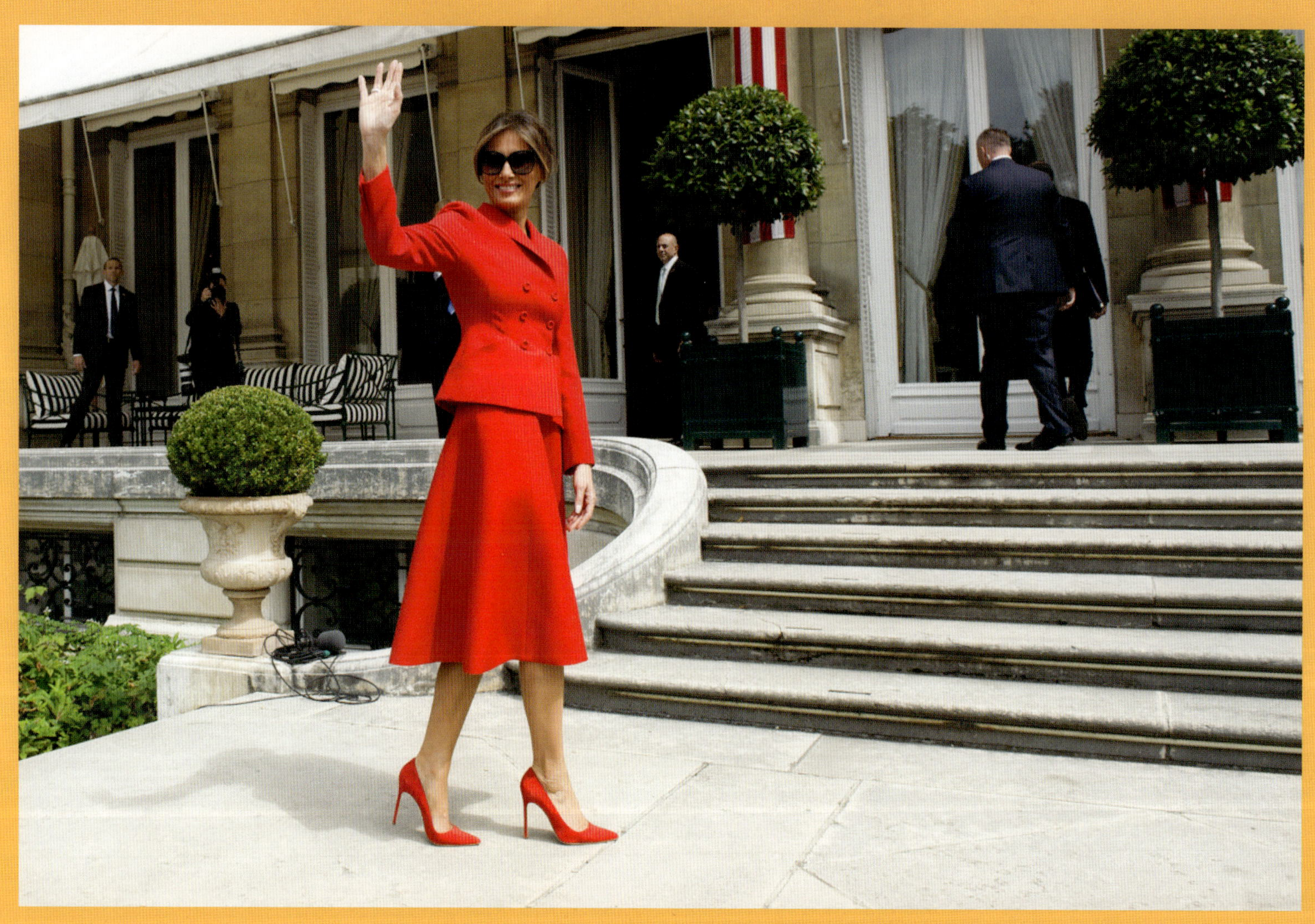

Melania Trump bringing elegance back to France as well![6]

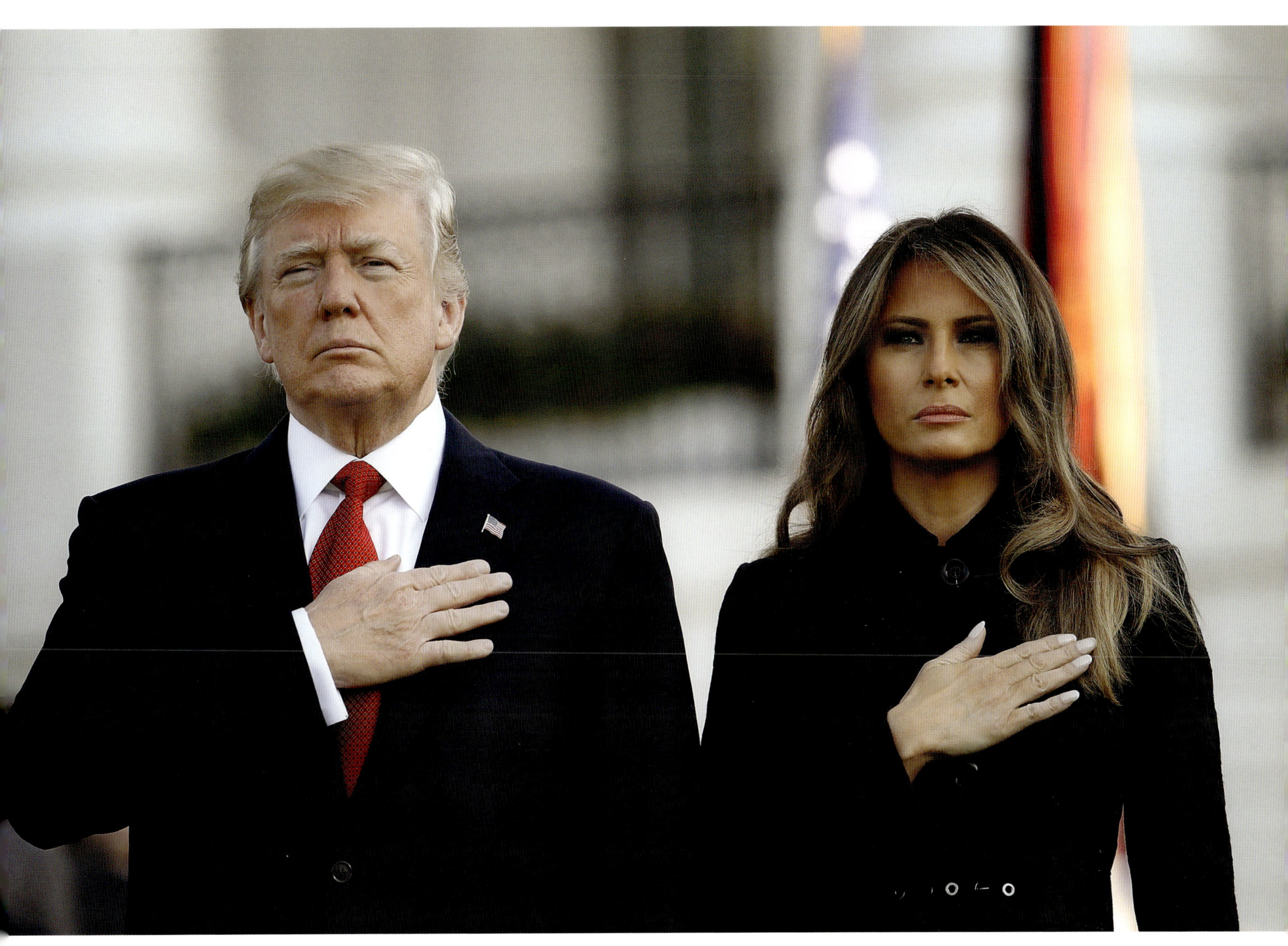

Taps plays in the background as the President and First Lady lead a moment of silence on the anniversary of the 9/11 assaults on the United States.[11]

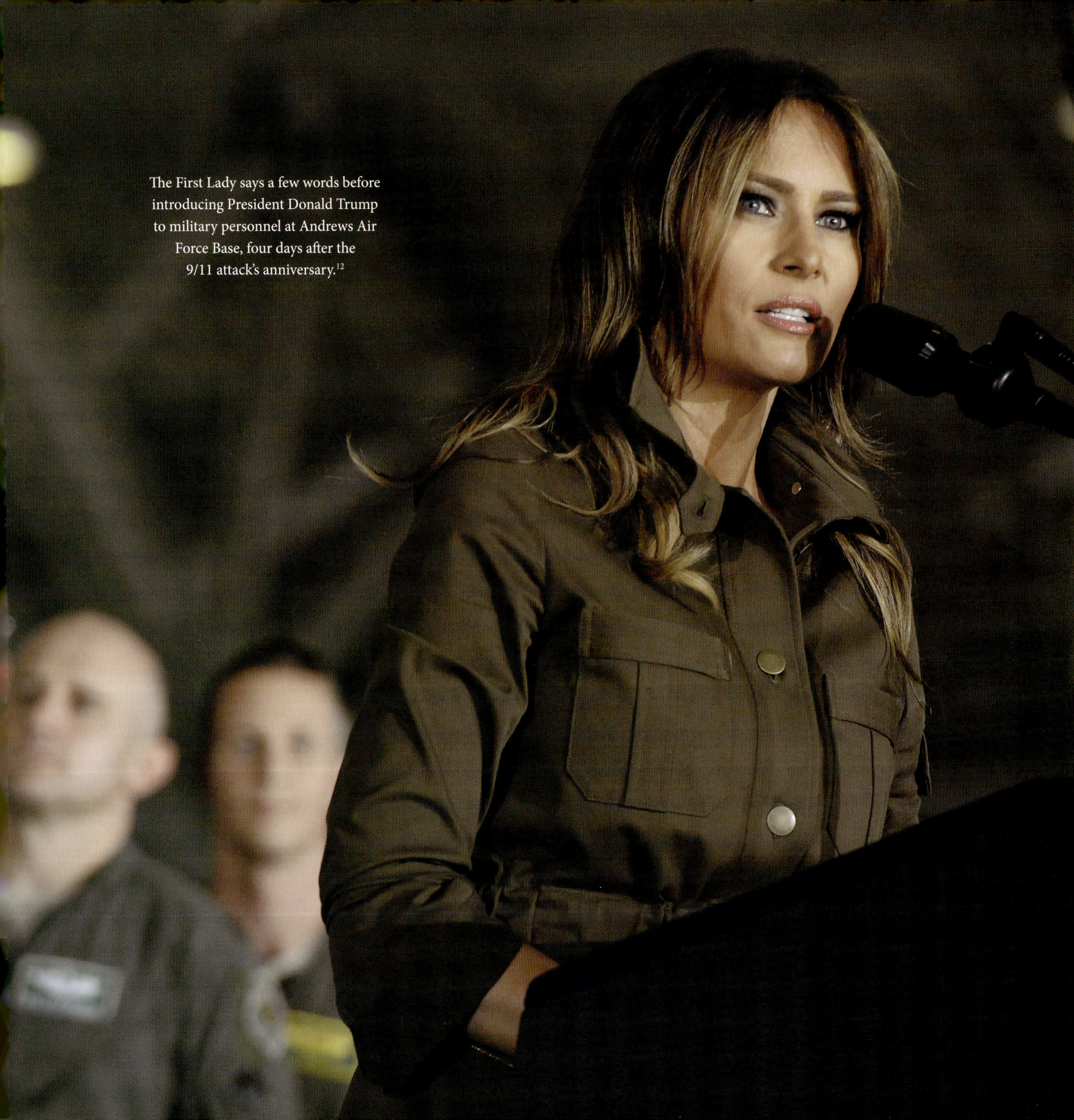

The First Lady says a few words before introducing President Donald Trump to military personnel at Andrews Air Force Base, four days after the 9/11 attack's anniversary.[12]

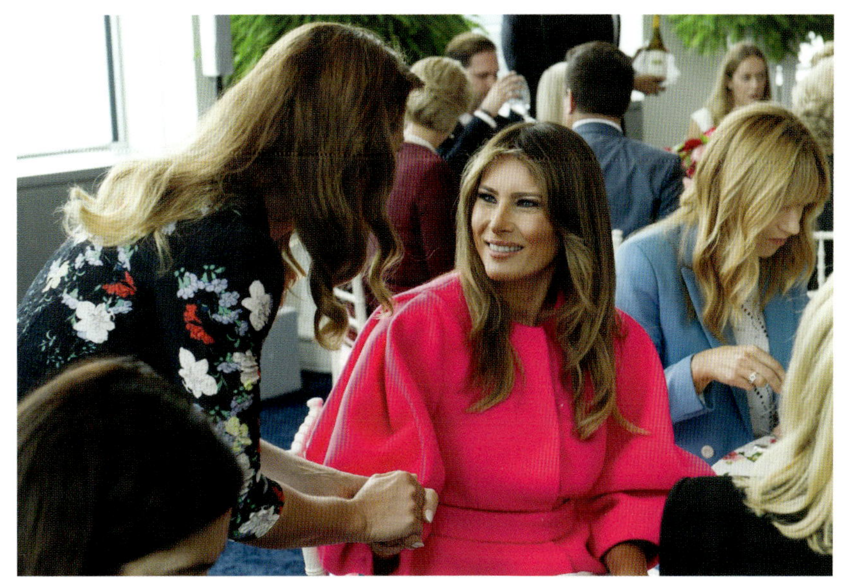

At the United Nations.[6]

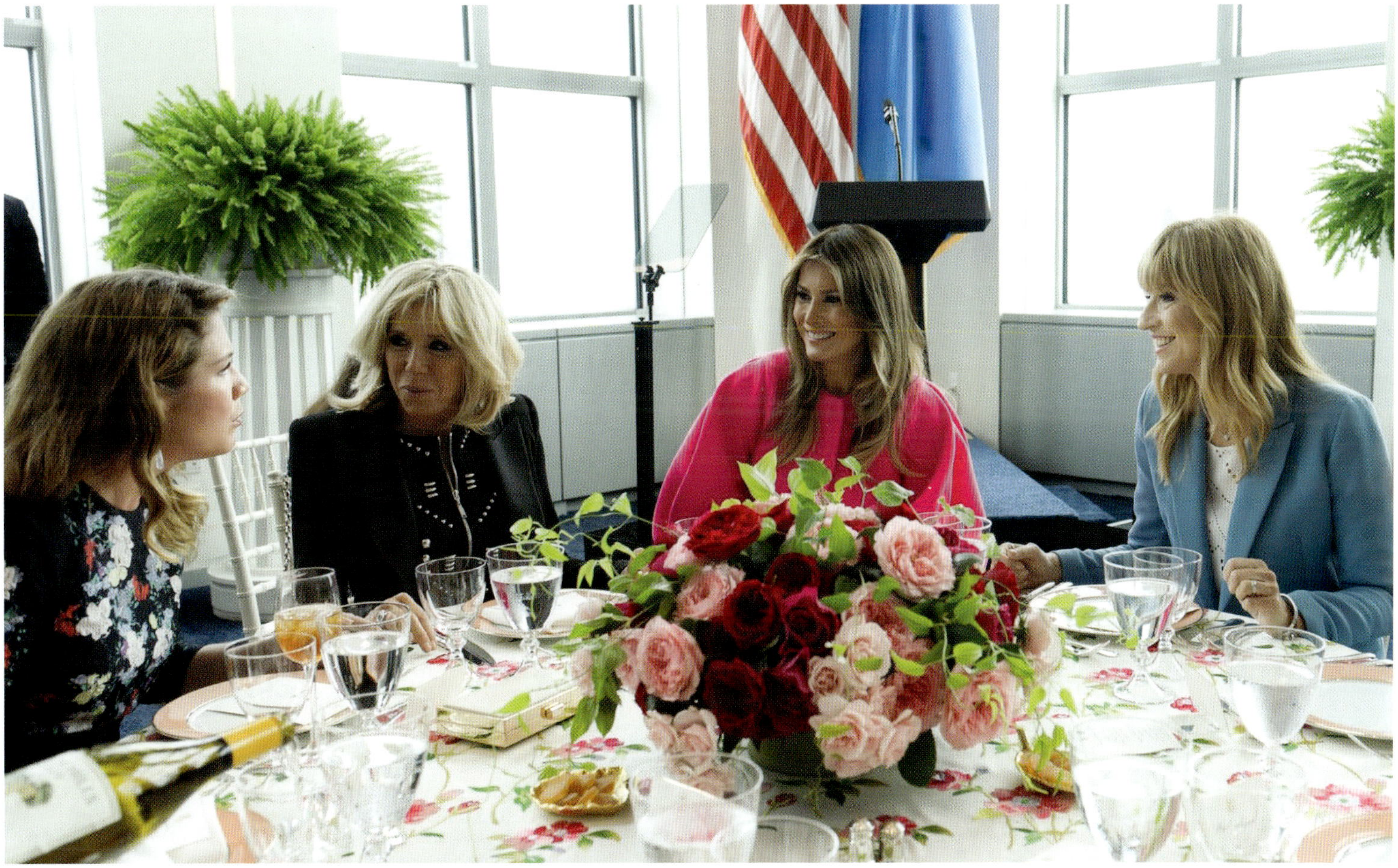

United Nations Luncheon.[6]

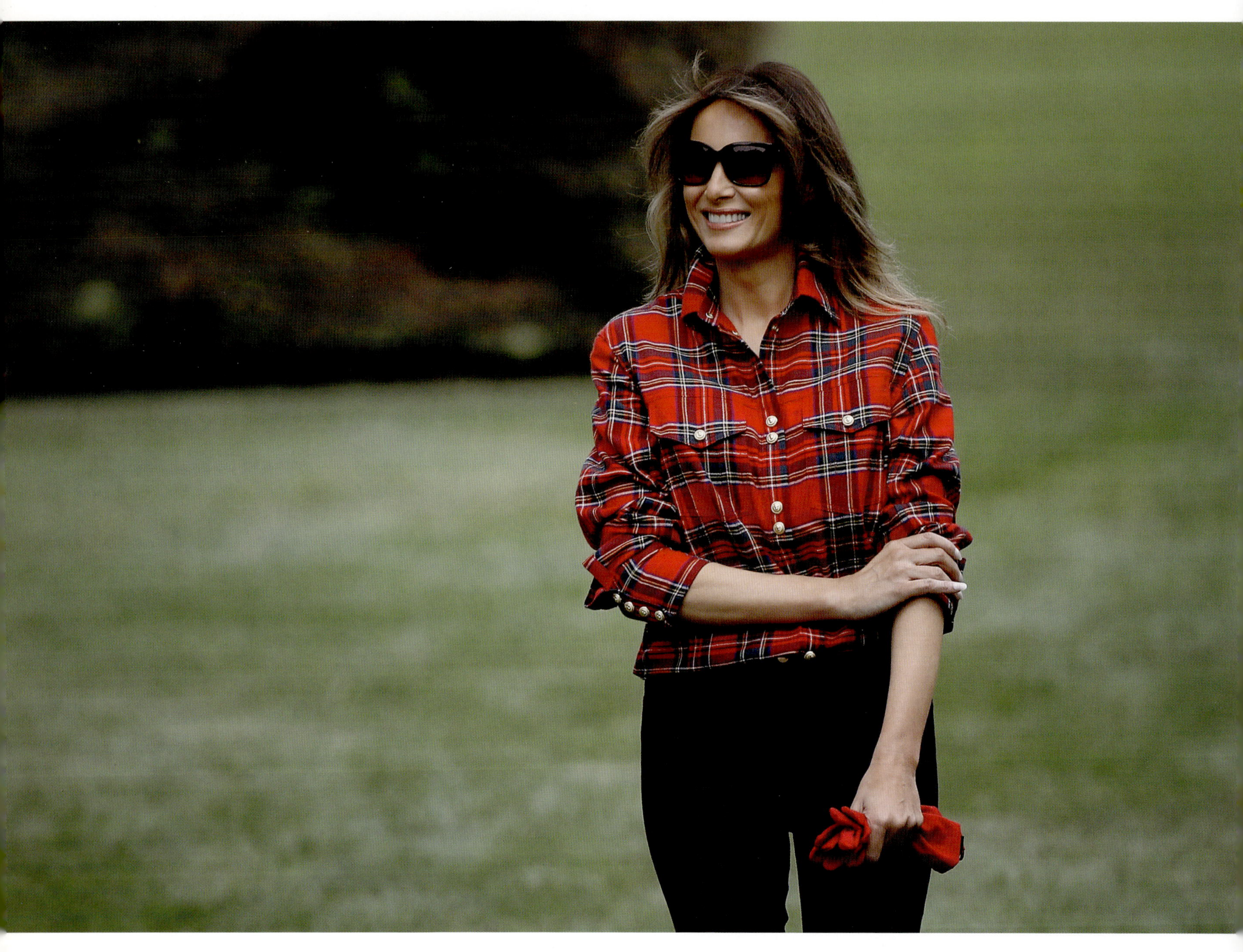

Following up on a tradition started by Michelle Obama, Melania Trump meets with the Boys & Girls Club of Washington to plant and harvest vegetables for the White House Kitchen Garden.[11]

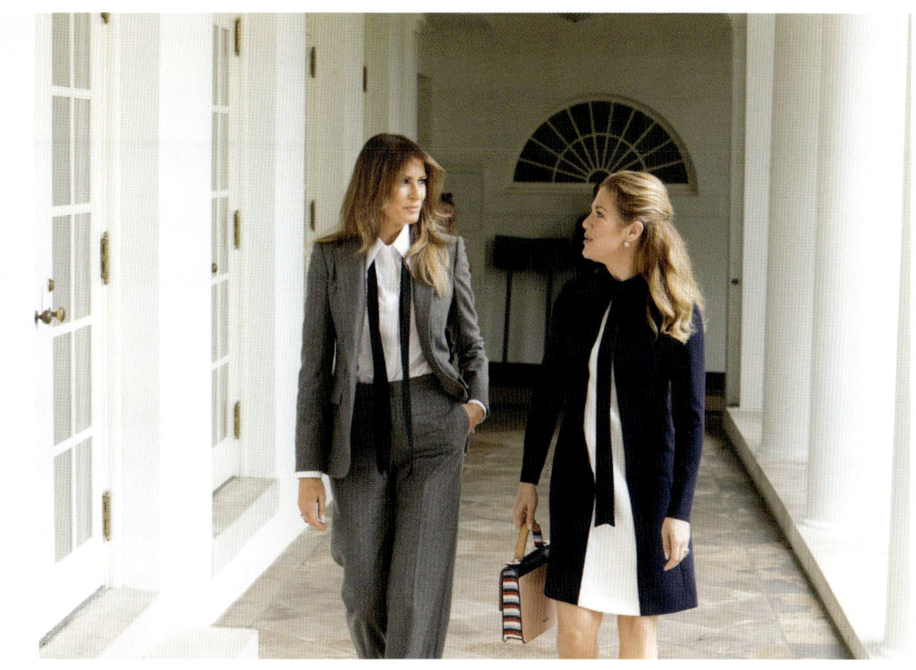

First Lady Melania Trump and Mrs. Sophie Grégoire Trudeau of Canada.[6]

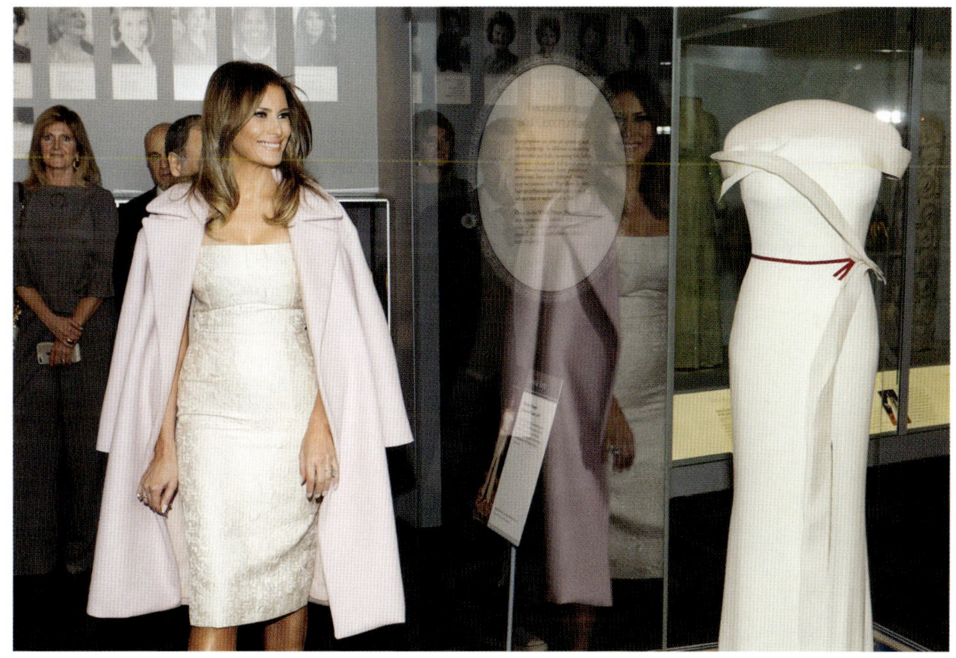

The First Lady presents her elegant inaugural gown to the Smithsonian National Museum of American History.[6]

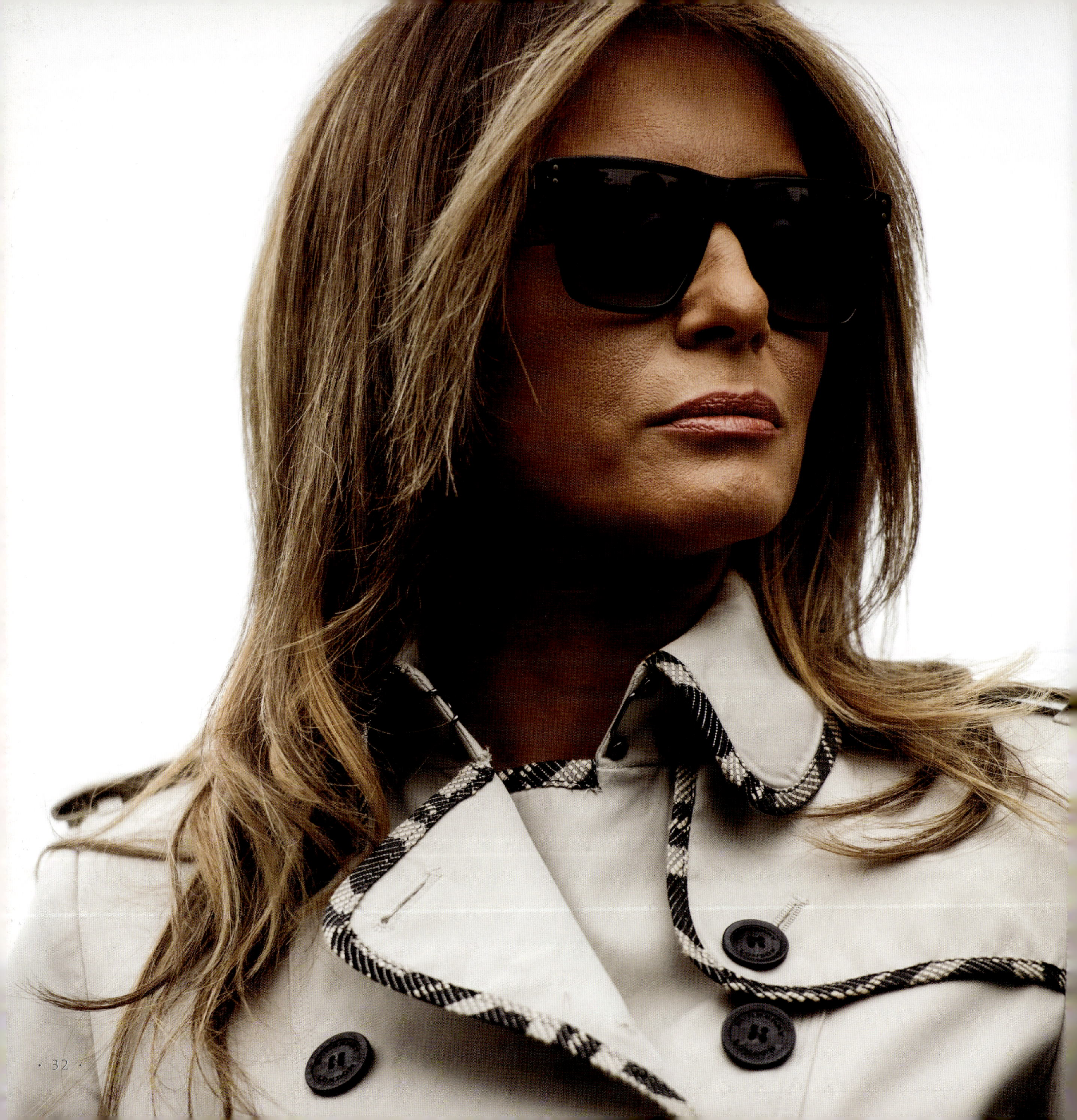

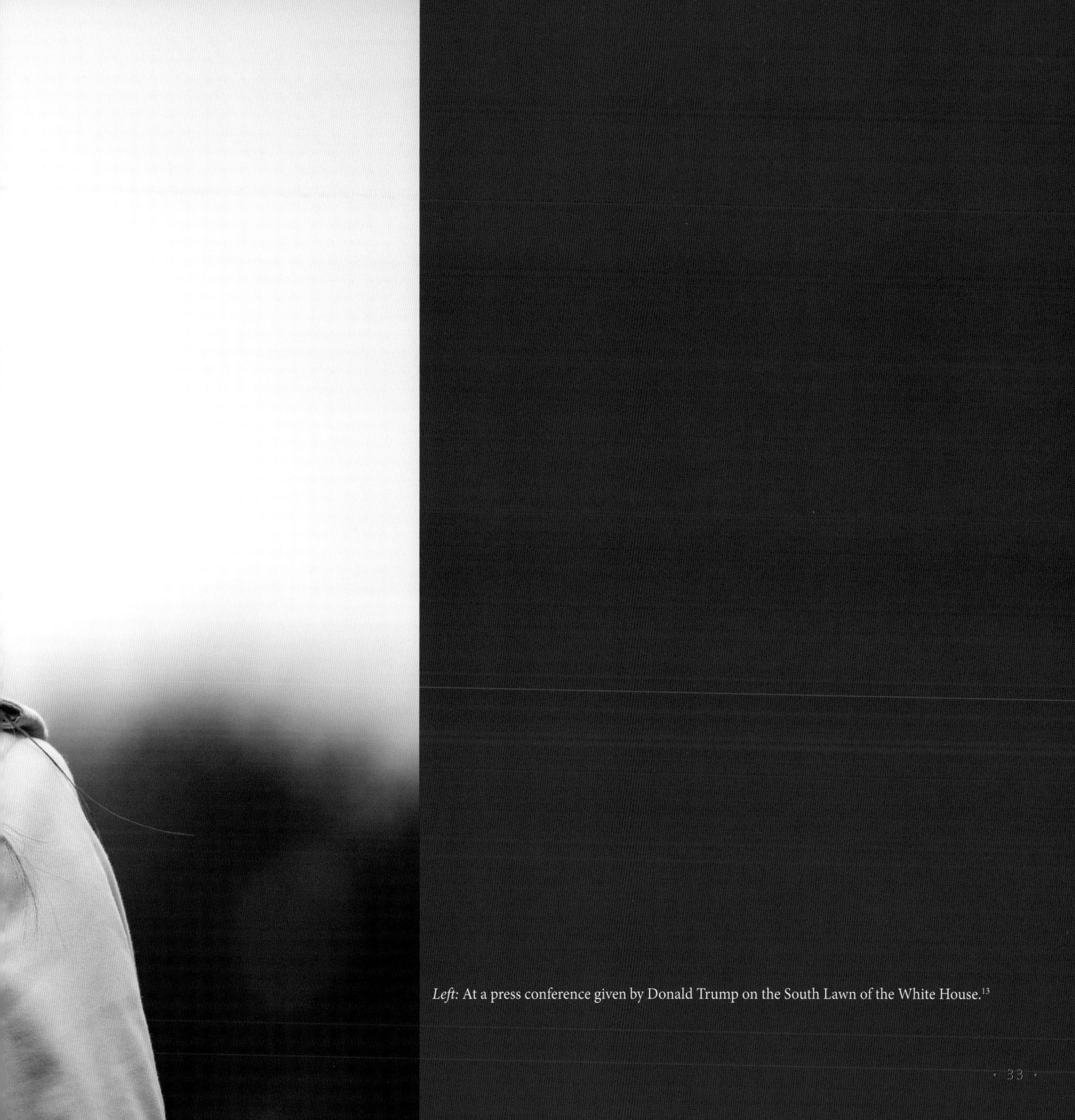

Left: At a press conference given by Donald Trump on the South Lawn of the White House.[13]

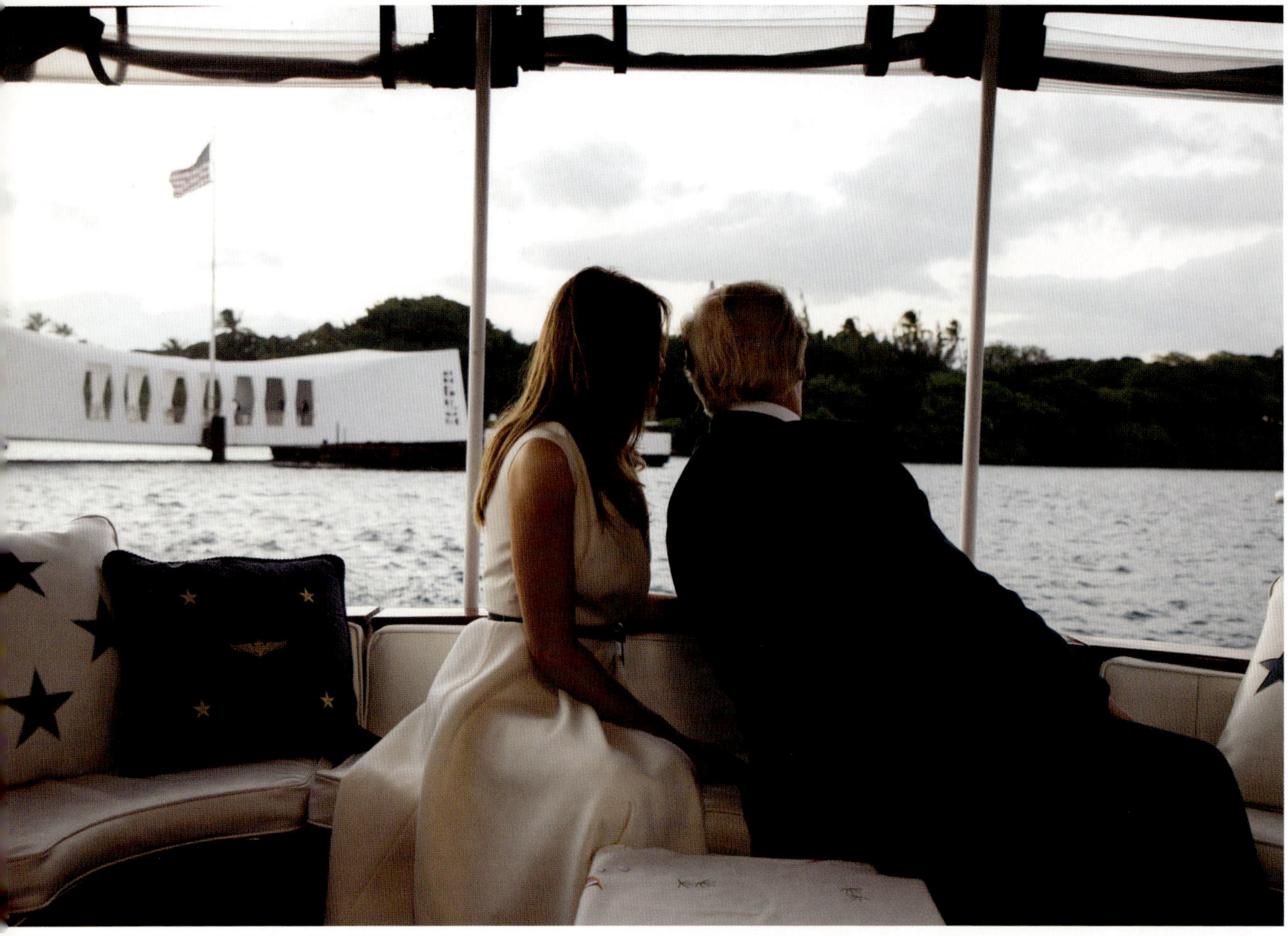

The first couple tour the USS Arizona Memorial in Pearl Harbor Hawaii.[5]

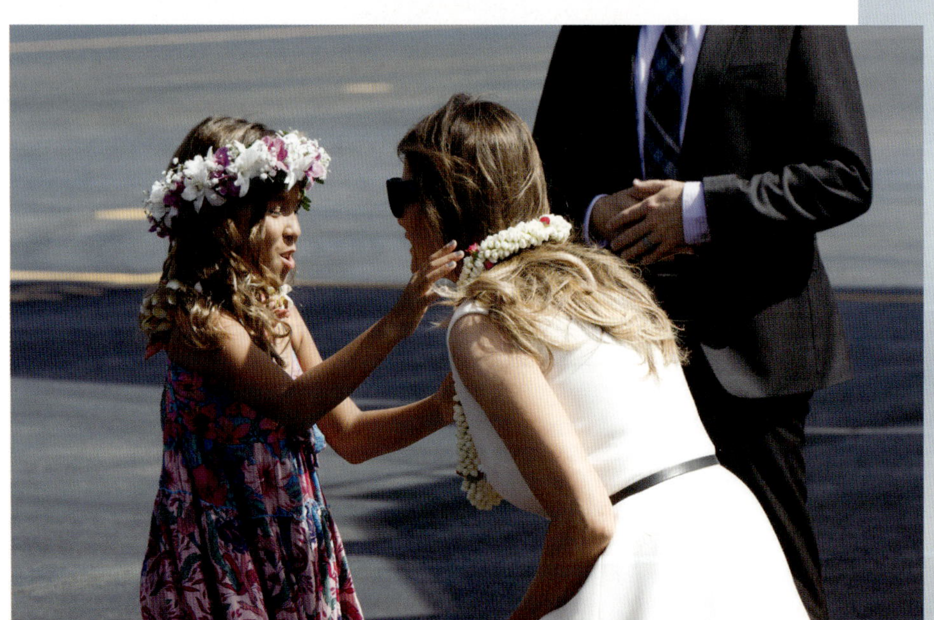

Aloha, Melania! As the Trumps arrive in Hawaii.[6]

Right: Paying homage at the USS Arizona, Pearl Harbor, Honolulu, Hawaii.[14]

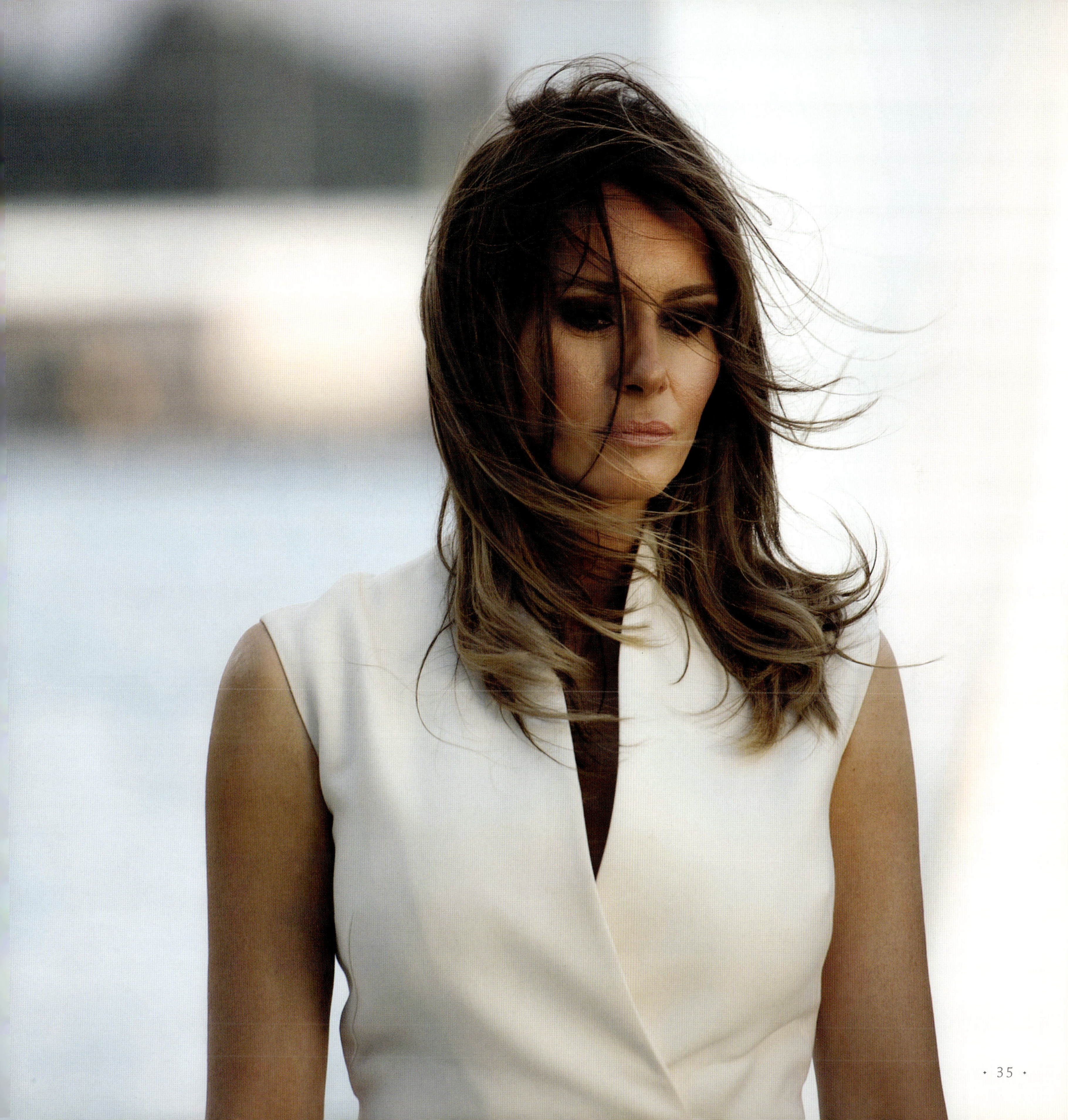

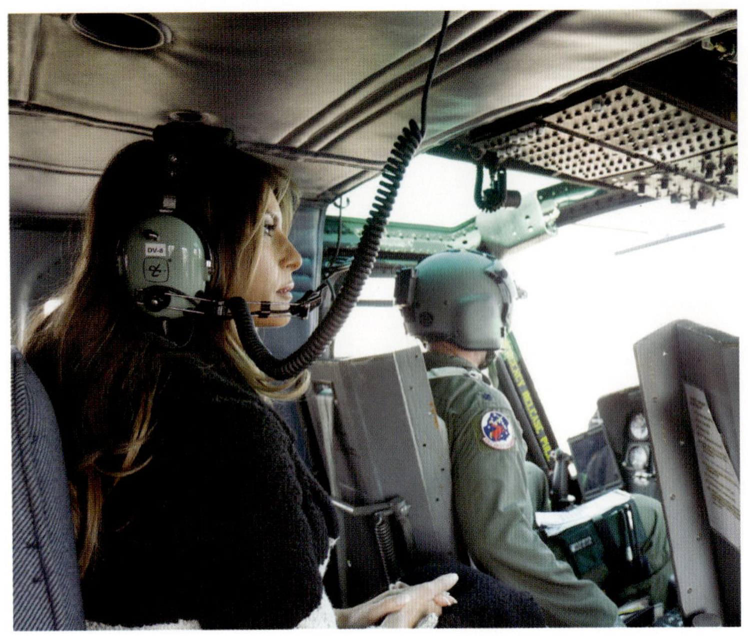

Harbor Chopper Rides![6]

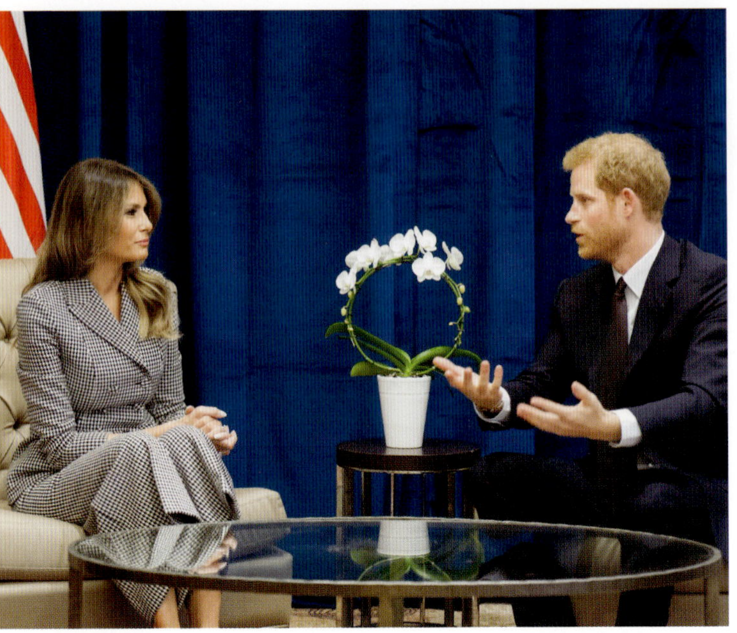

First Lady Melania Trump and Prince Harry at the Invictus Games, which were started by Prince Harry for wounded and ill soldiers from all over the world.[6]

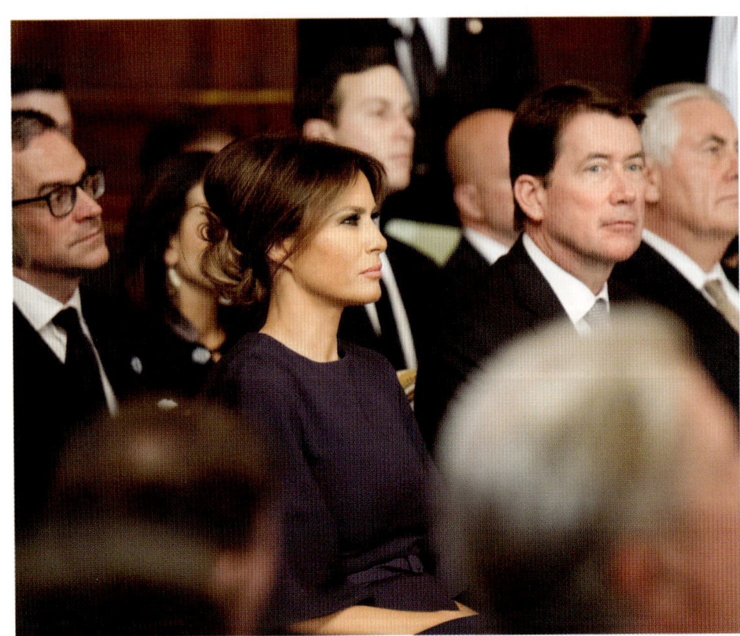

Sitting with dignitaries in Japan.[6]

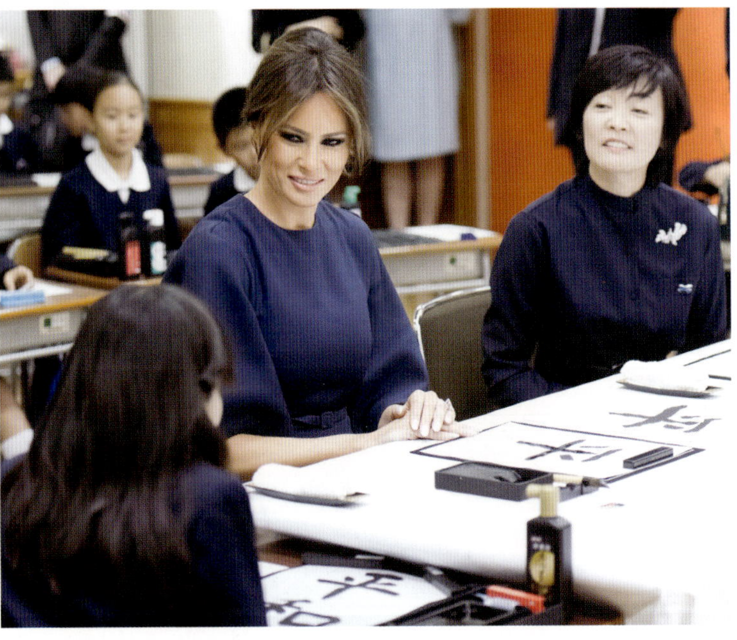

Melania goes back to school in Japan![6]

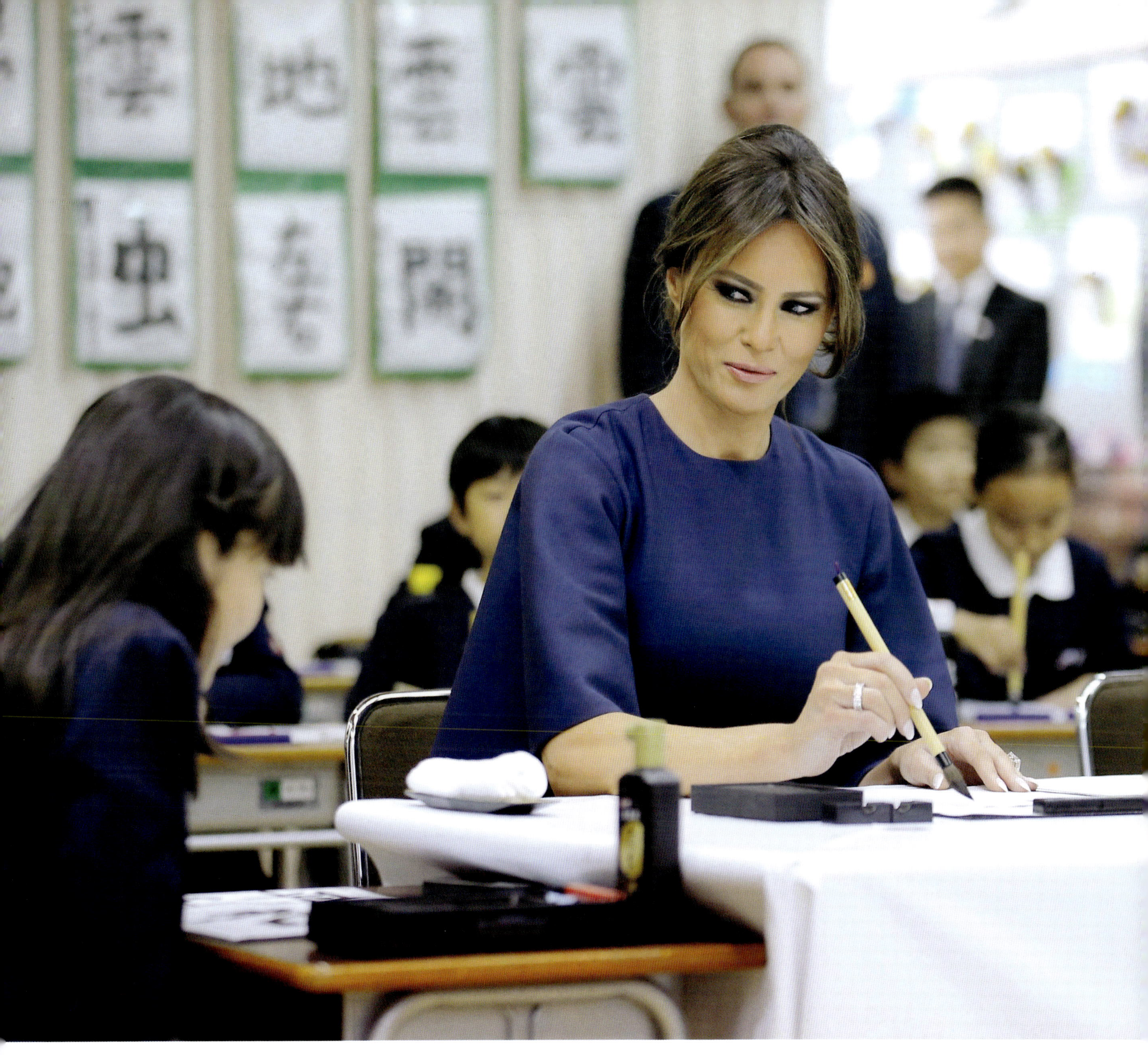

The First Lady learns calligraphy from students in Japan.[15]

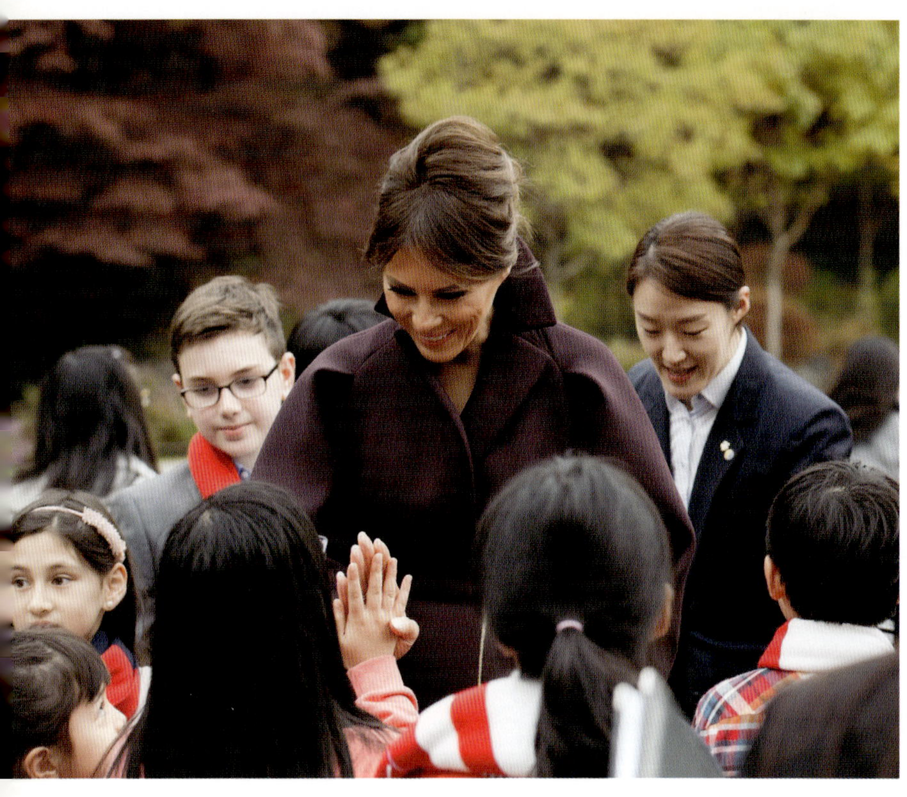

High fives and smiles with children in Asia.[6]

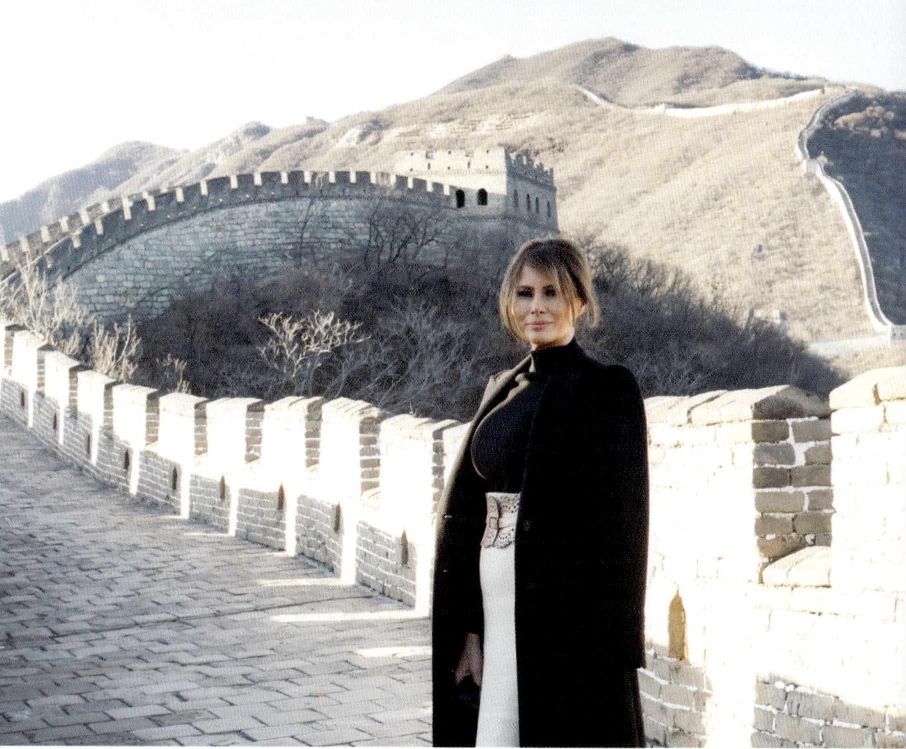

Melania visits China.[6]

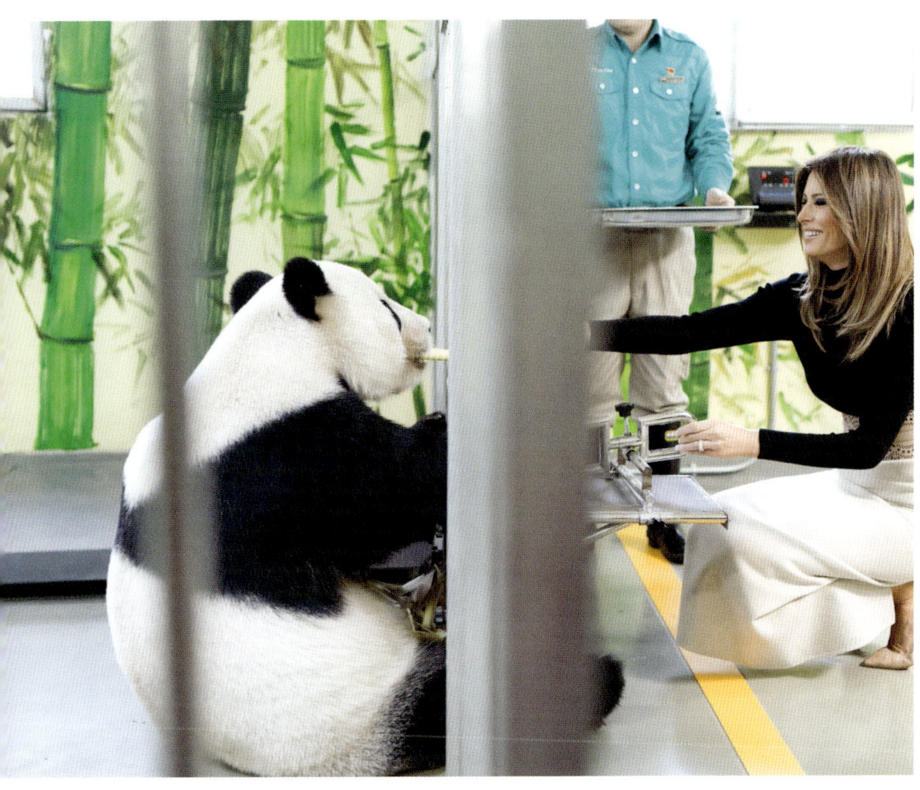

Party time with pandas.[6]

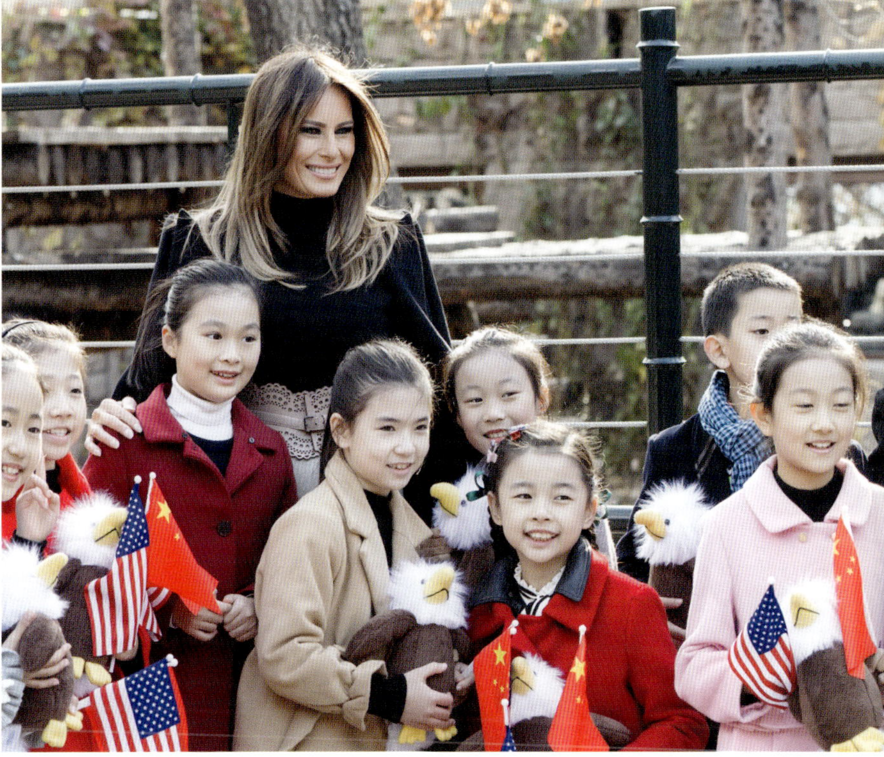

Eagles, smiles, and flags.[6]

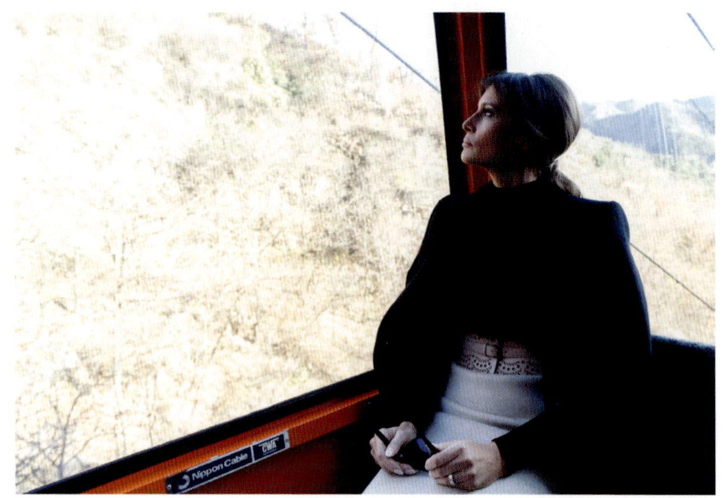

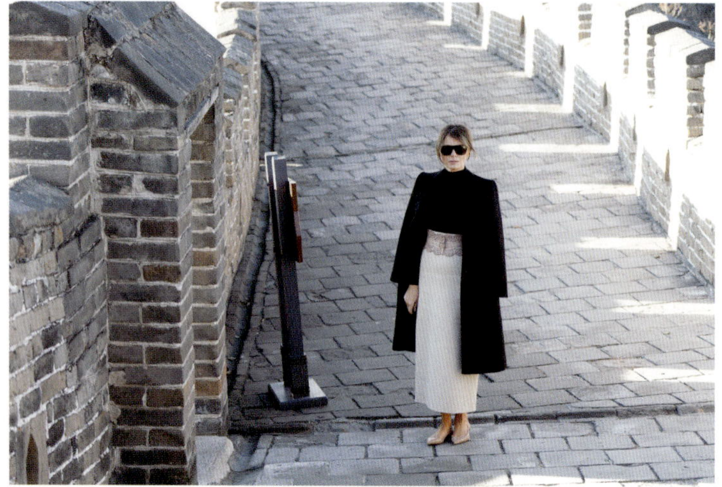

Contemplation.[6]

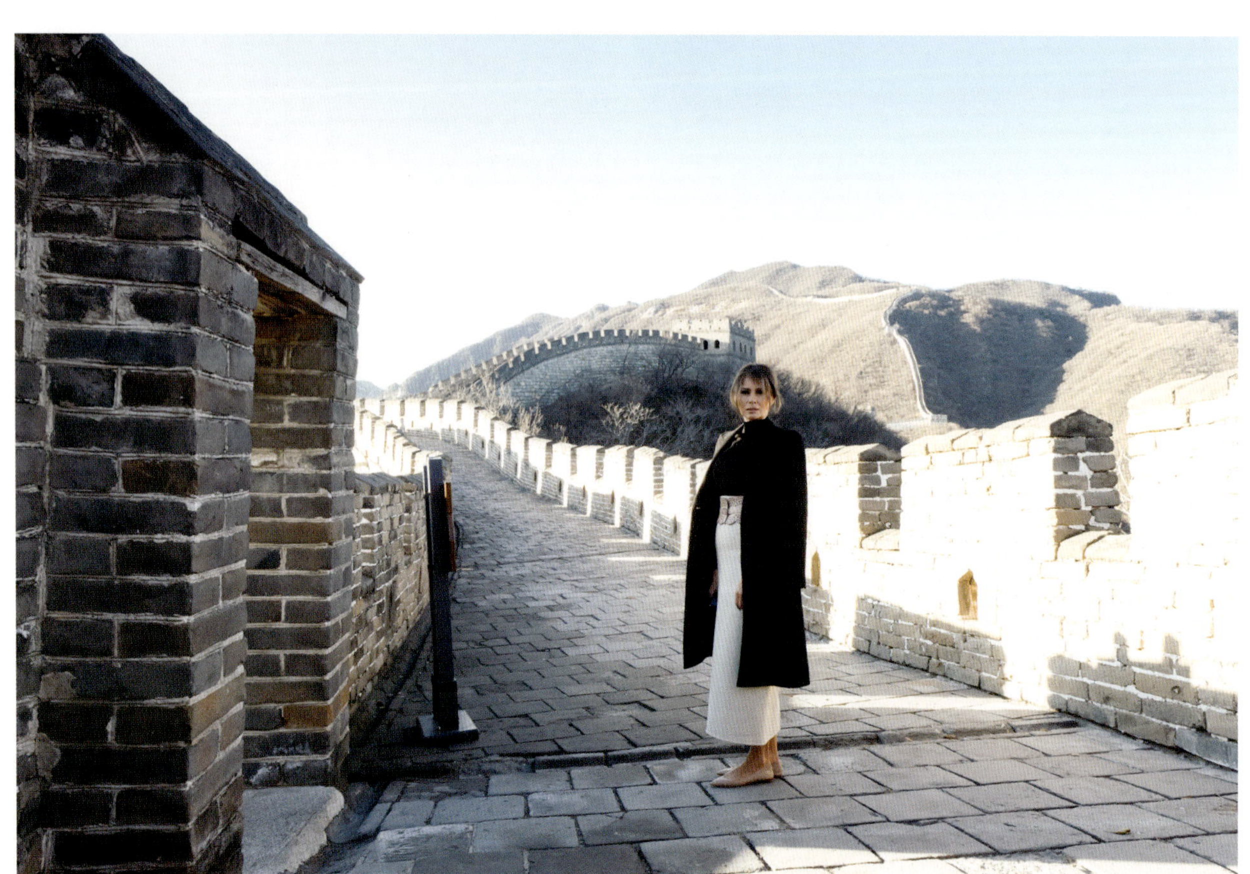

On the Great Wall.[6]

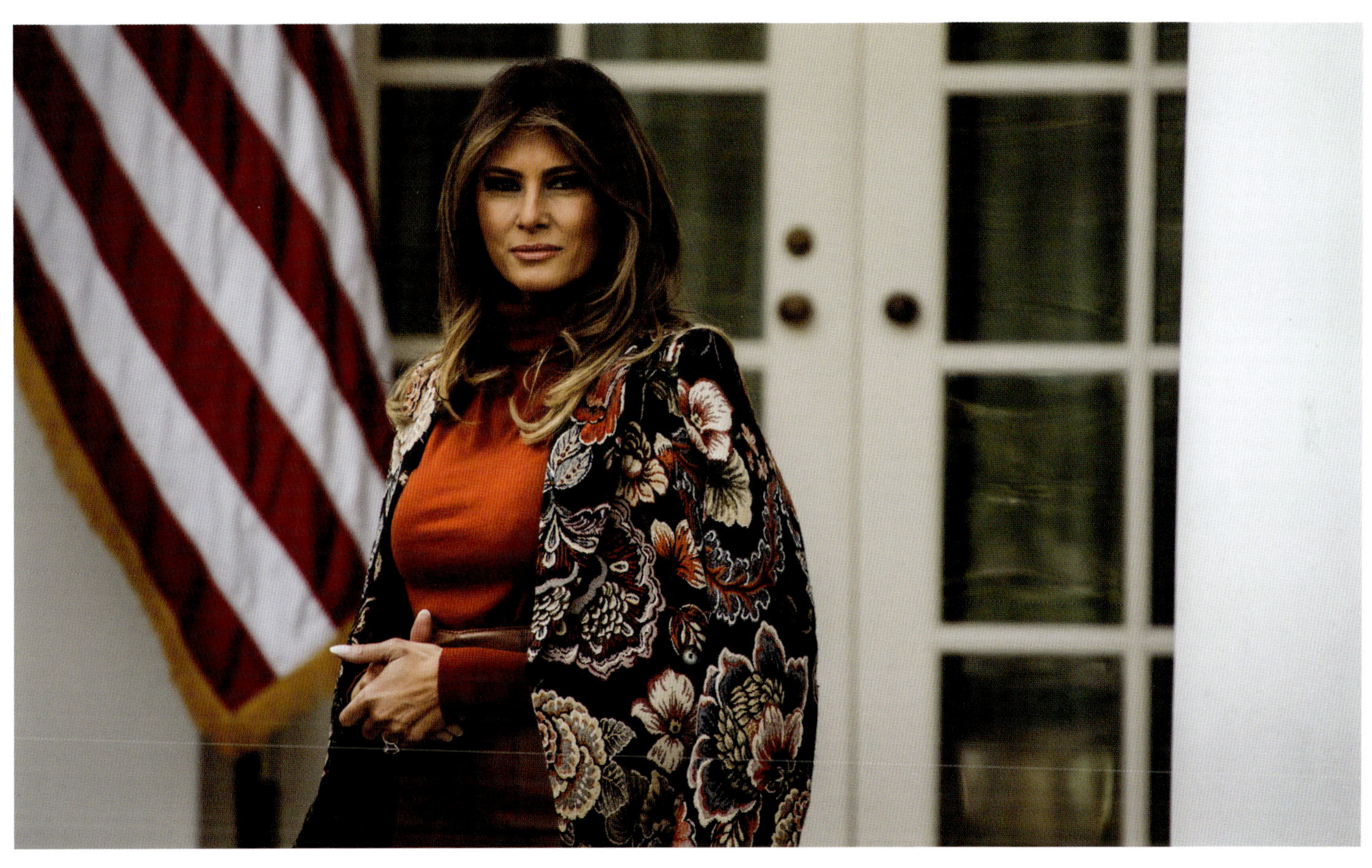

On Thanksgiving, a turkey is pardoned on Melania's watch during the annual pardoning ceremony at the White House.[16]

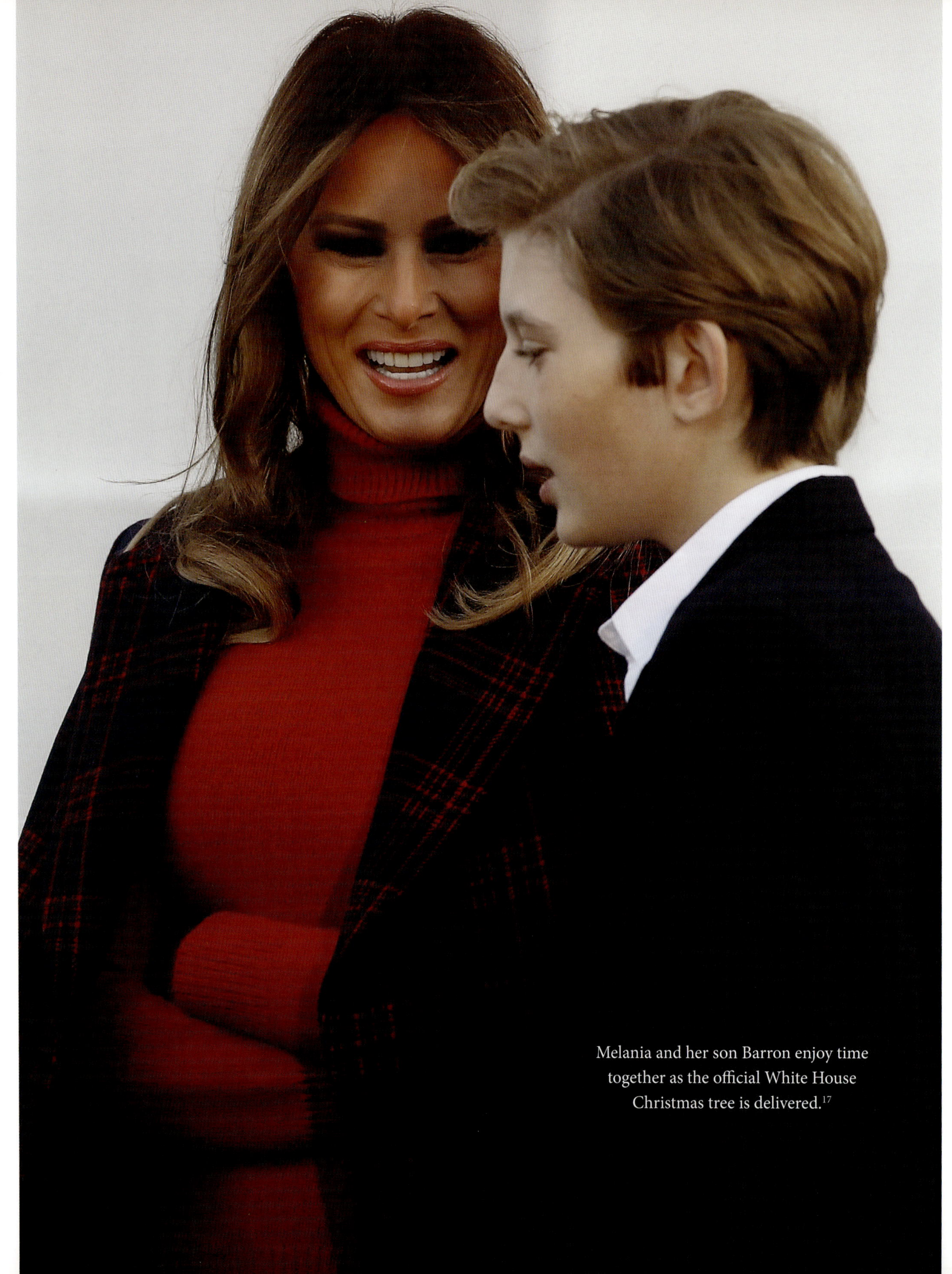

Melania and her son Barron enjoy time together as the official White House Christmas tree is delivered.[17]

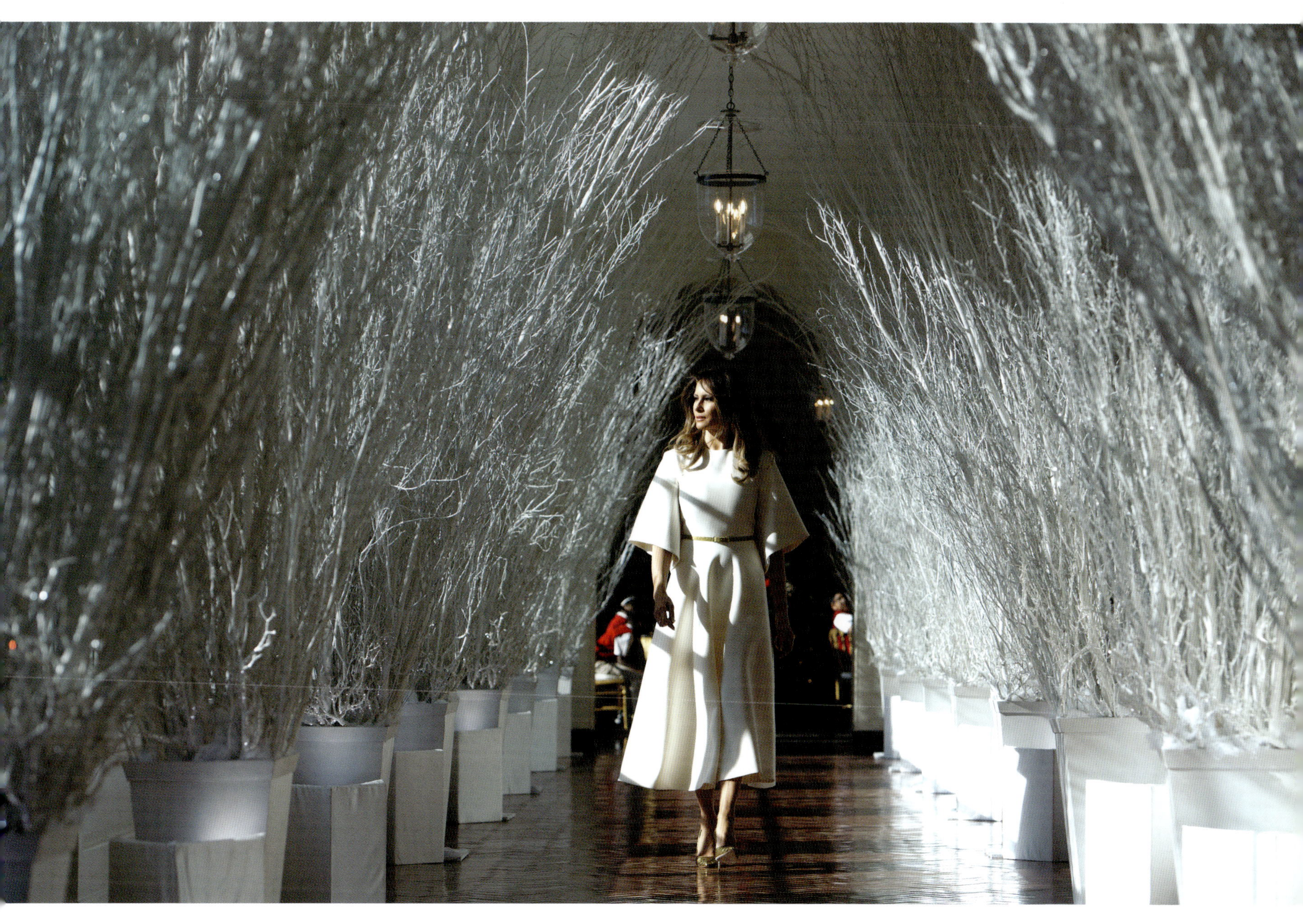

Mrs. Trump inspects the new Christmas decorations in the White House.[18]

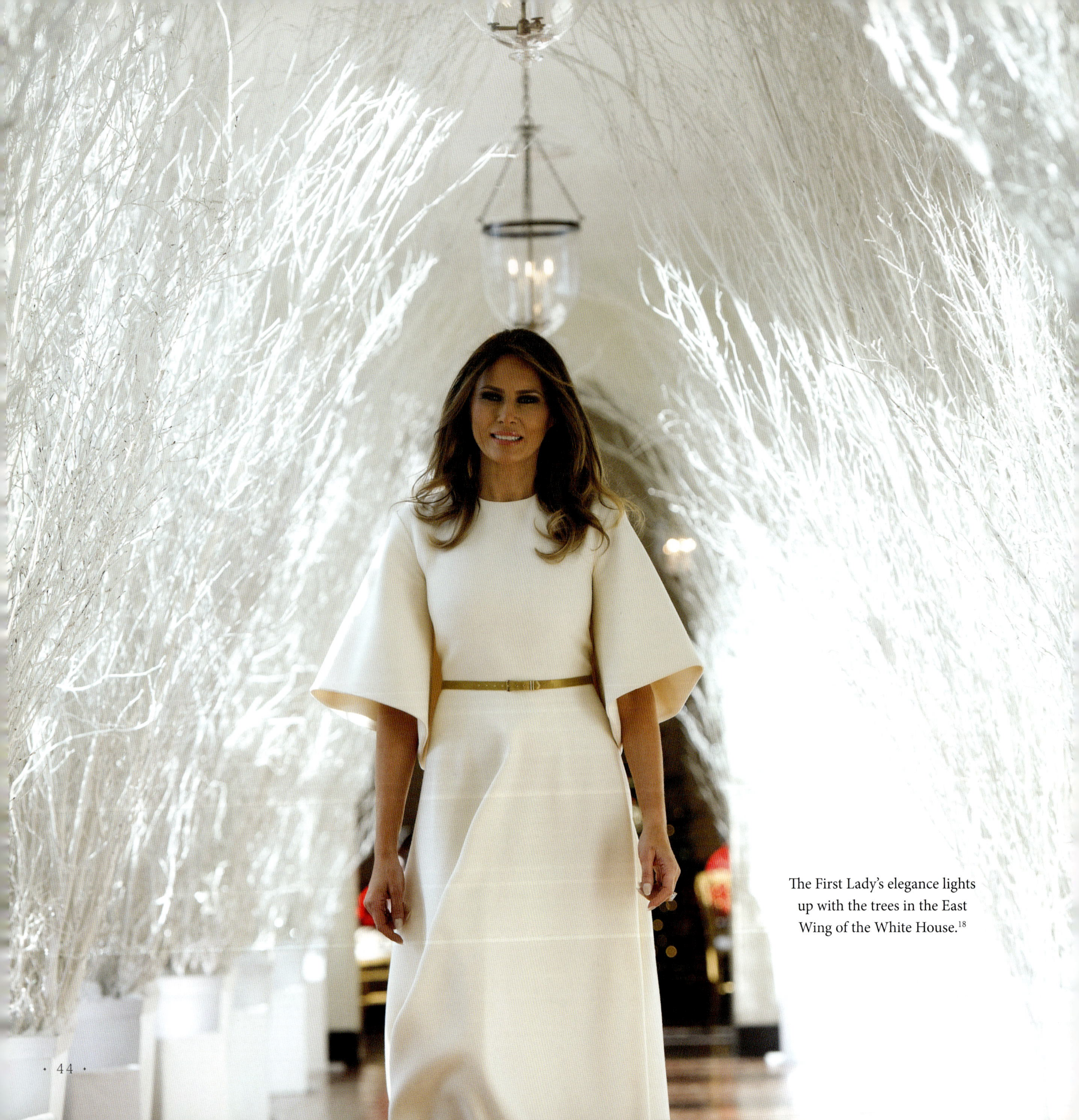

The First Lady's elegance lights up with the trees in the East Wing of the White House.[18]

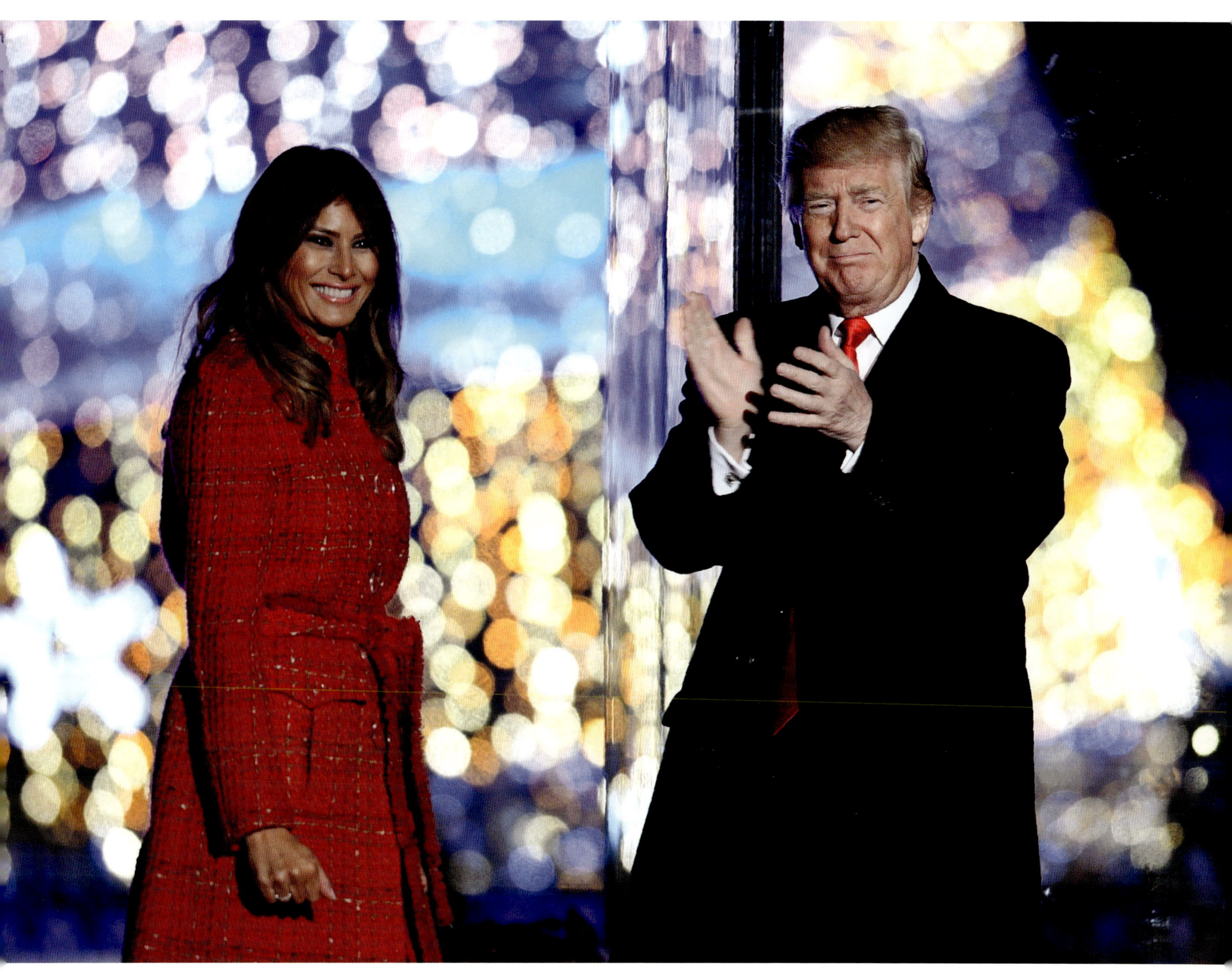

The President and First Lady preside over the annual Christmas tree lighting ceremony.[14]

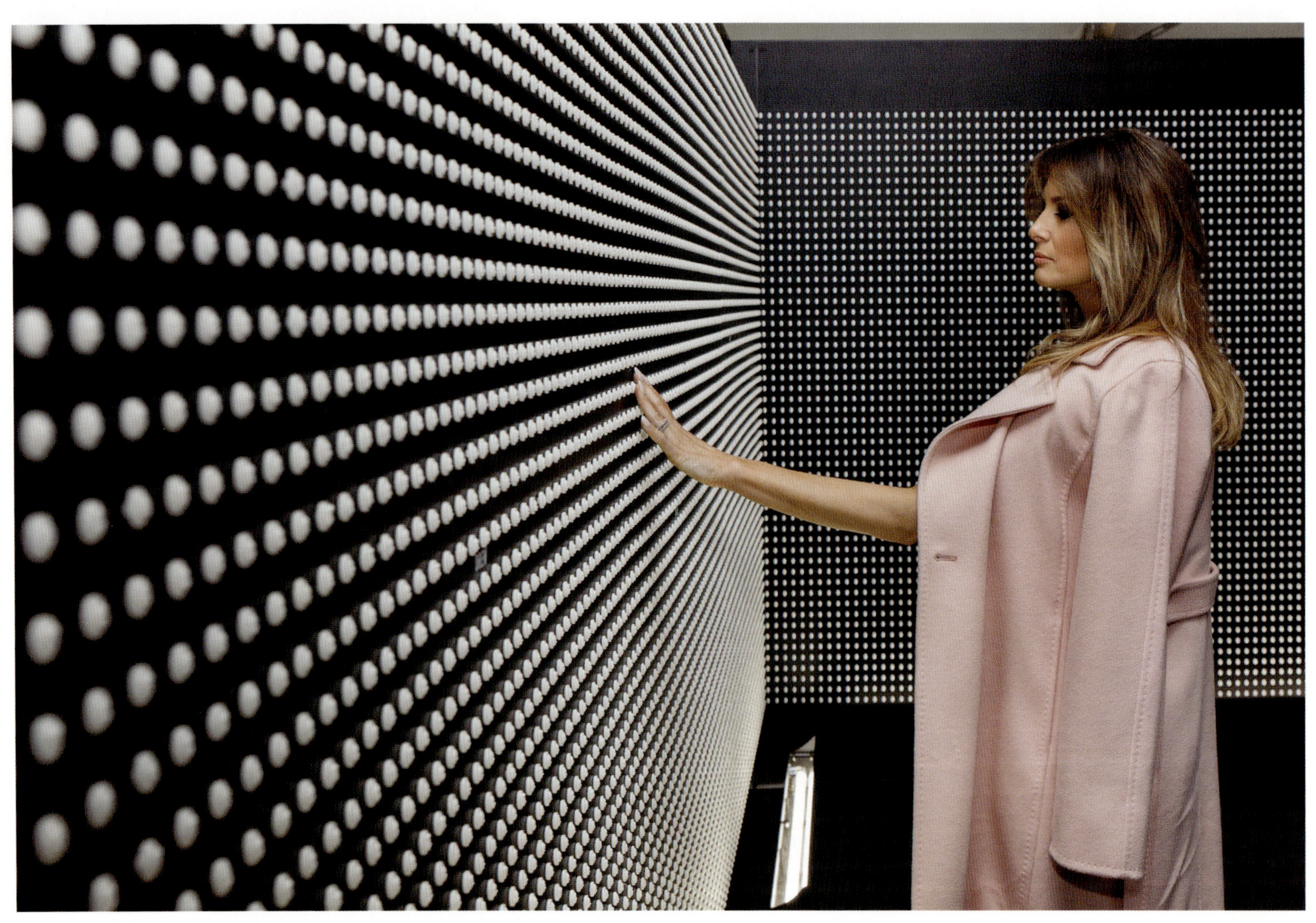

At the "Prescribed to Death" opioid memorial.[6]

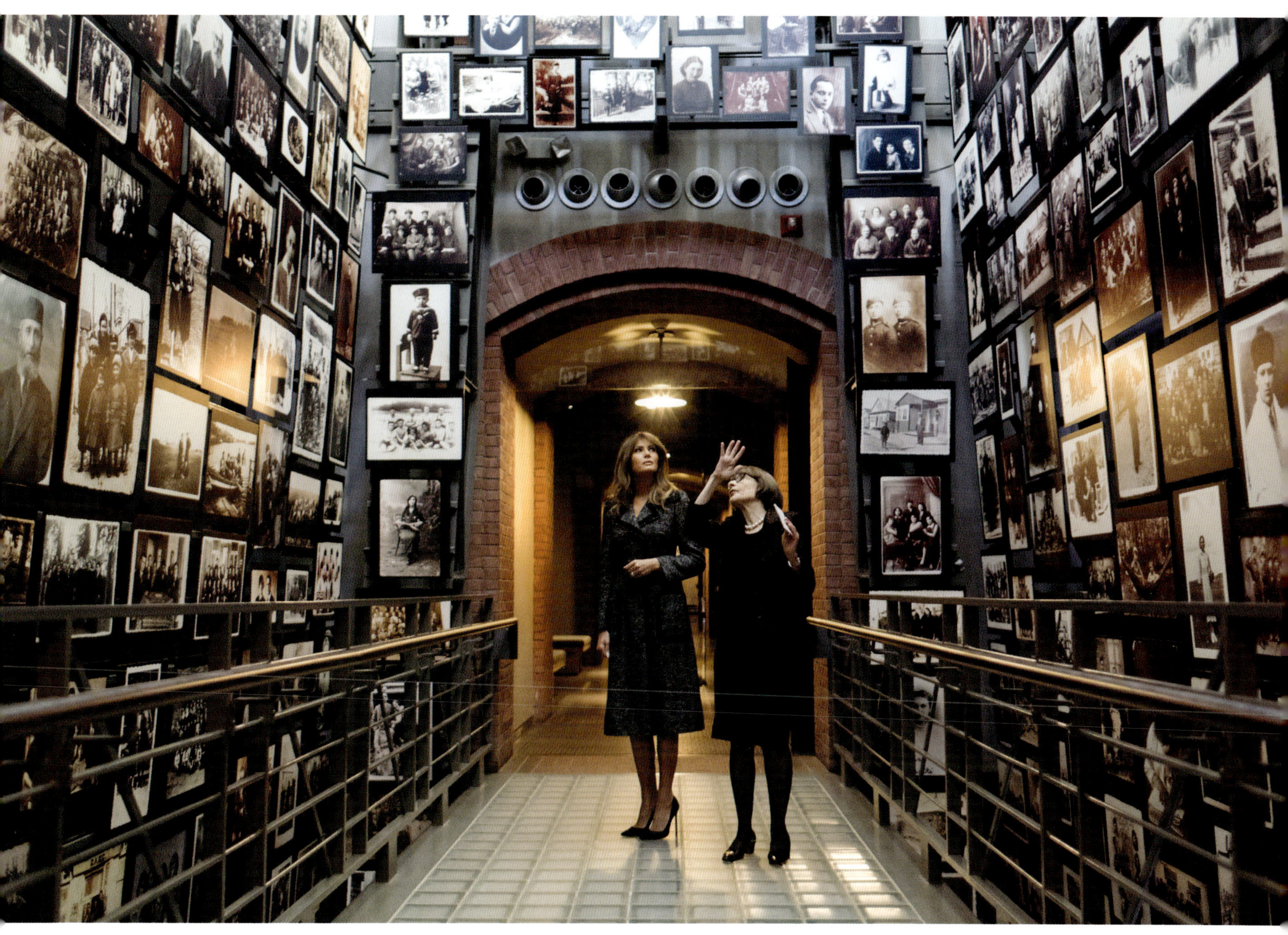

Visiting the Holocaust Memorial Museum.[6]

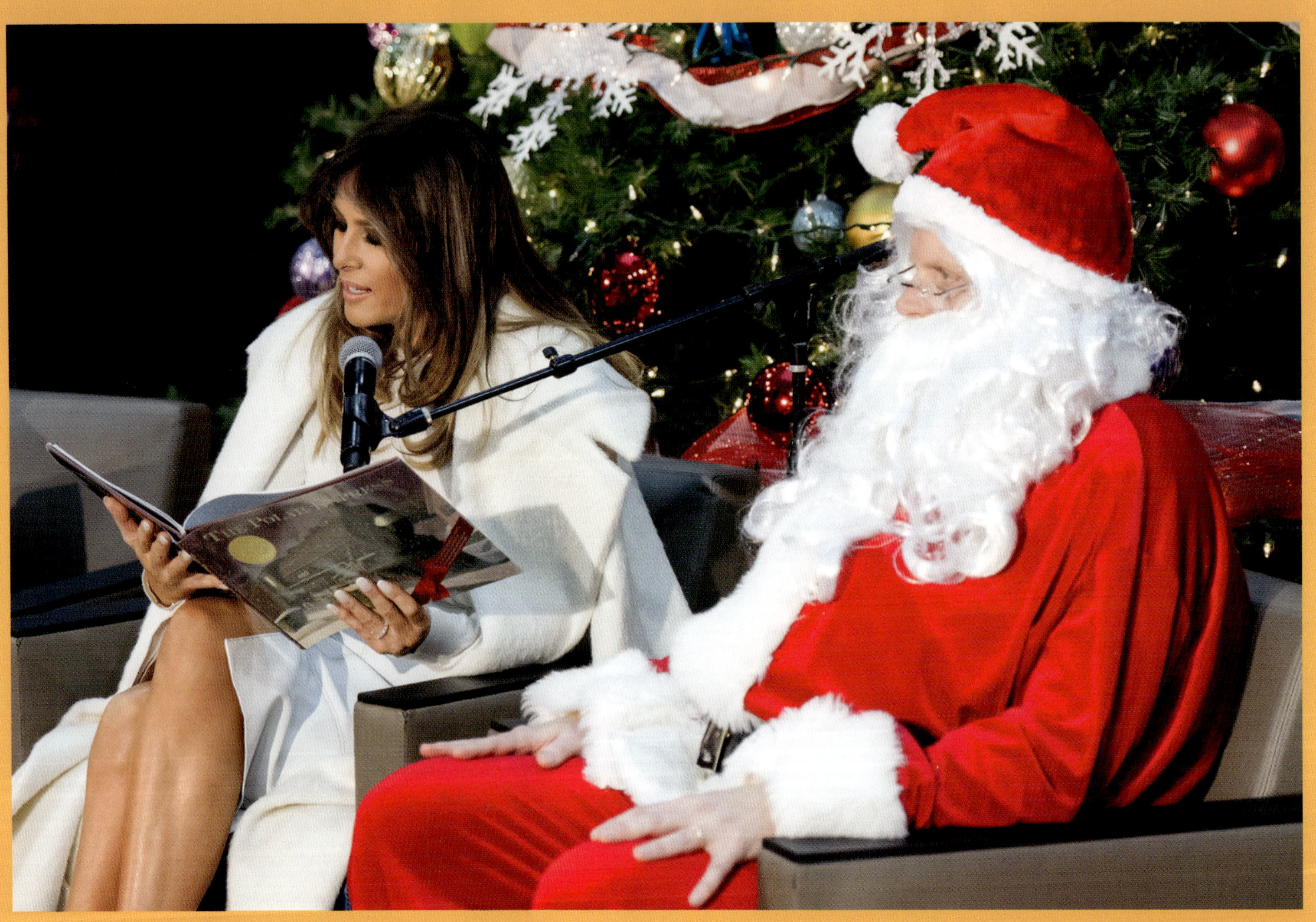

Reading *The Polar Express* with Santa Claus for Christmas at Children's National Hospital.[6]

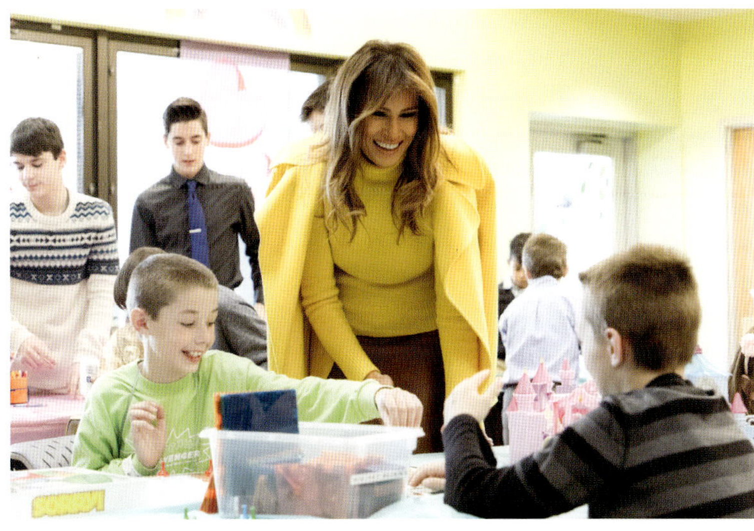

Arts, crafts, and smiles at Cincinnati Memorial Hospital.[6]

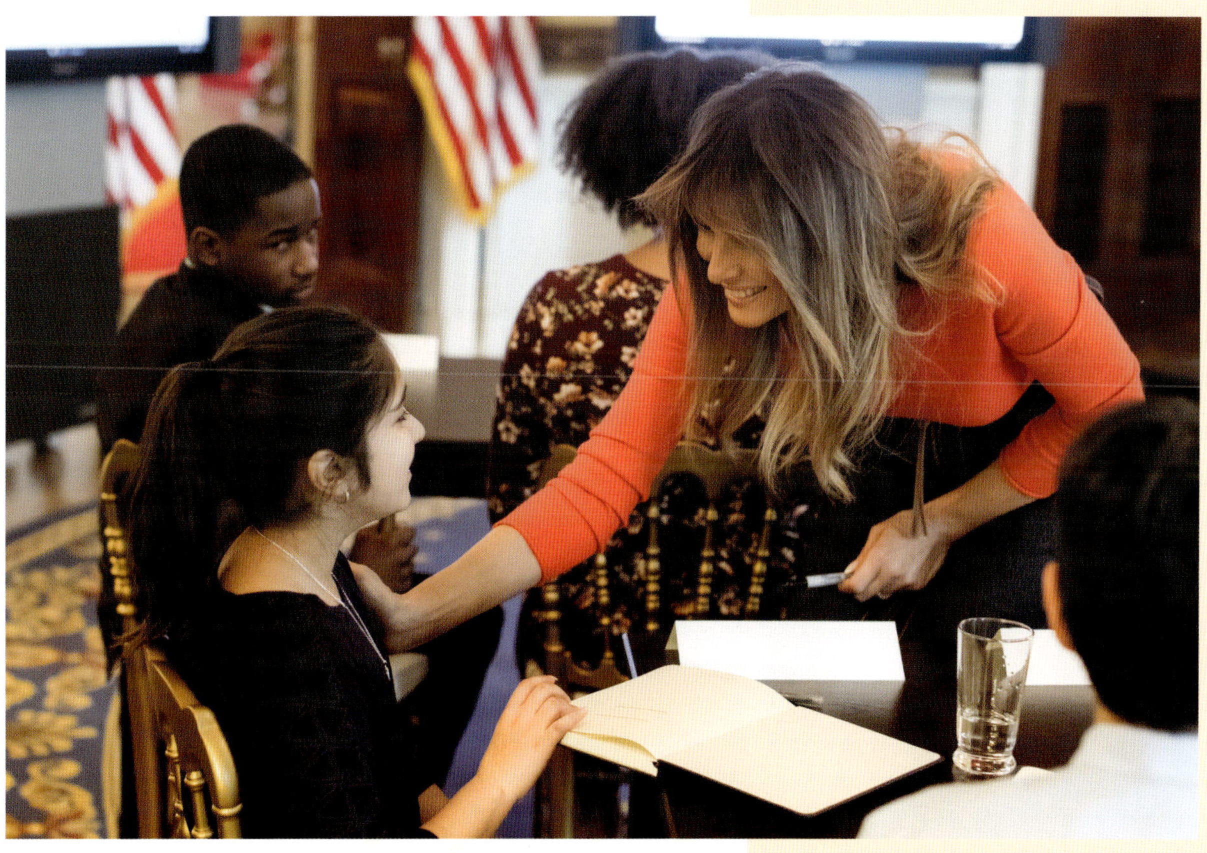

Chatting with students.[6]

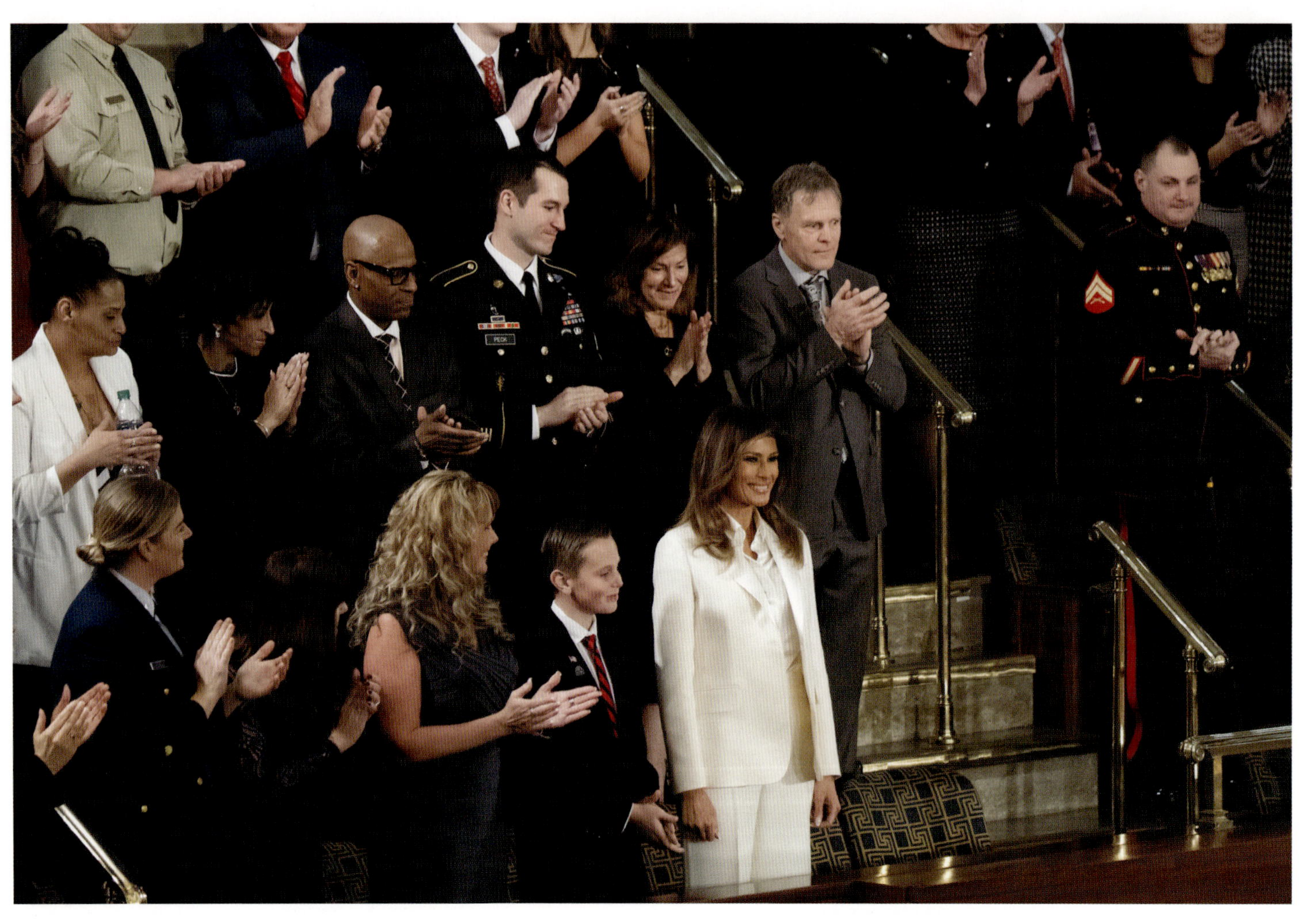

Elegance wears Dior and a tan at the 2018 State of the Union Address.[6]

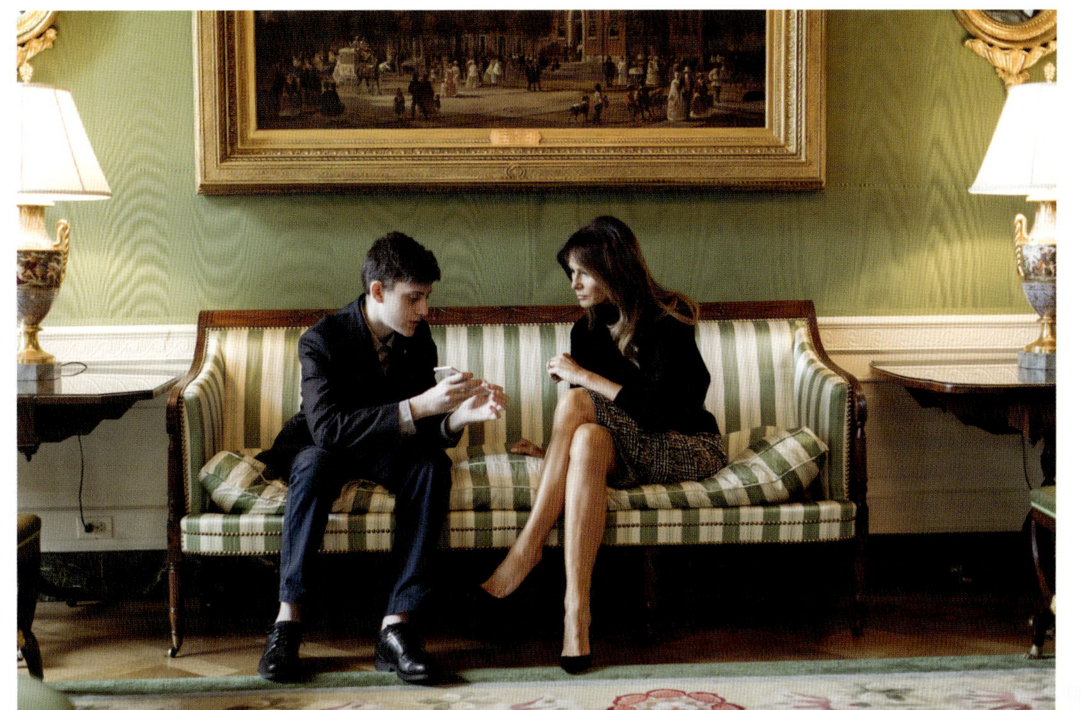

The First Lady and Marjory Stoneman Douglas High School shooting survivor, Kyle Kashuv.[6]

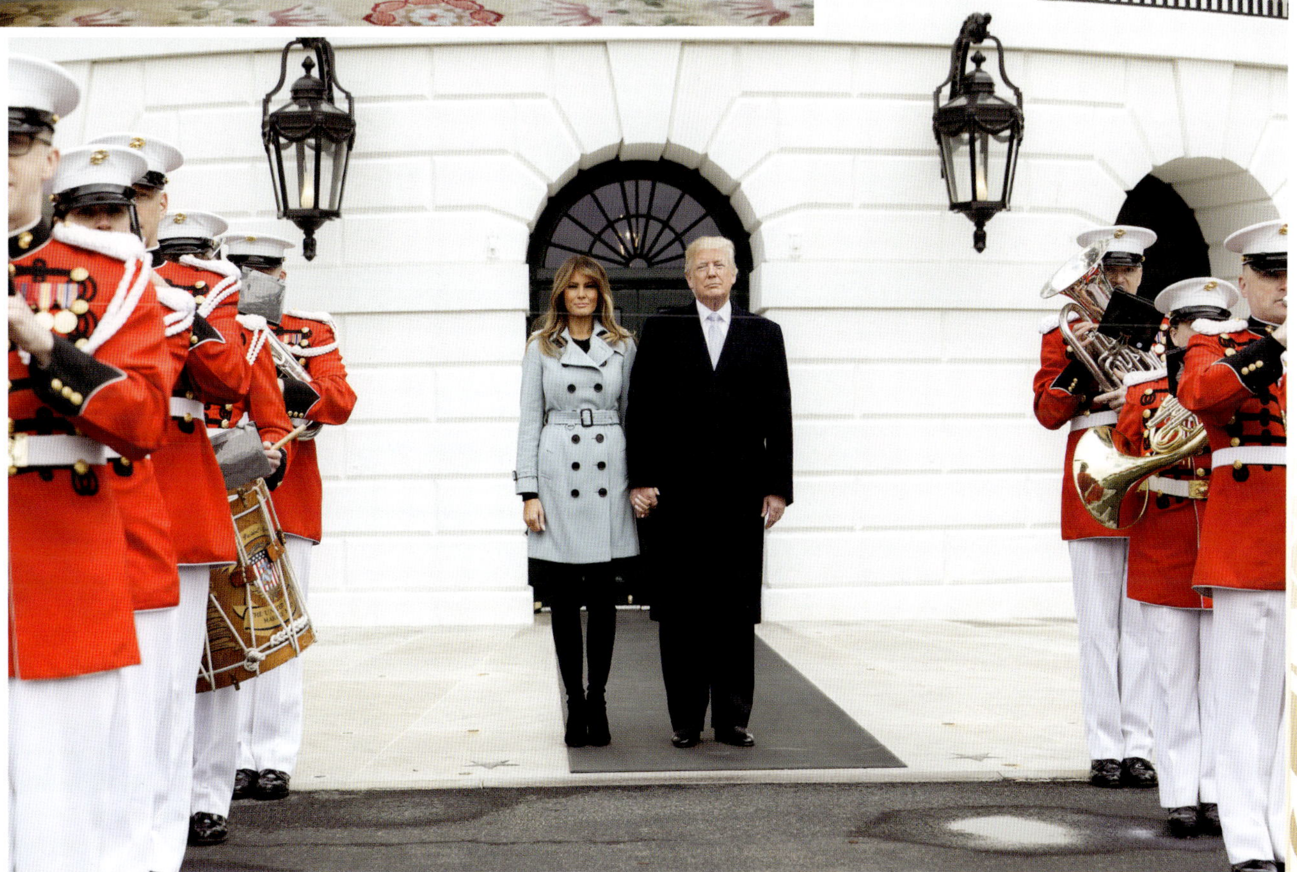

Another year of Easter Egg Rolling![6]

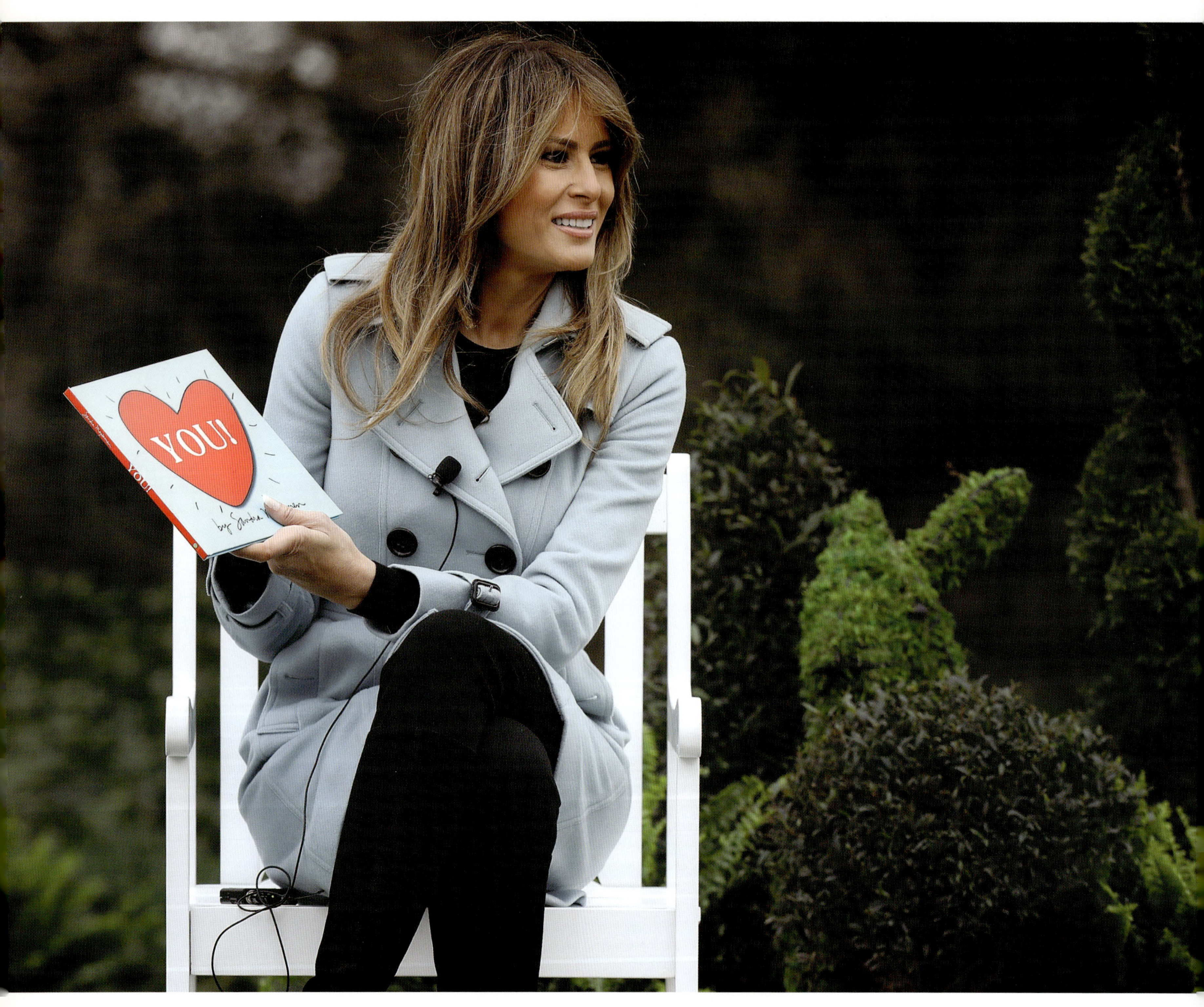

Melania has her heart on her sleeve and a gorgeous smile.[19]

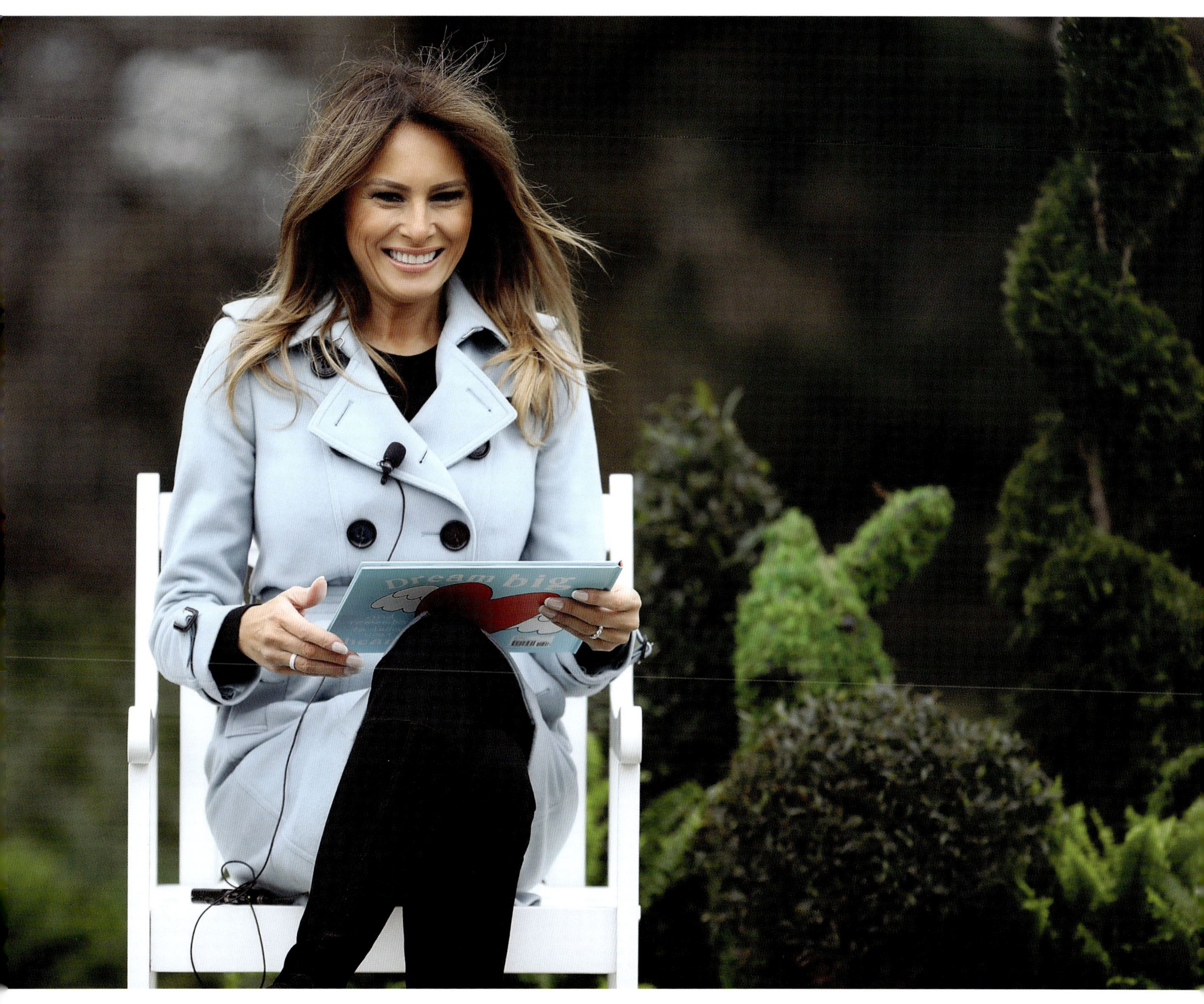

Mrs. Trump reads the book *You!* by Sandra Magsamen during the 140th annual Easter Egg Roll on the South Lawn of the White House, April 2, 2018, in Washington, DC. The tradition was begun in 1878 by President Rutherford B. Hayes.[3]

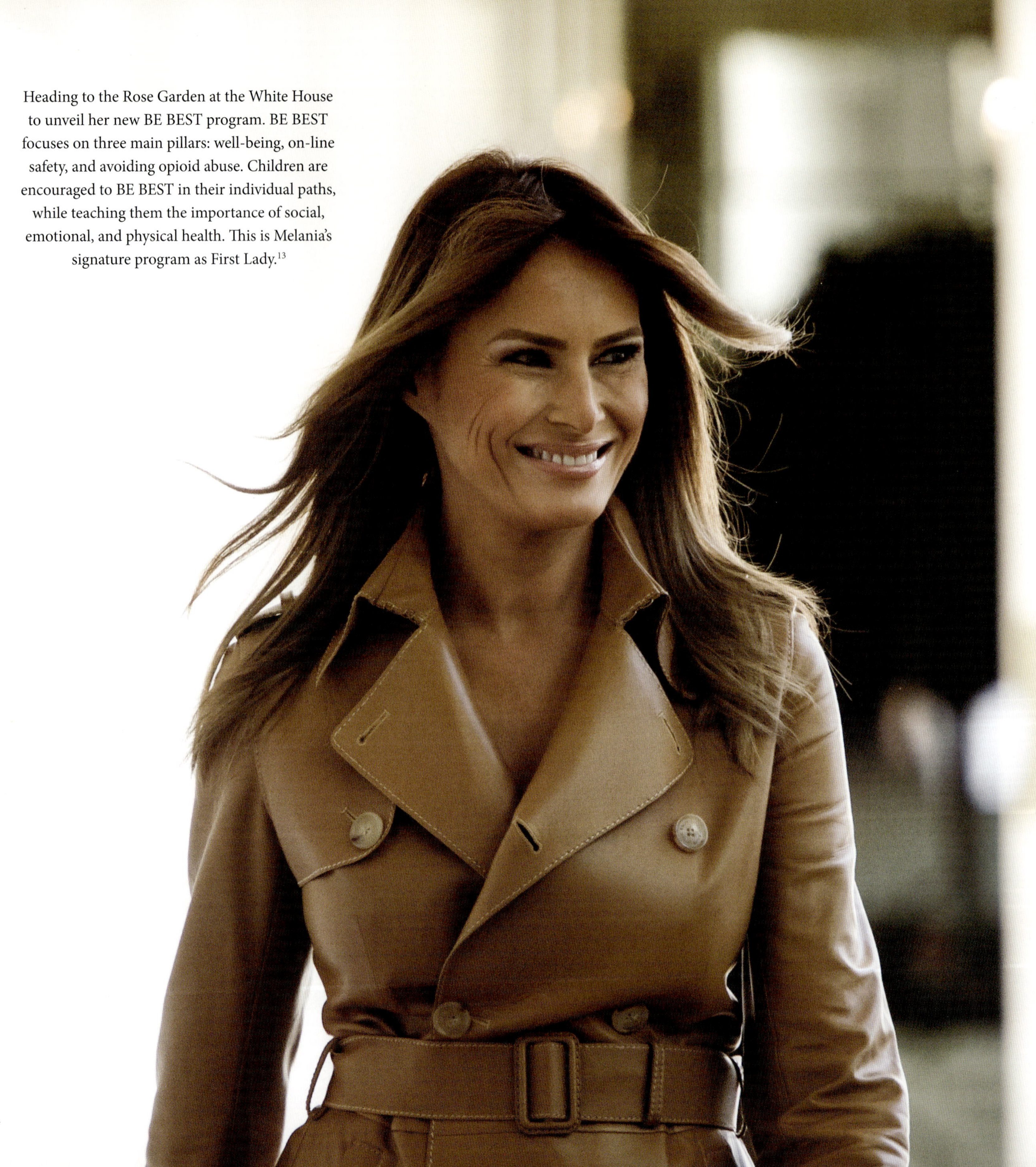

Heading to the Rose Garden at the White House to unveil her new BE BEST program. BE BEST focuses on three main pillars: well-being, on-line safety, and avoiding opioid abuse. Children are encouraged to BE BEST in their individual paths, while teaching them the importance of social, emotional, and physical health. This is Melania's signature program as First Lady.[13]

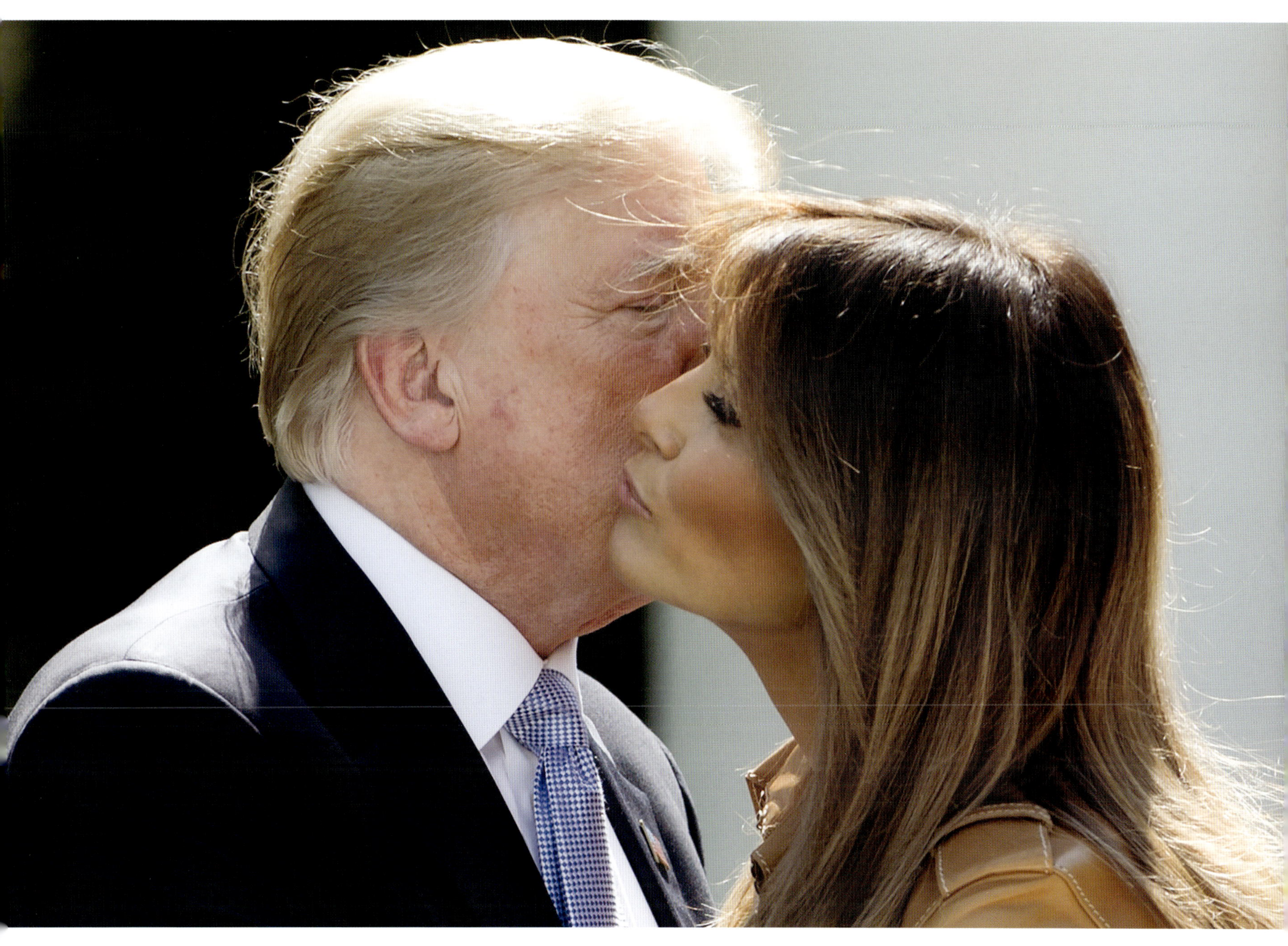

The President gives Melania some moral support before she unveils her BE BEST program.[18]

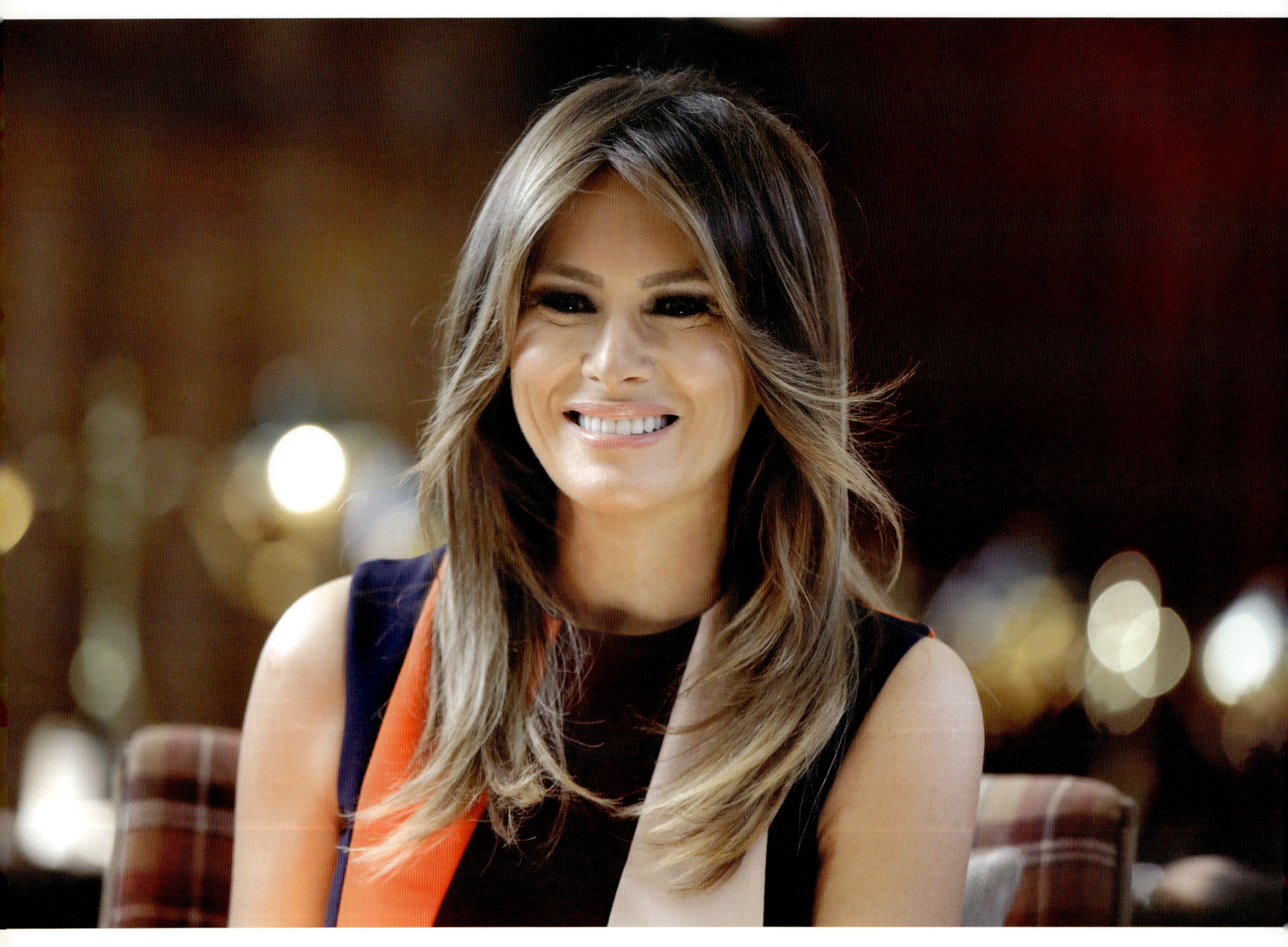

Visiting the Chelsea Pensioners, British Army Personnel who are retired and taken care of at the Royal Hospital in London.[21]

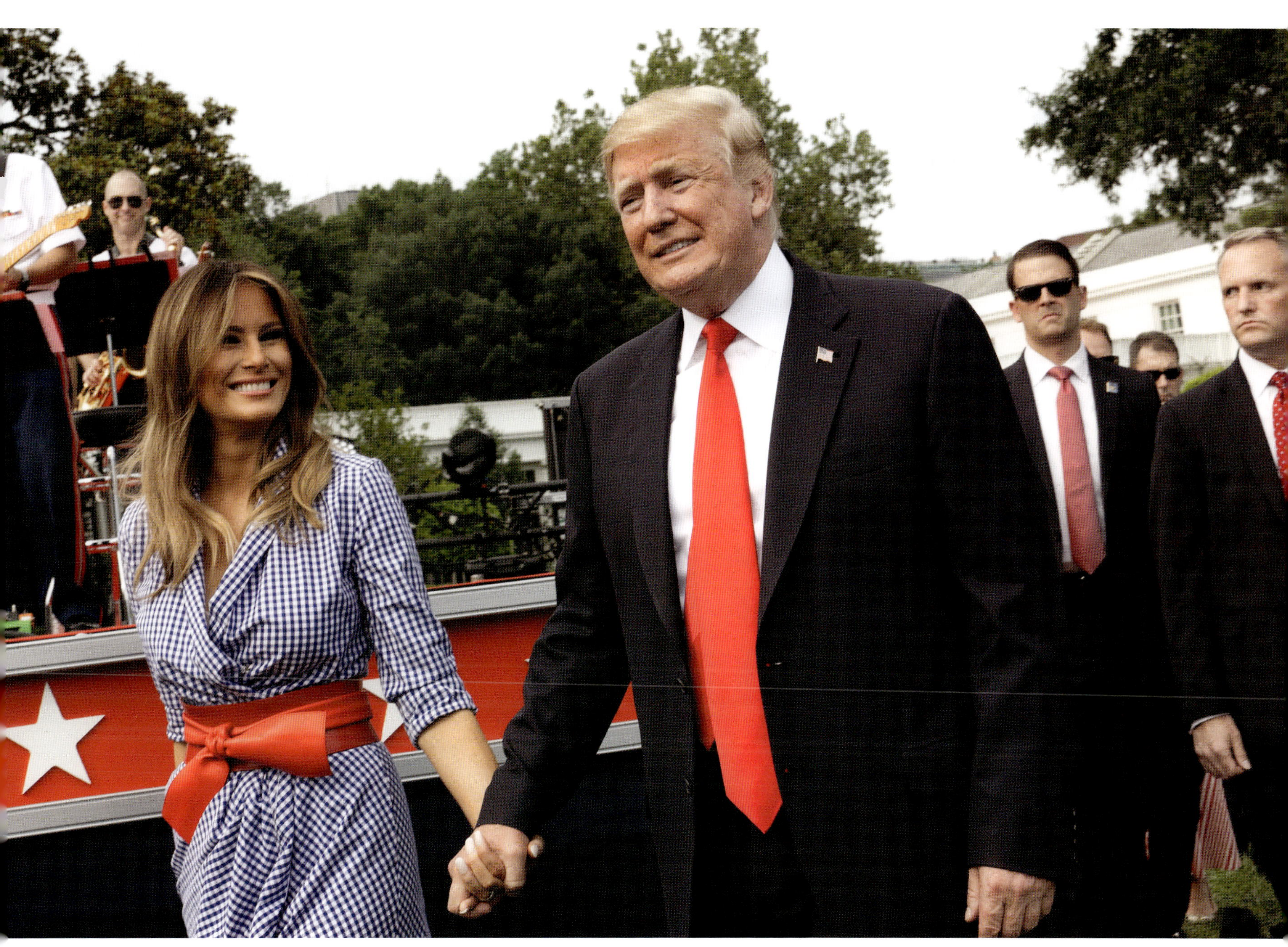

President Donald J. Trump and First Lady Melania Trump participate in a Fourth of July picnic with military families at the White House, July 4, 2018.[6]

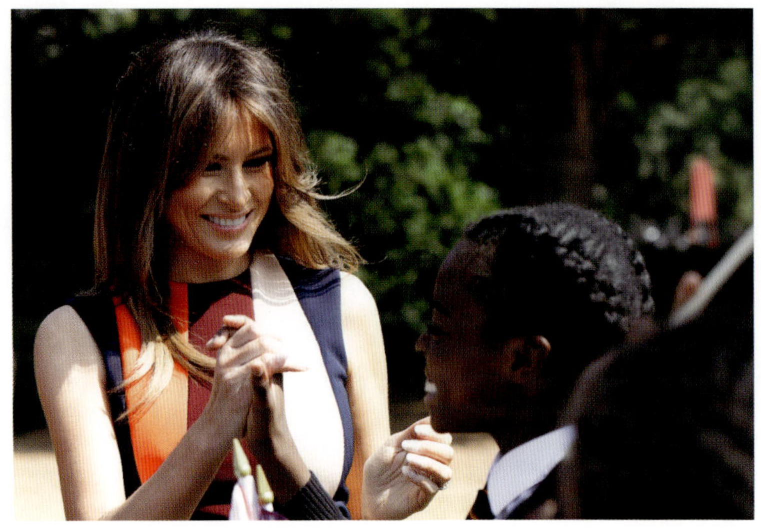

Smiles all around at the Royal Hospital London.[6]

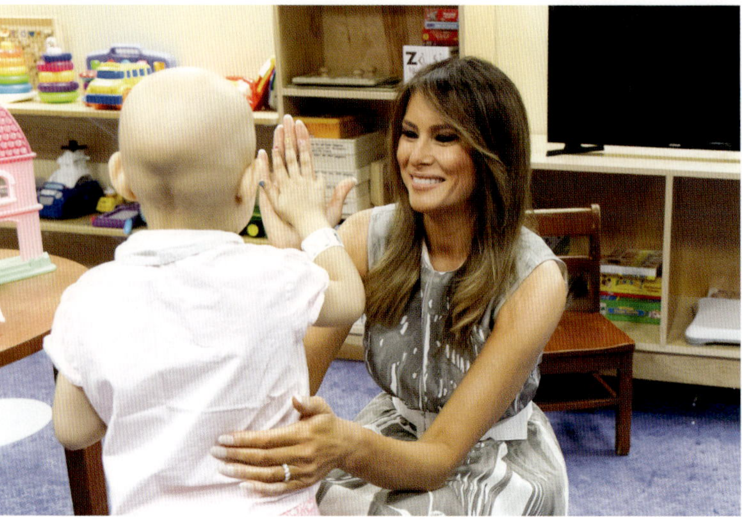

Four-year-old Essence Overton and the First Lady share a high five at the Monroe Carell Jr. Children's Hospital in Nashville, Tennessee.[6]

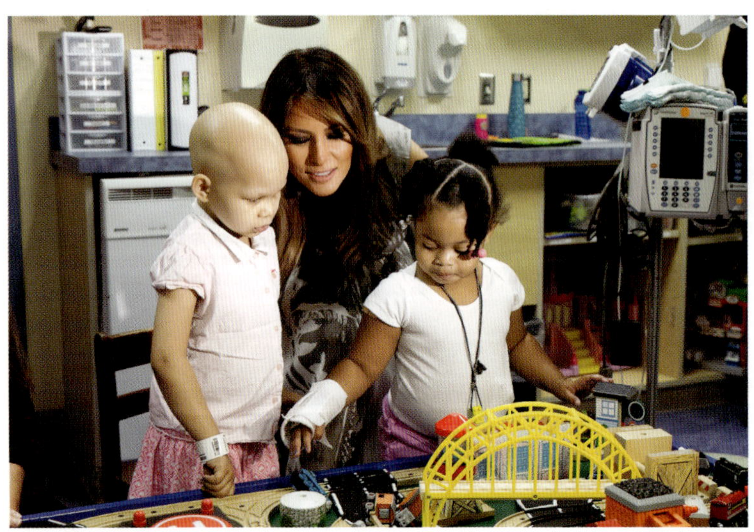

Essence and Natalayah Fields get some quality time with Mrs. Trump at an activities table.[6]

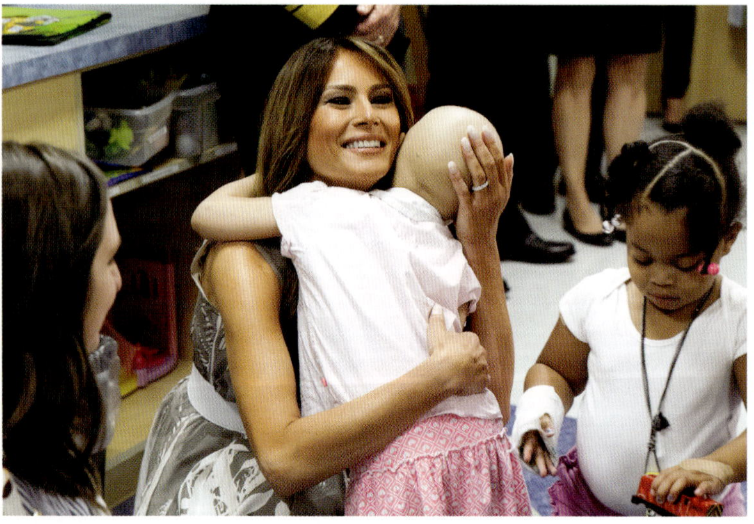

Hugs![6]

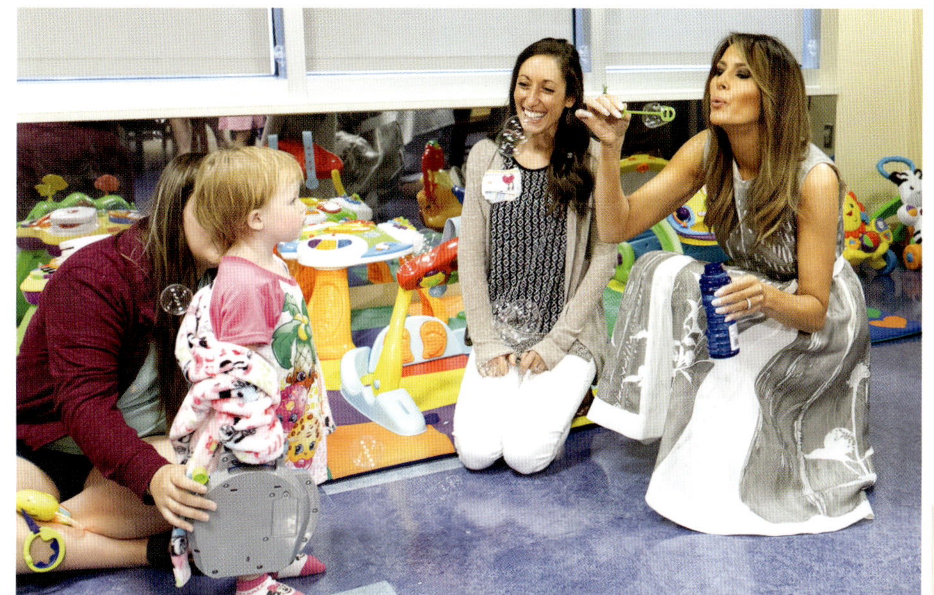

Double bubbles with Elliegh Rasmussen.[6]

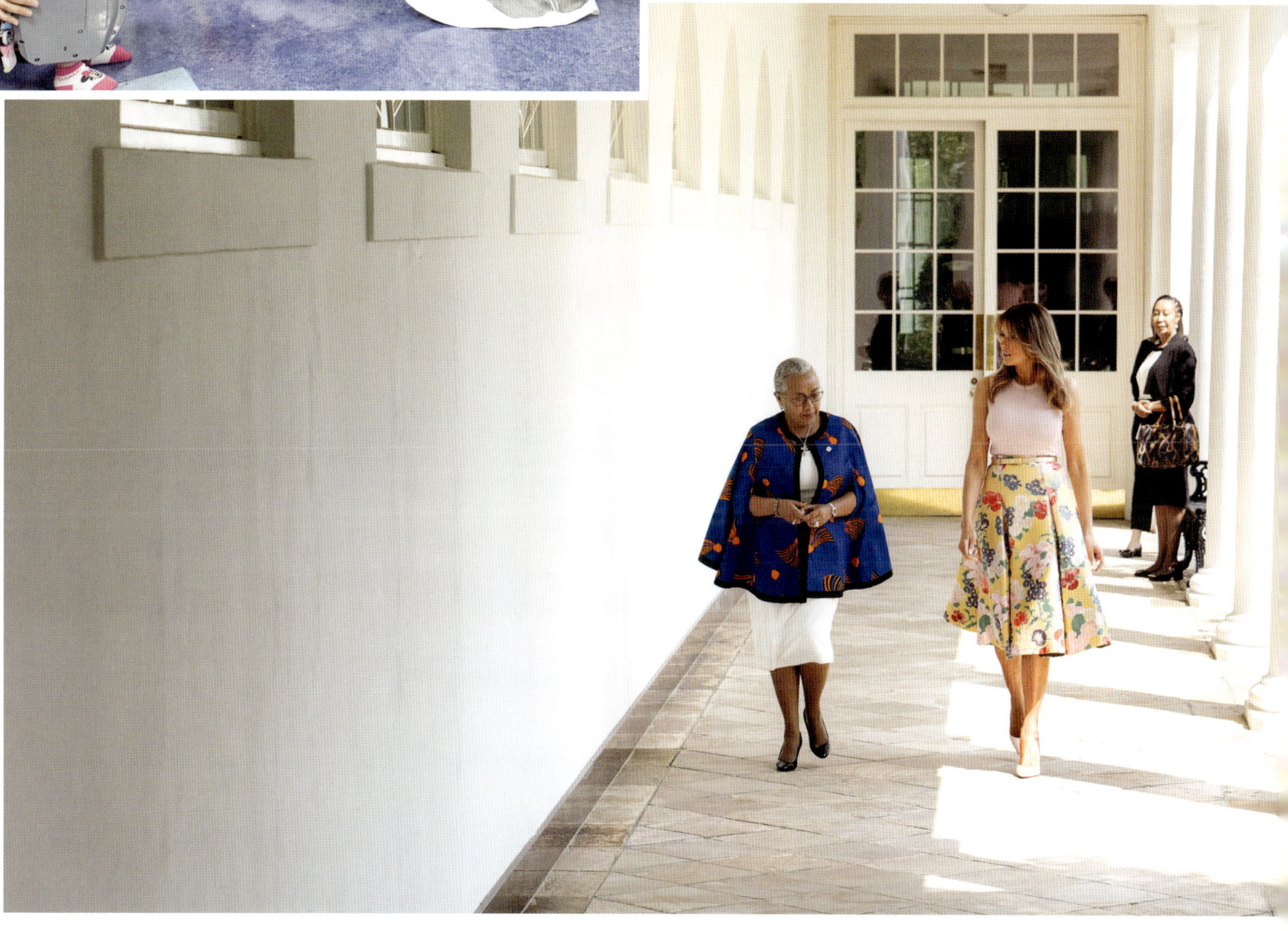

First Lady Melania Trump and Mrs. Kenyatta of the Republic of Kenya.[6]

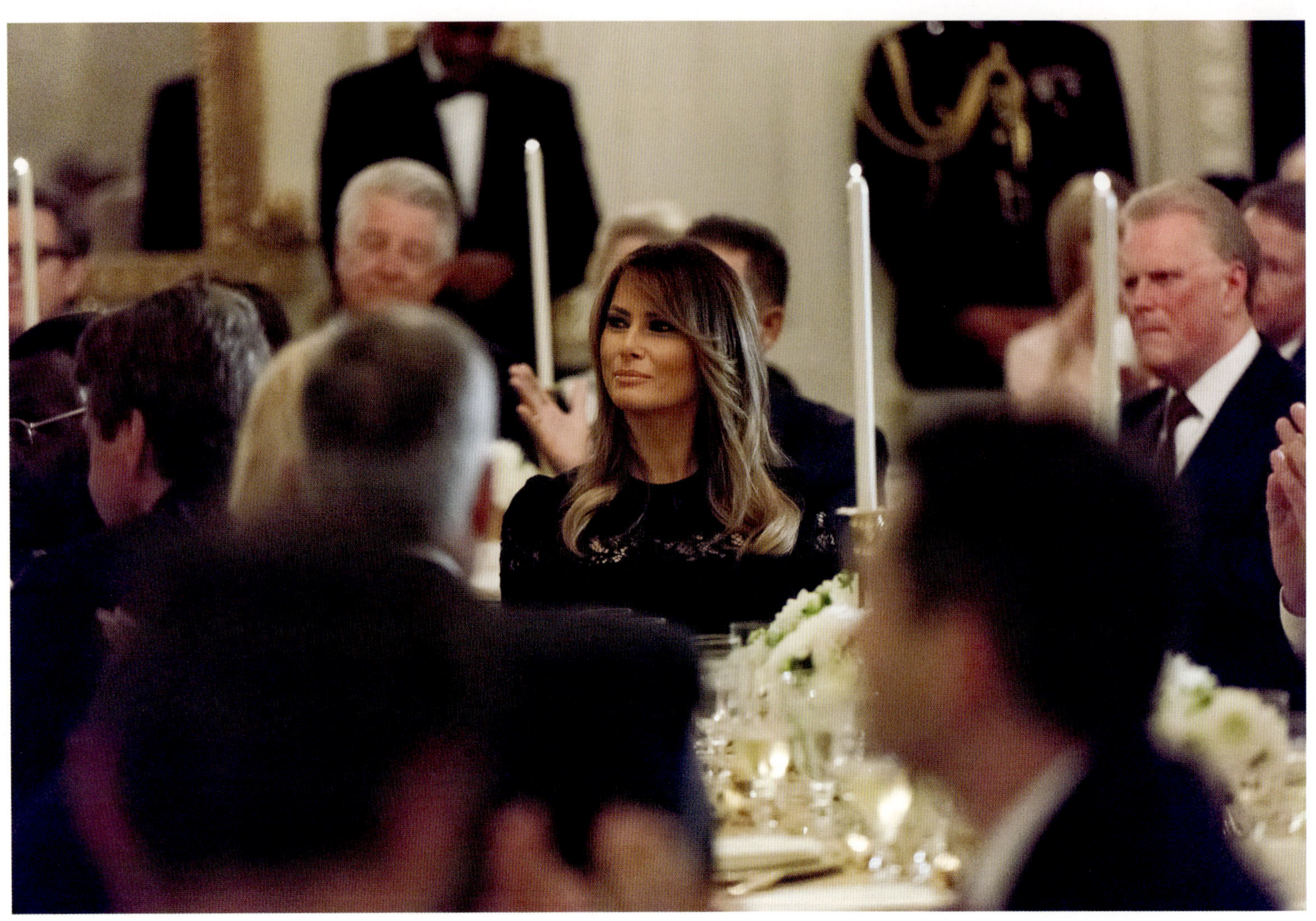

Elegance and Evangelicals.[6]

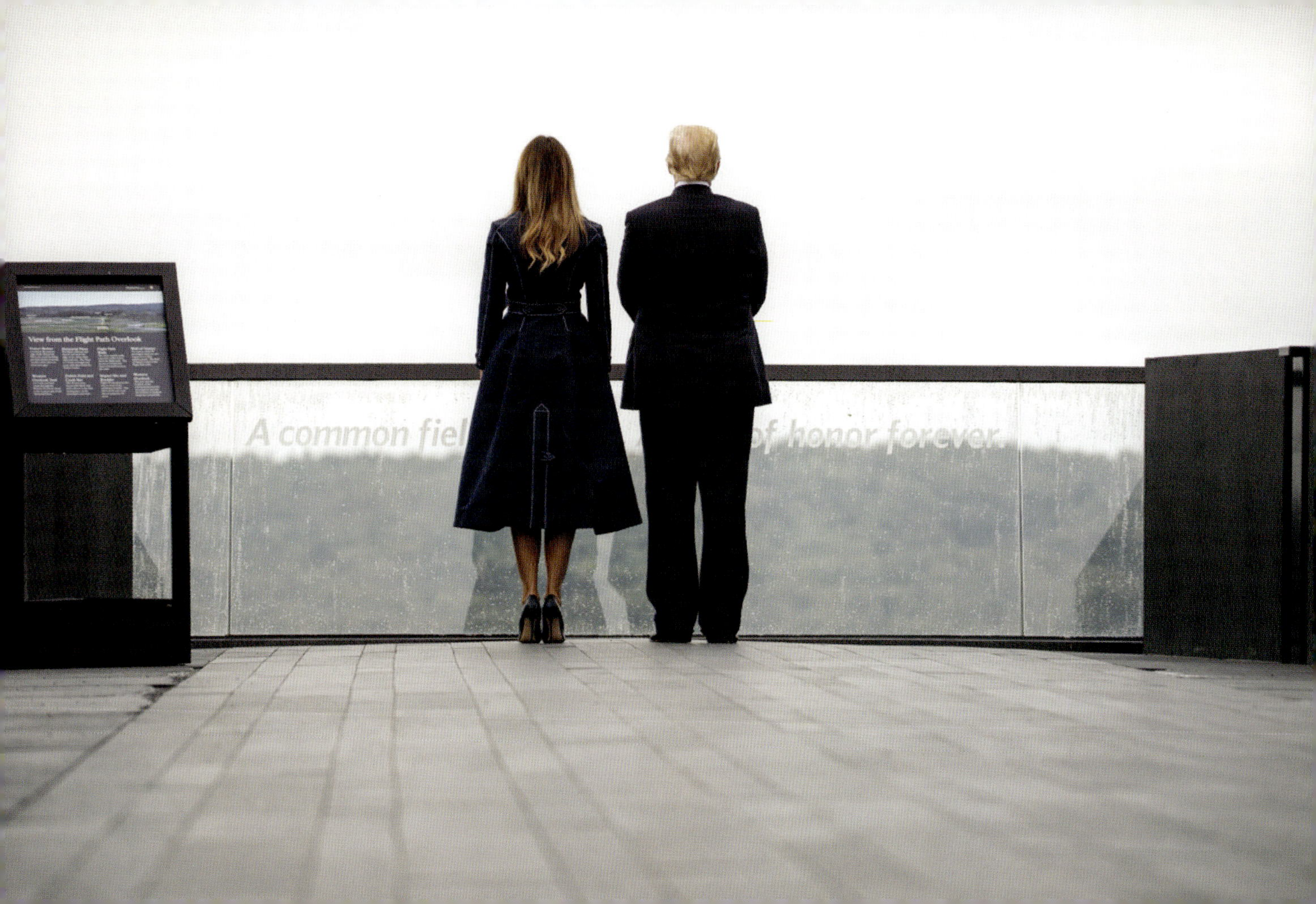
View from the Flight Path Overlook
A common fiel
of honor forever.

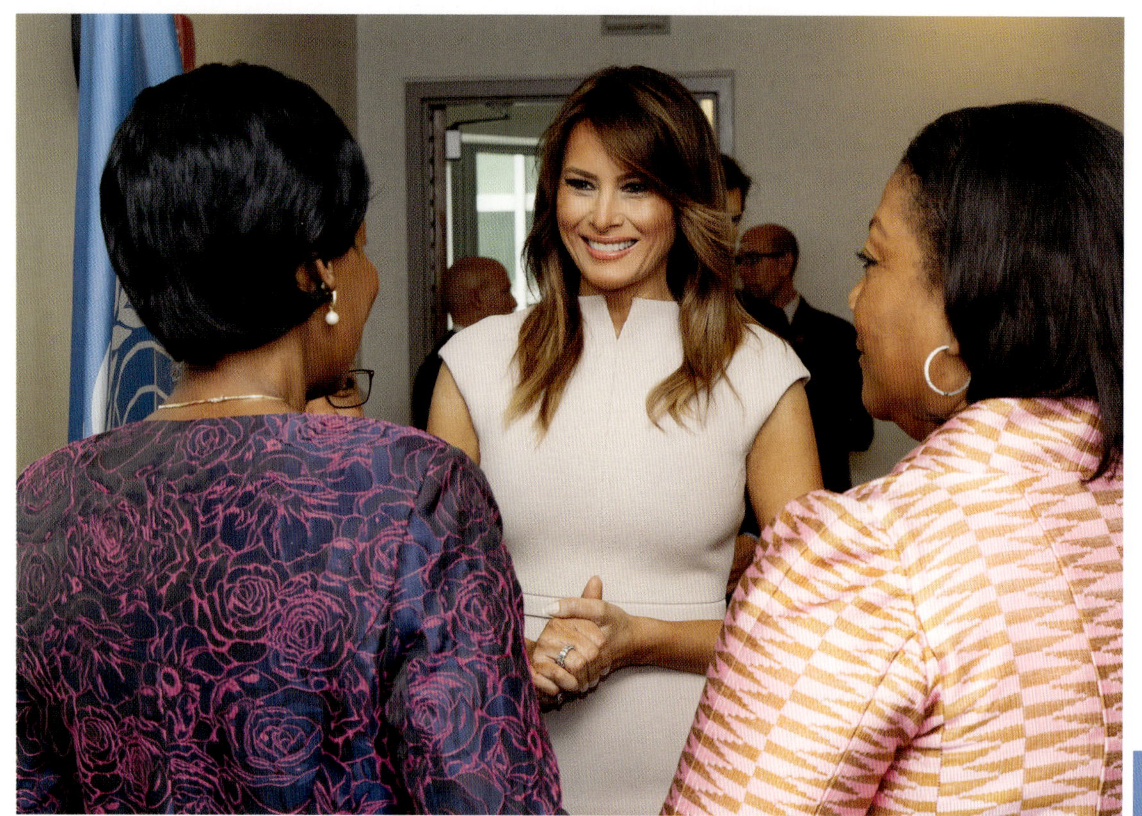

The First Lady speaks with Gertrude Mutharika, the First Lady of Malawi, Rebecca Akufo-Addo, the First Lady of the Republic of Ghana, and Margaret Kenyatta, the First Lady of Kenya while hosting a United Nations reception.[6]

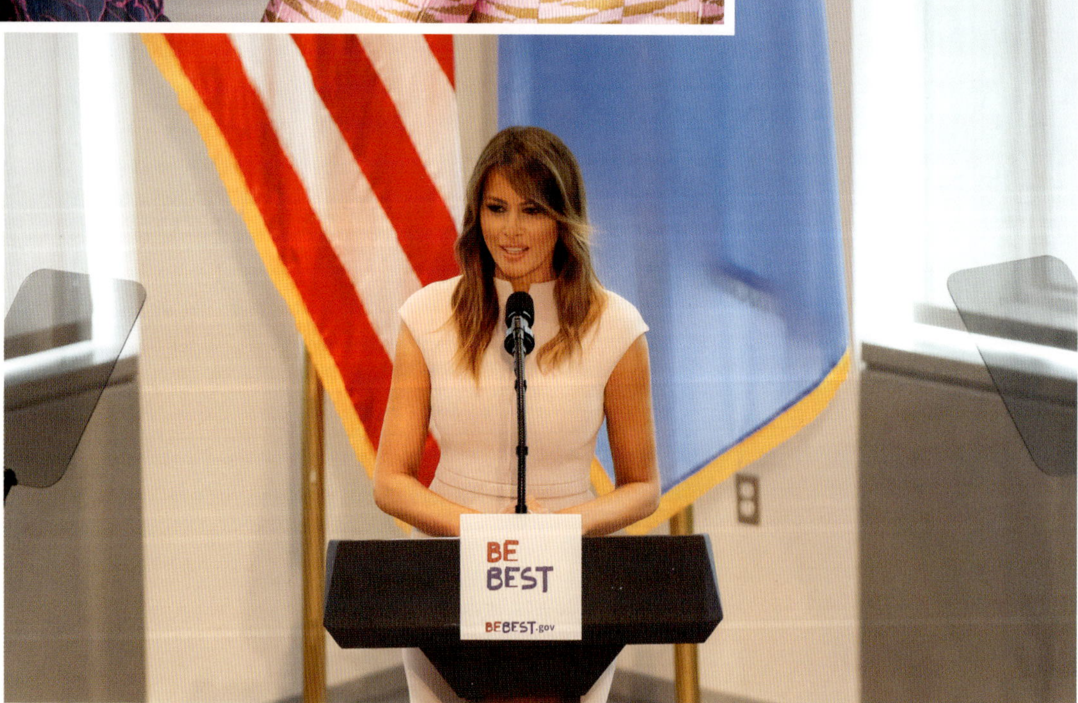

Elegance in Motion as the First Lady gives a presentation at a United Nations reception she hosted.[6]

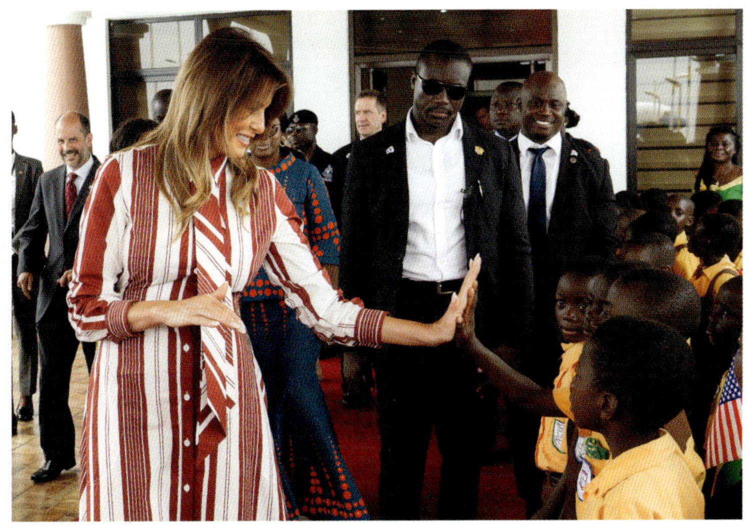

The First Lady is welcomed to Ghana, Africa with a ceremony led by Rebecca Akufo-Addo, the First Lady of the Republic of Ghana, and local schoolchildren at Kotoka International Airport.[6]

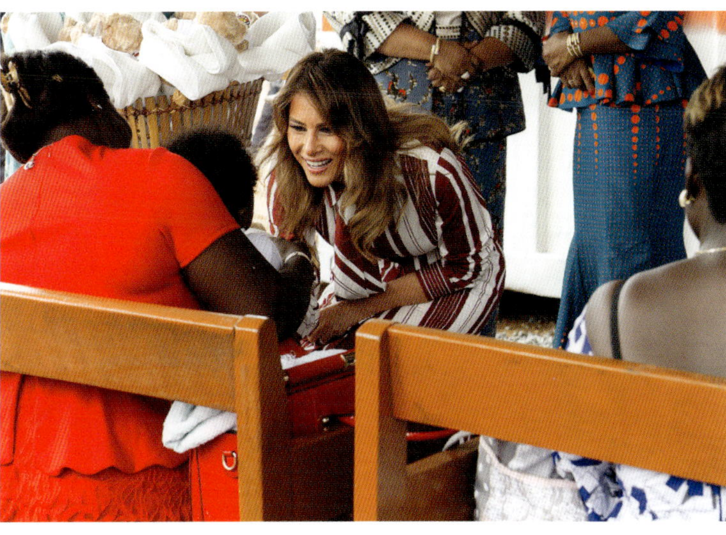

The two First Ladies meet with mothers and children at the Child Welfare Clinic inside the Greater Accra Regional Hospital.[6]

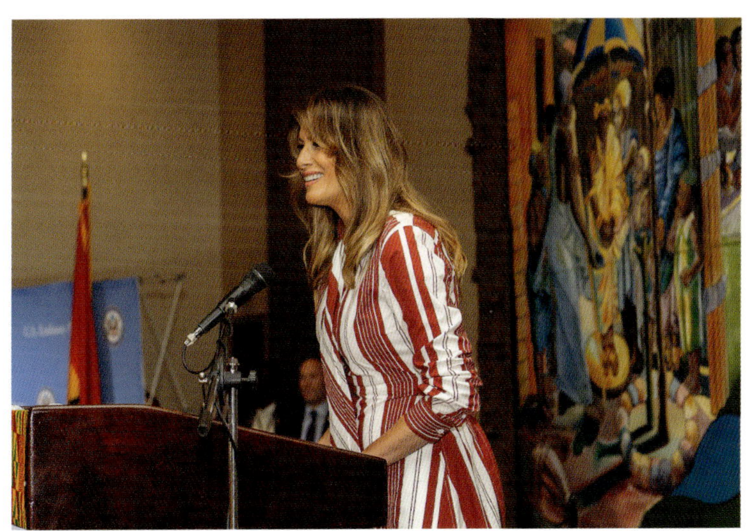

Mrs. Trump speaks to United States Embassy Ghana staff and families.[6]

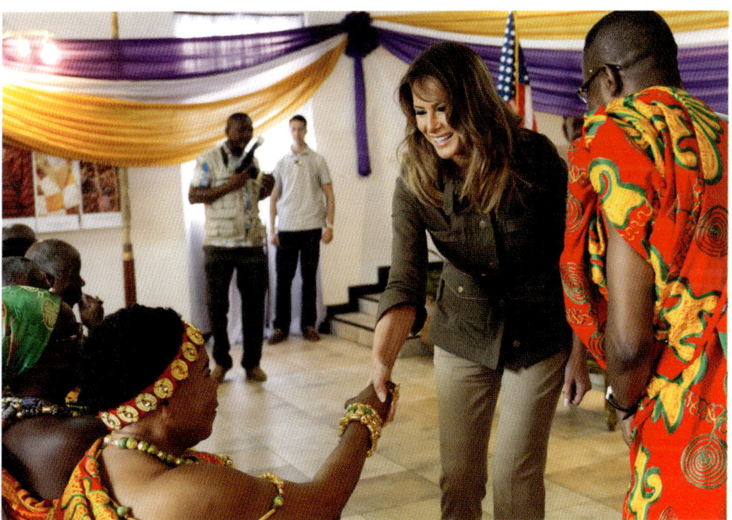

Melania shakes hands with Ghana chieftains at the Emintsimadze Palace in Cape Coast, Ghana.[6]

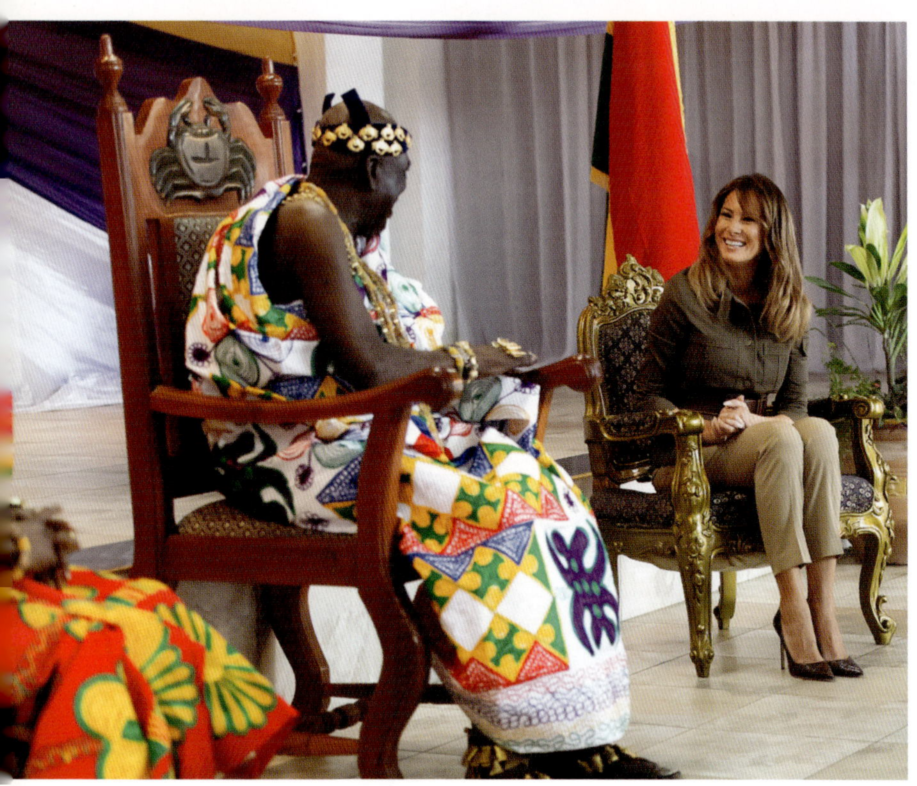

The First Lady Meets Cape Coast's head Chief, Osabarimba Kwesi Atta II for permission to visit the Cape Coast Castle on her African Trip. The Cape Coast Castle was a large slavery trading outpost in Ghana built by European traders. Originally built for trade in goods, it eventually became a major holding area for slaves before the captives were placed on ships.[6]

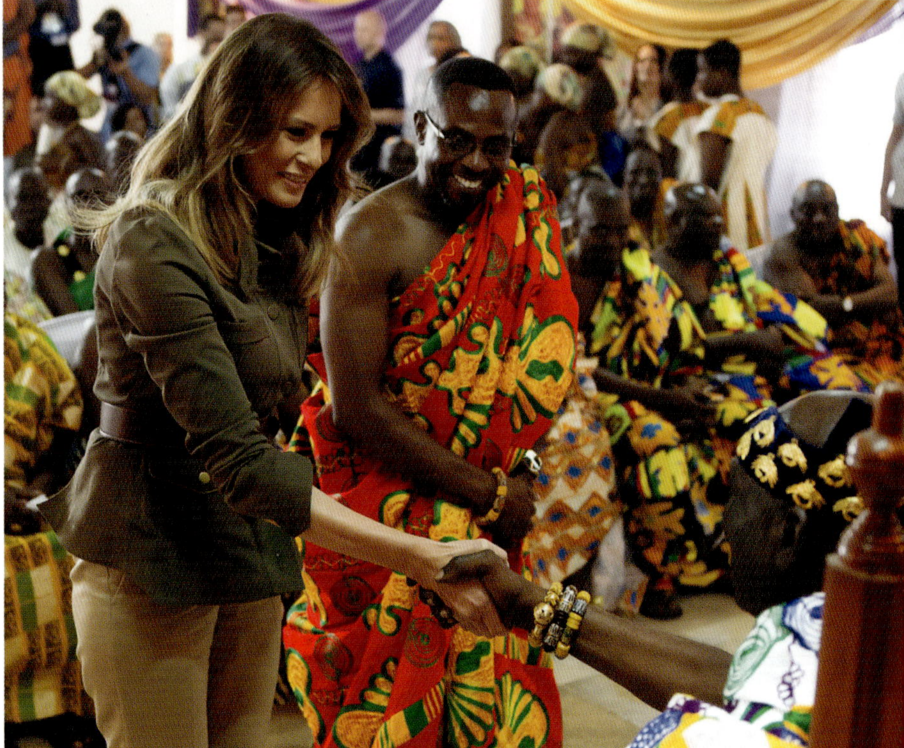

Shaking hands with the Chief.[6]

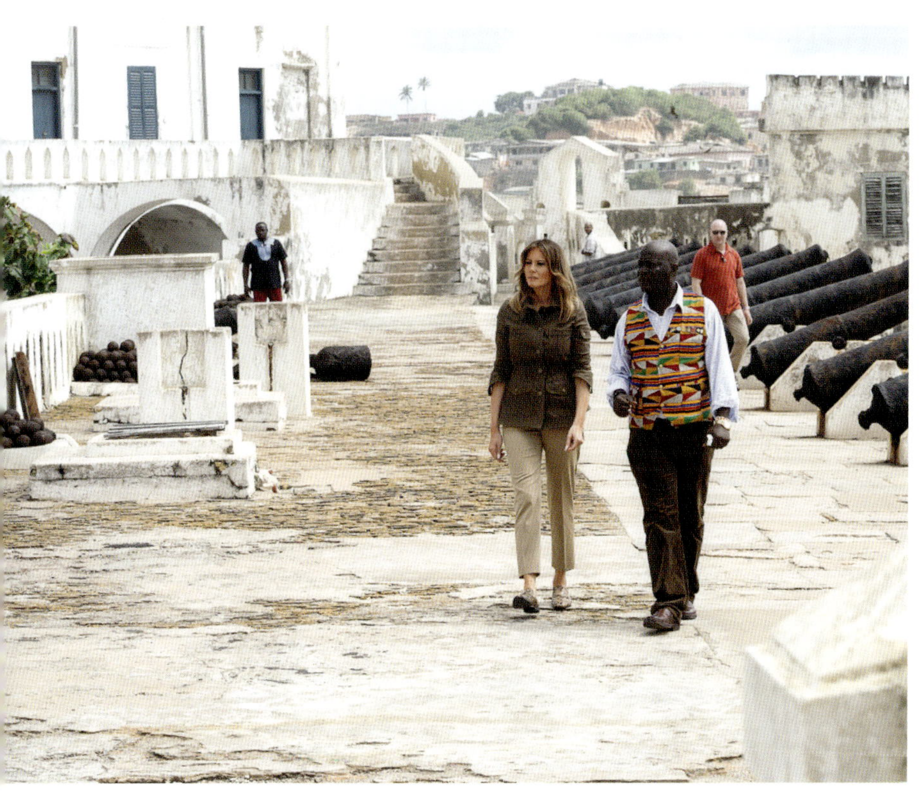

Touring the remnants of Cape Coast Castle.[6]

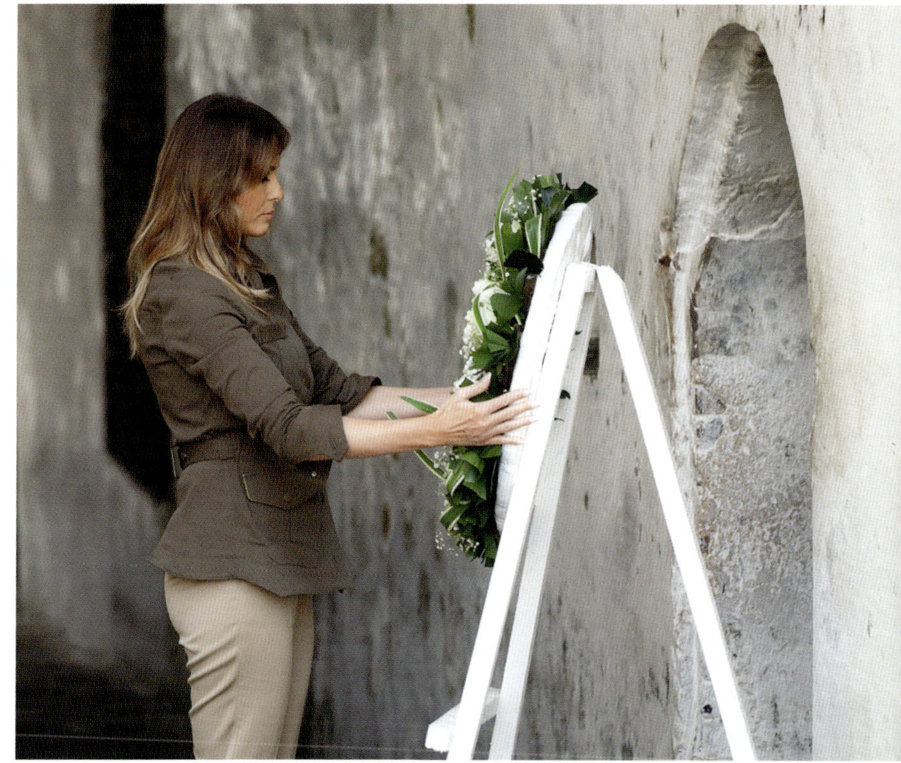

Mrs. Trump places a wreath at the Door of No Return. After passing through the Door slaves would be lowered into boats and rowed out to ships, never to return to their homeland again.[6]

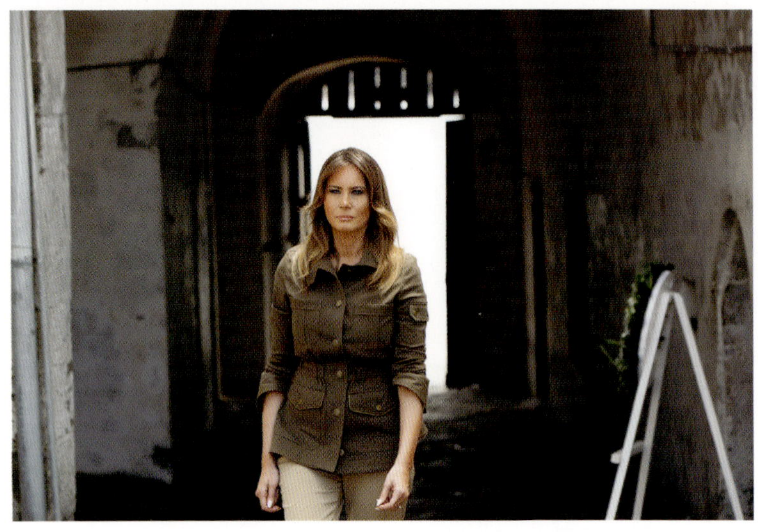

The First Lady walks through the Door of No Return after placing a wreath there.[6]

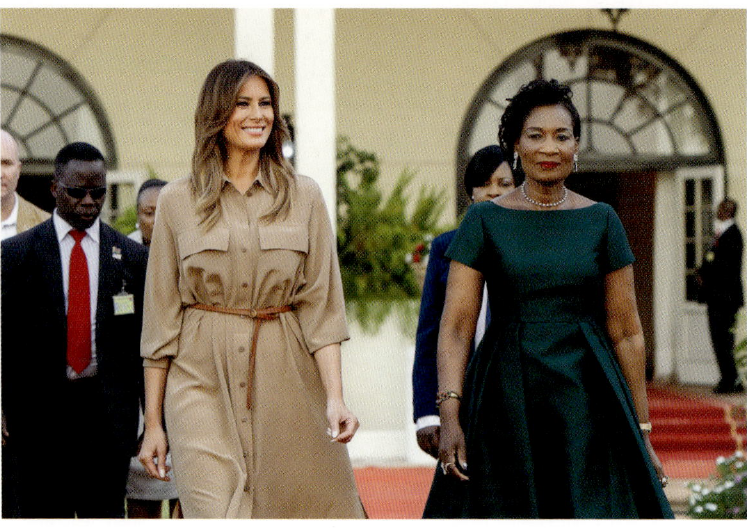

Being met by Gertrude Mutharika, First Lady of Malawi.[6]

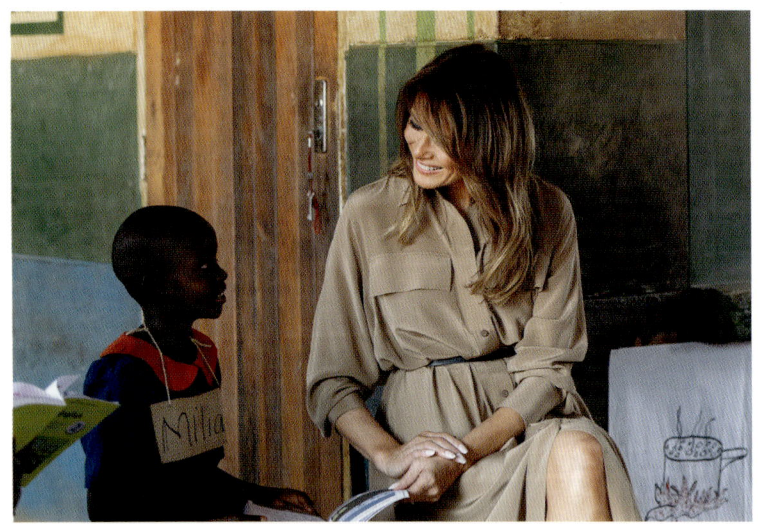

Mrs. Trump makes a new friend at the Chipala Primary School in Lilongwe, Malawi.[6]

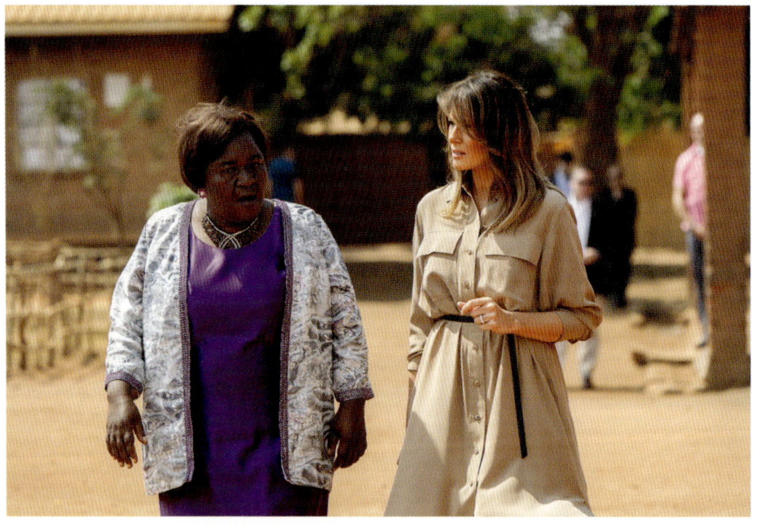

Chatting with Maureen Masi, Head Teacher of Chipala Primary School.[6]

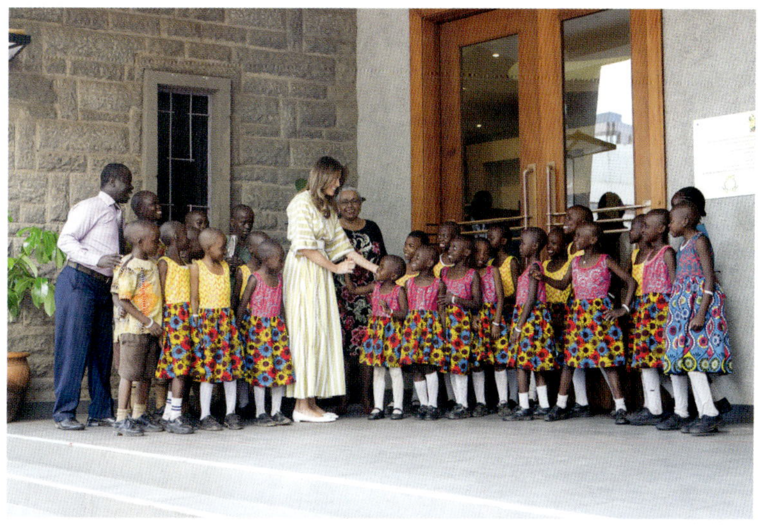

First Lady Melania Trump and Margaret Kenyatta, First Lady of Kenya listen to a welcoming song performed by local children.[6]

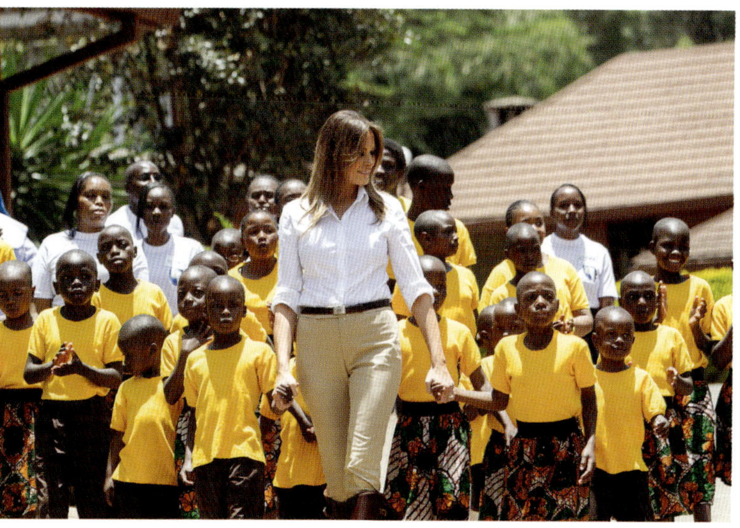

Visiting The Nest Children's home in Kenya. The Nest is for children ages two to seventeen whose mothers are imprisoned. Some were abandoned as babies. Most stay until they are reunited with their mothers or find new places to live. Regardless, each child receives care and an education.[6]

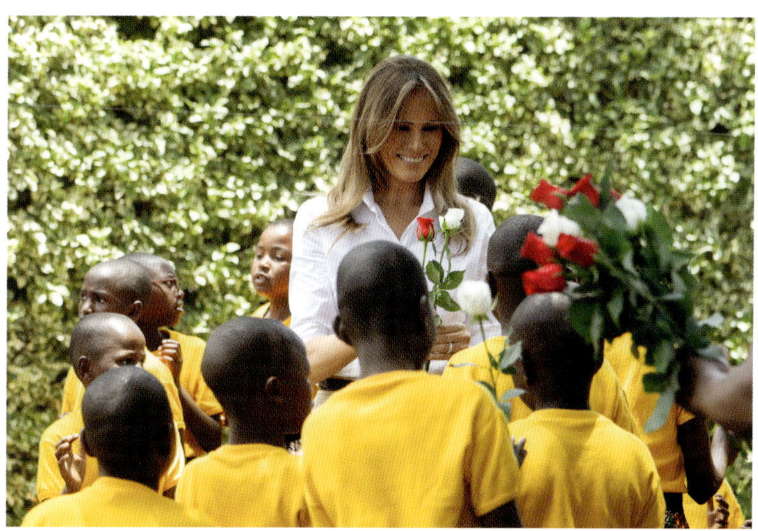

Elegance and roses in Africa.[6]

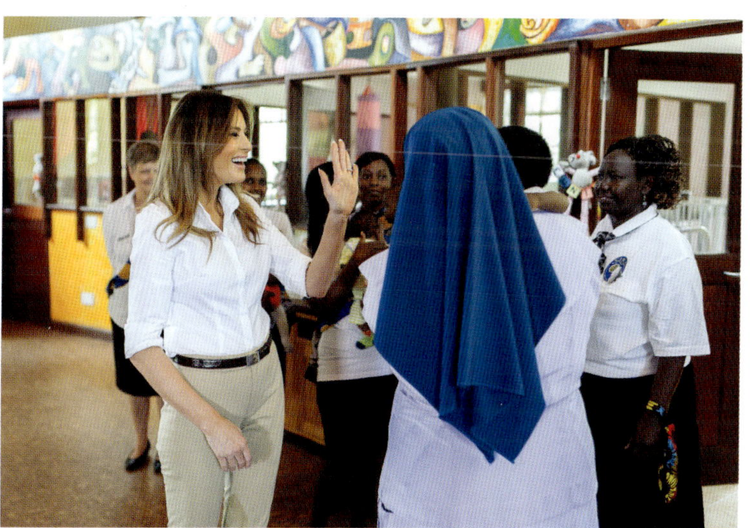

Meeting teachers at The Nest School.[6]

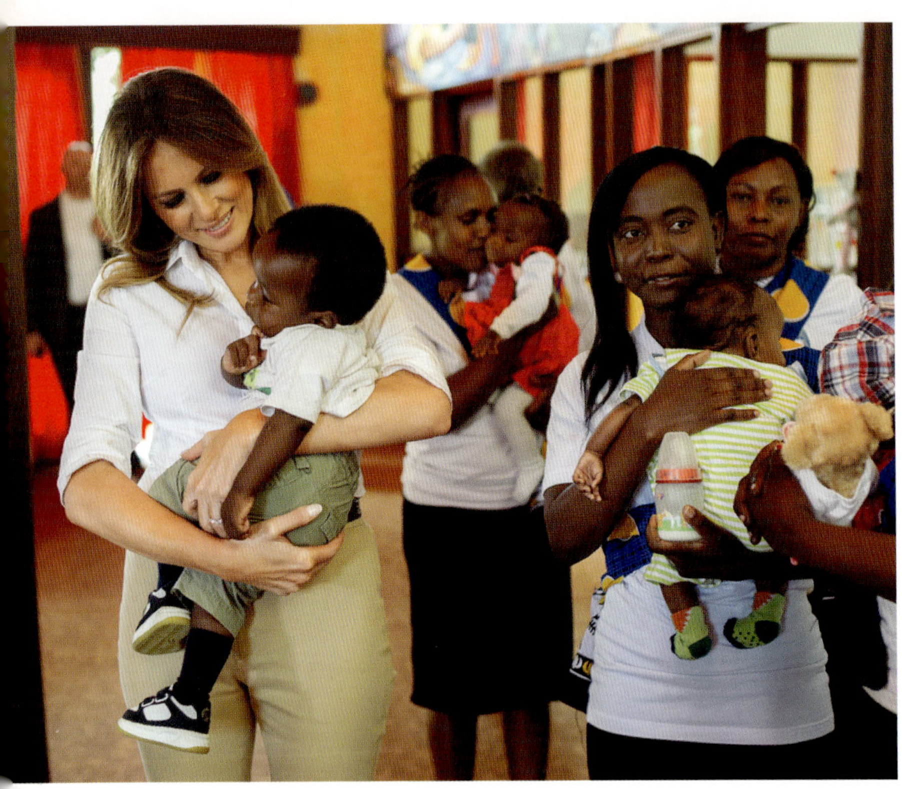

A moment shared.[6]

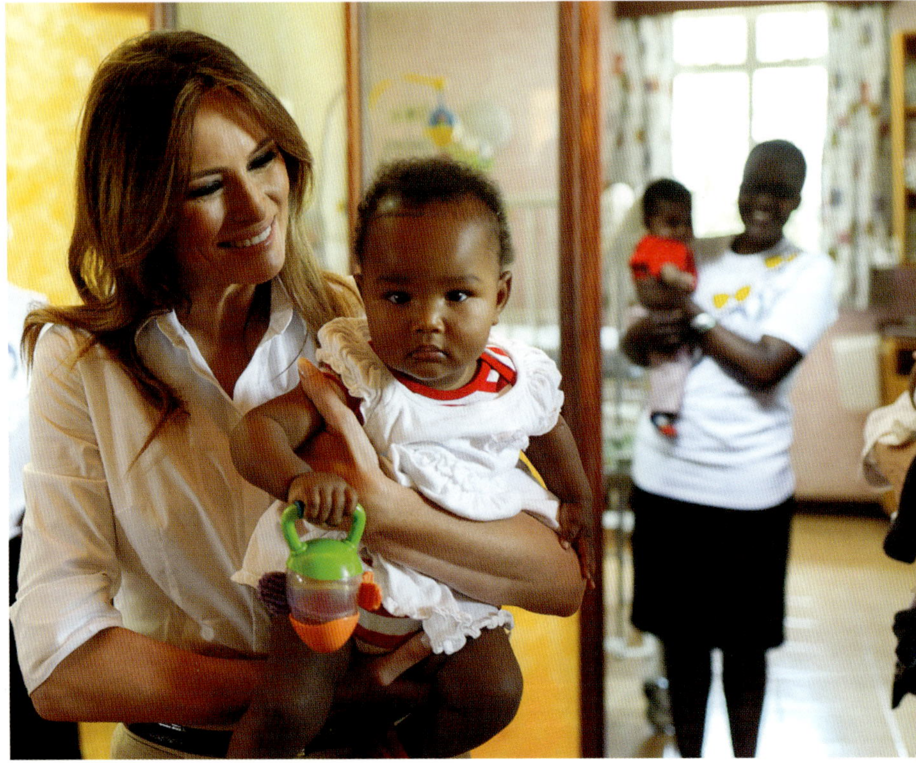

The First Lady is a mother as well as a representative of the United States. You can see the care in her eyes as she interacts with children.[6]

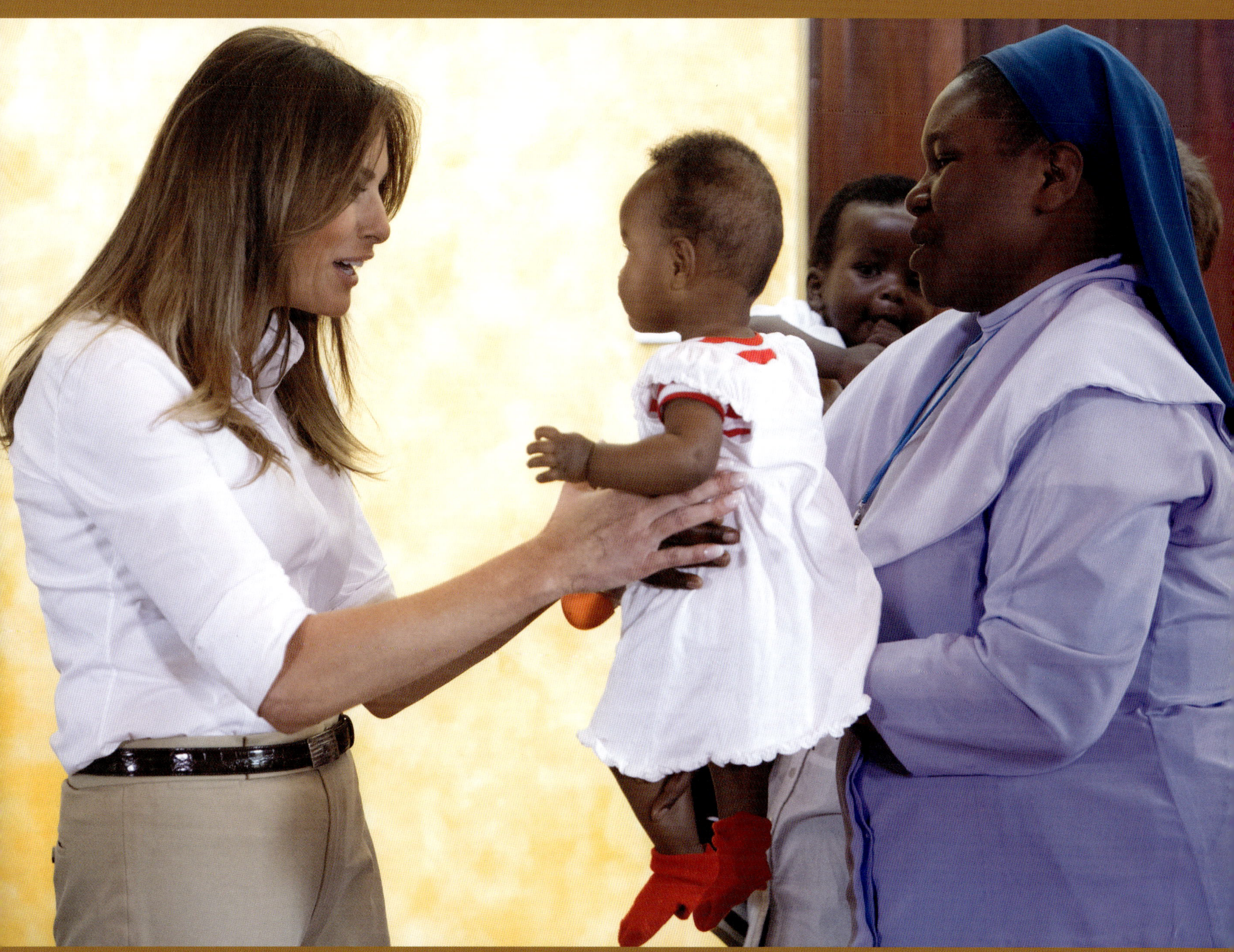

New friends, new smiles.[6]

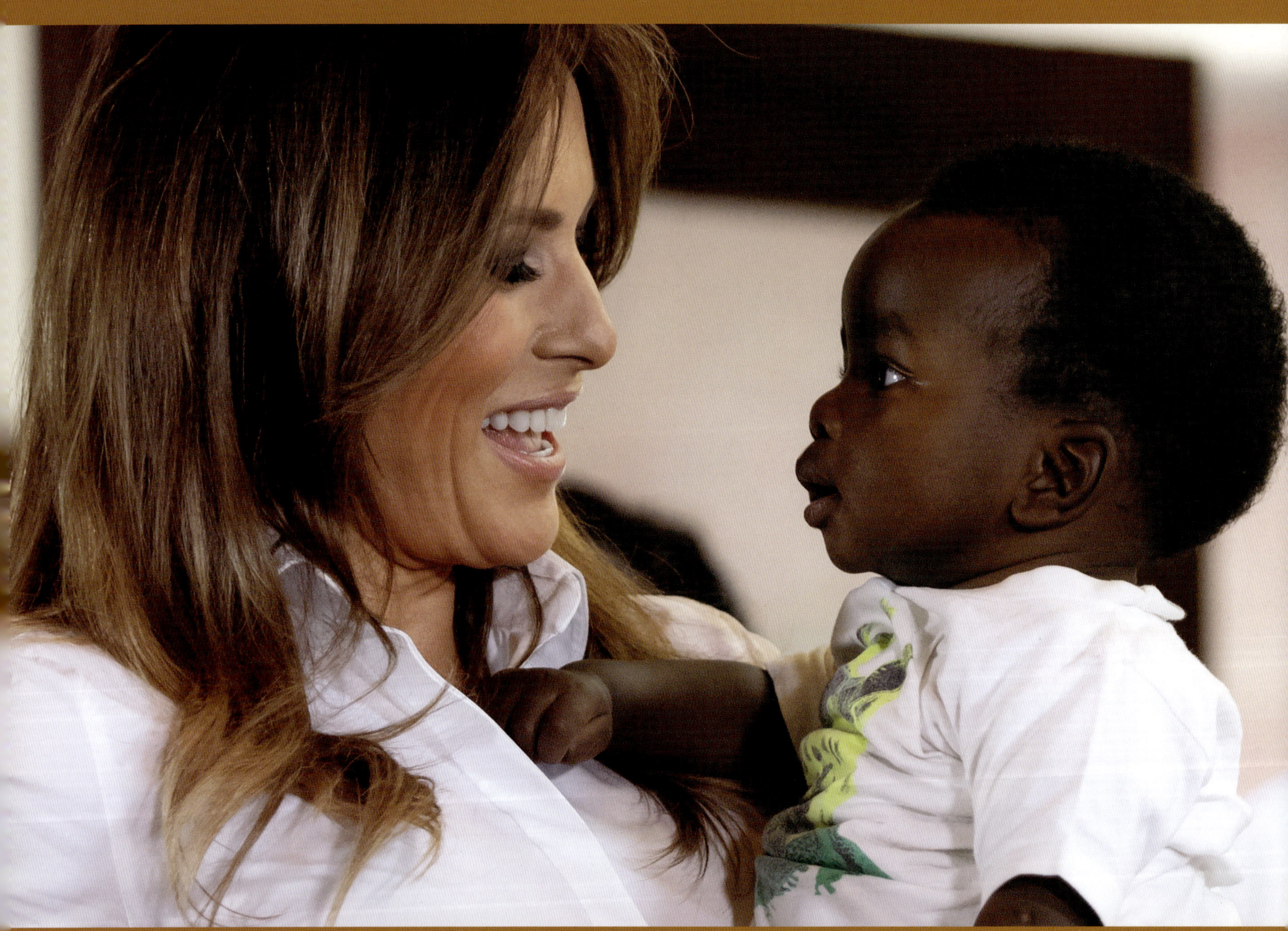

Elegance and Innocence.[18]

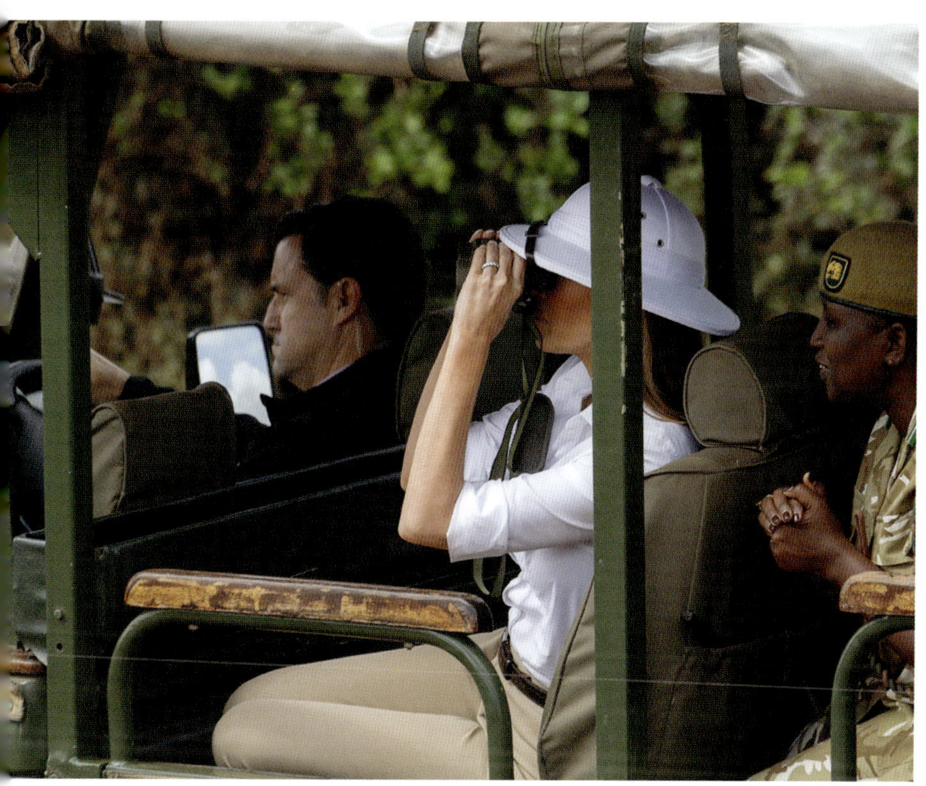

On Safari in Nairobi National Park with Nelly Palmeris, the Game Warden.[6]

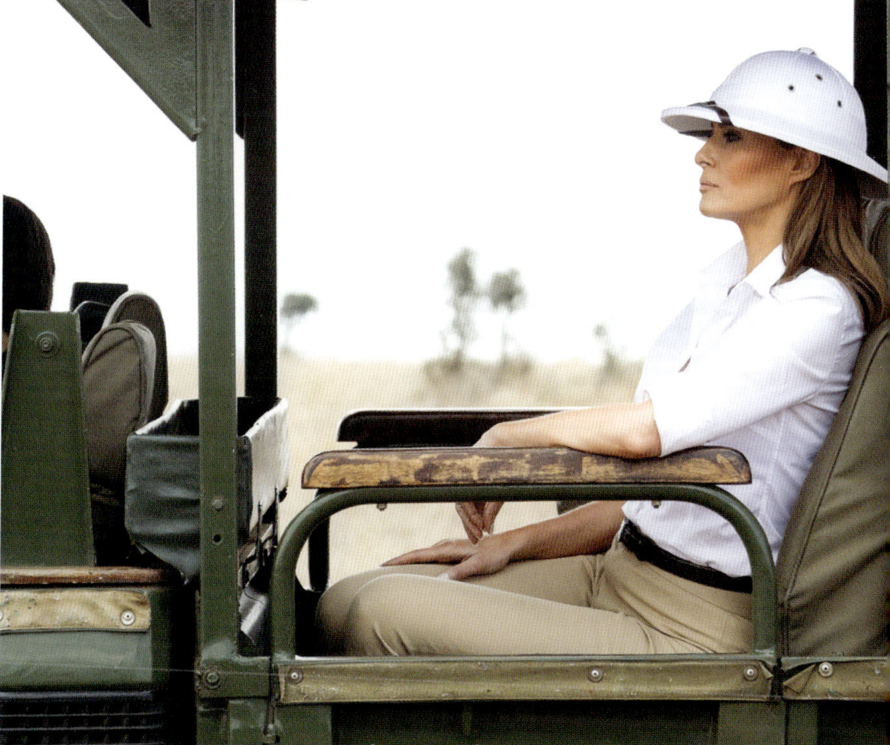

Elegance on safari.[6]

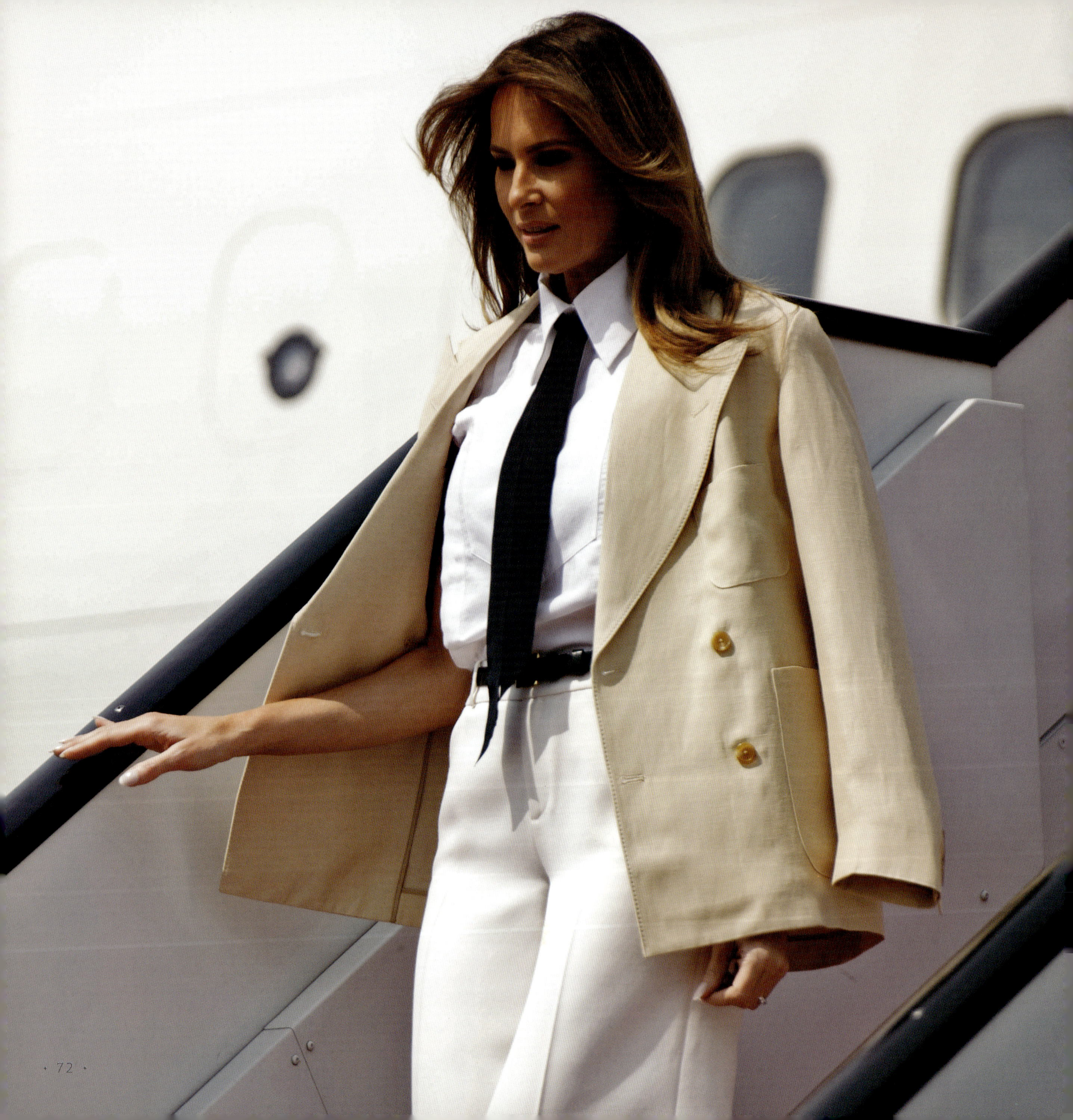

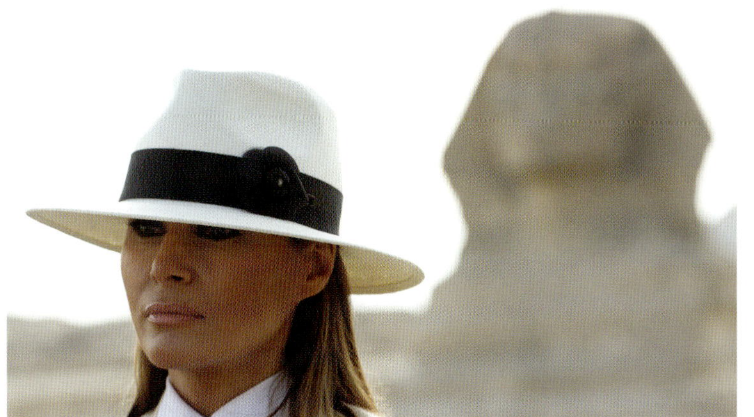

Two elegant enigmas.[6]

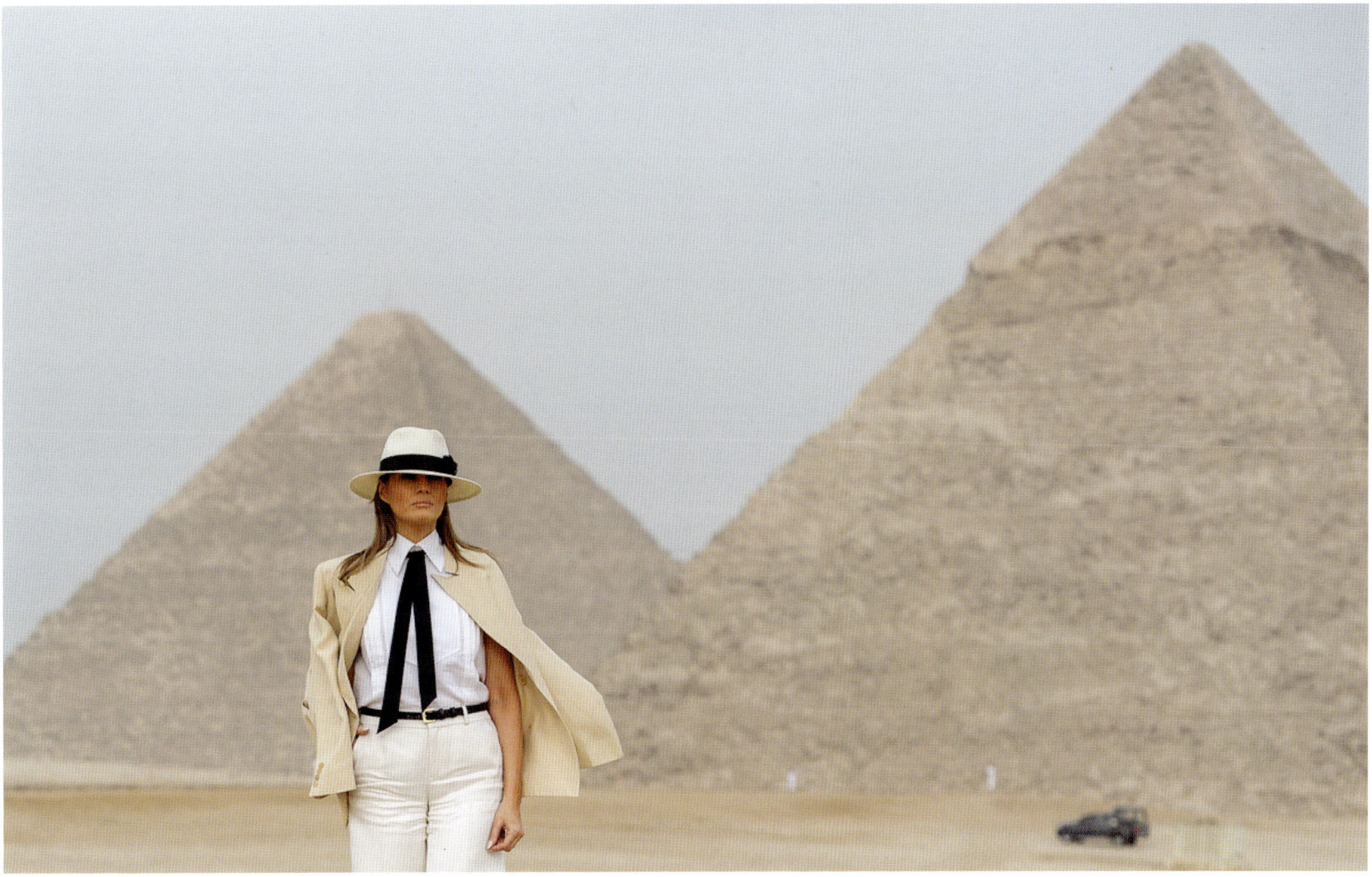

Pyramids at Giza, Oct 6, 2018, in Cairo.[6]

Left: The First Lady arriving in Cairo.[18]

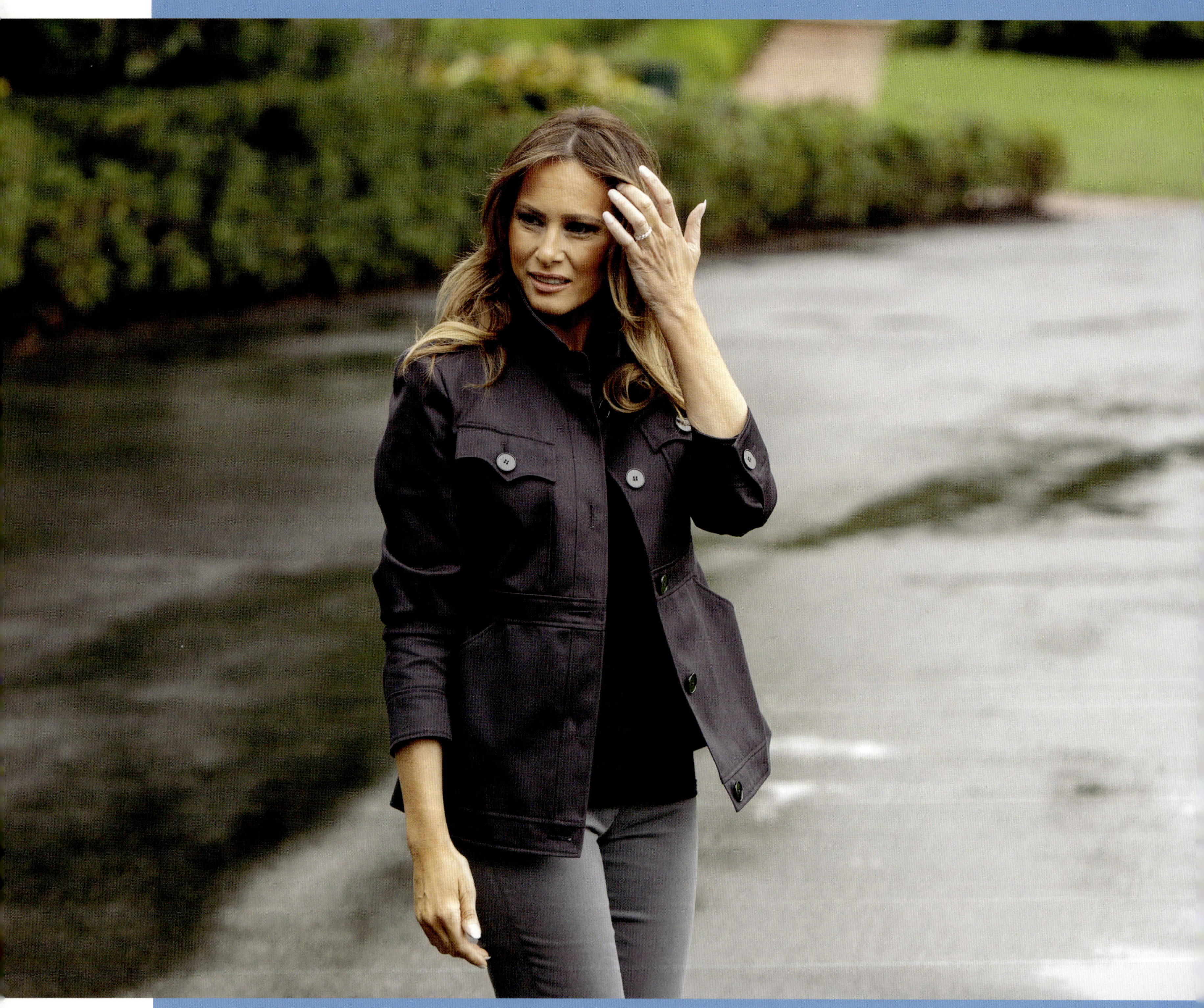

Getting ready to leave for Florida to view damage from Hurricane Michael.[22]

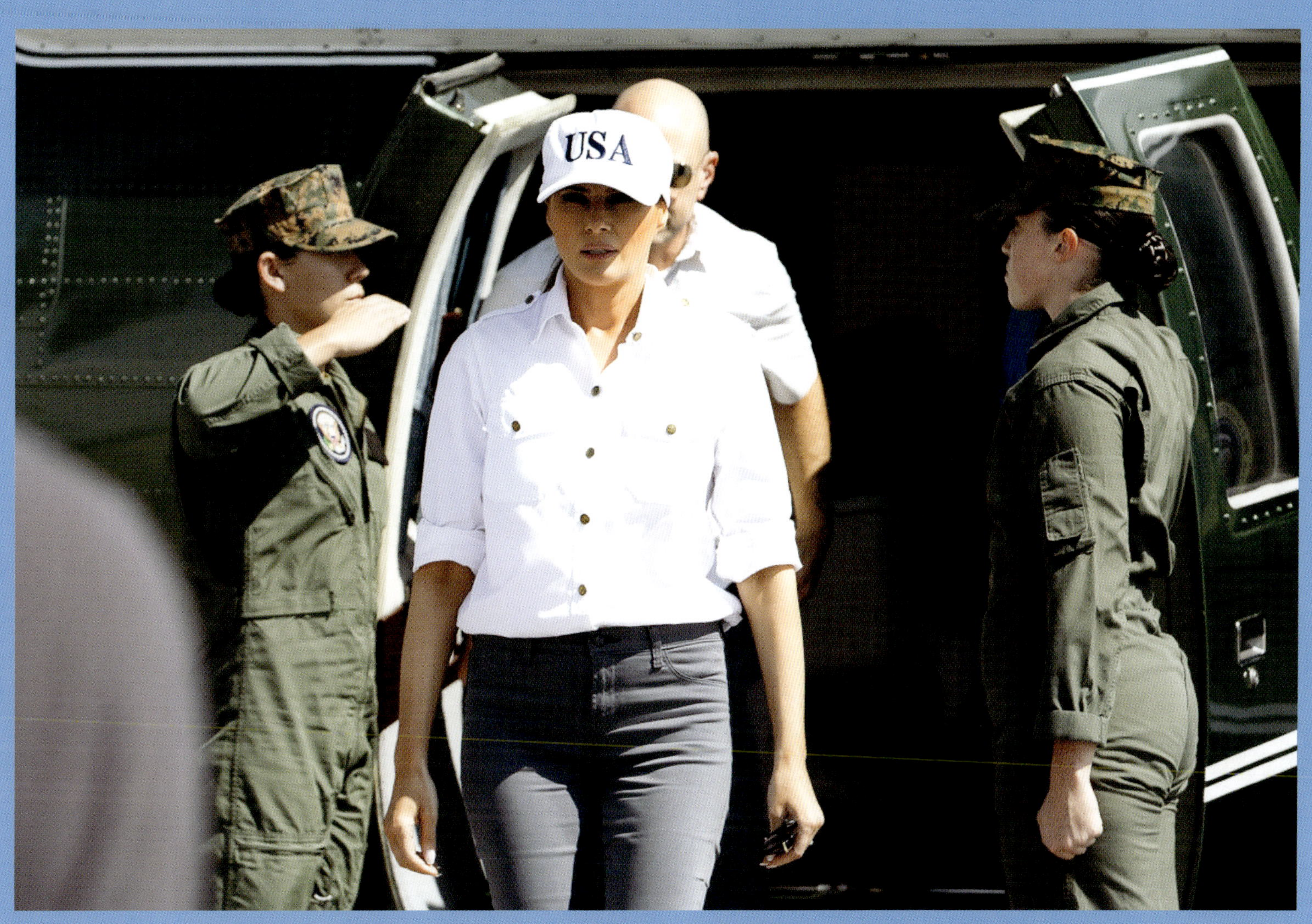

Deplaning from Marine One in Florida.

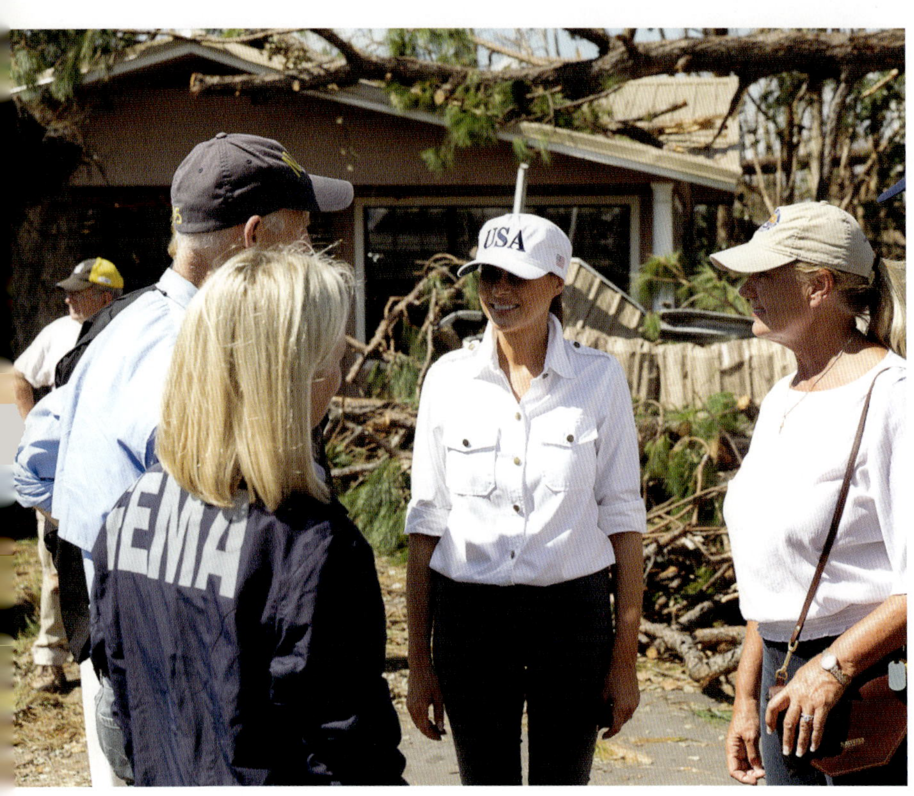

Working with the governor of Florida and his wife and meeting with residents impacted by Hurricane Michael.[6]

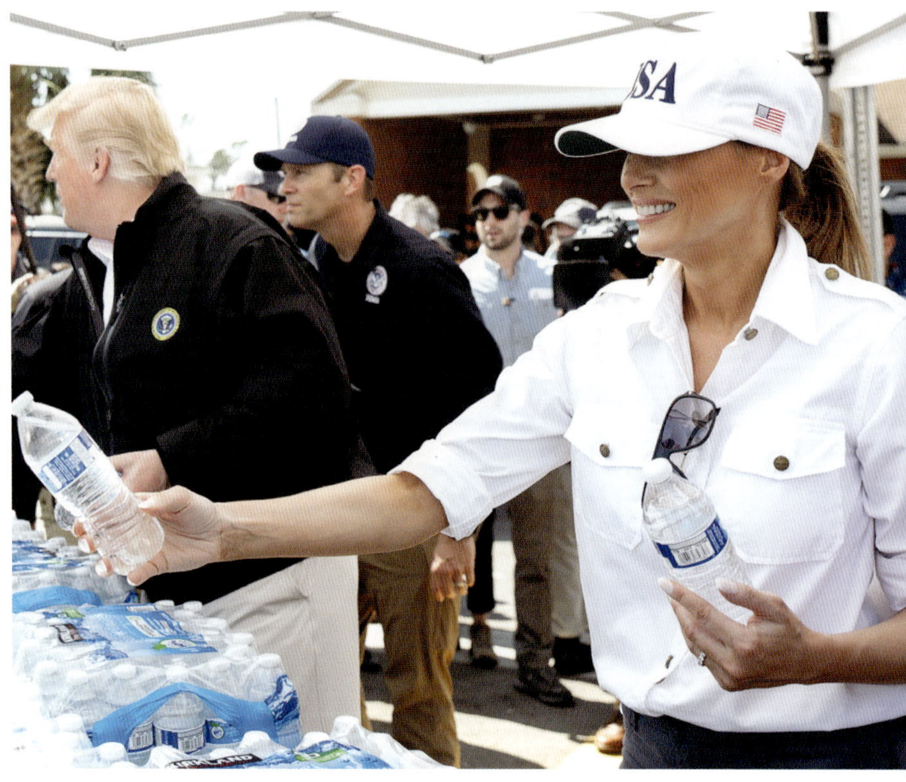

Passing out water bottles and aid to victims of the hurricane, in Lynn Haven, Florida.[6]

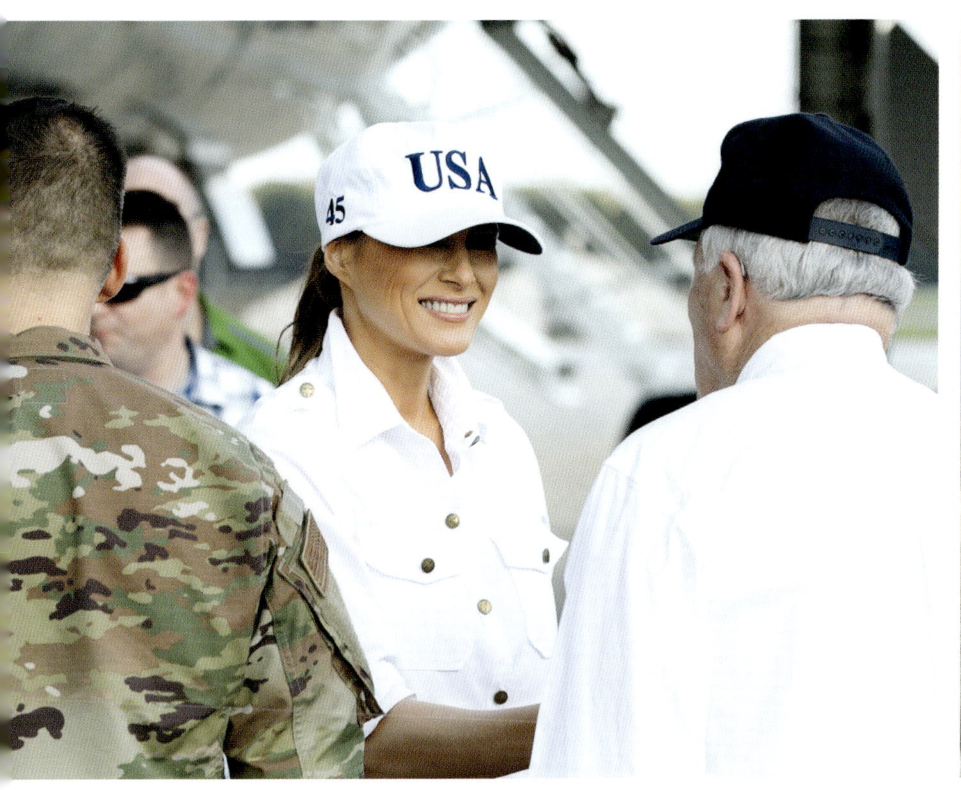

Meeting Georgia Governor Nathan Deal.[6]

On the ground in Georgia.[6]

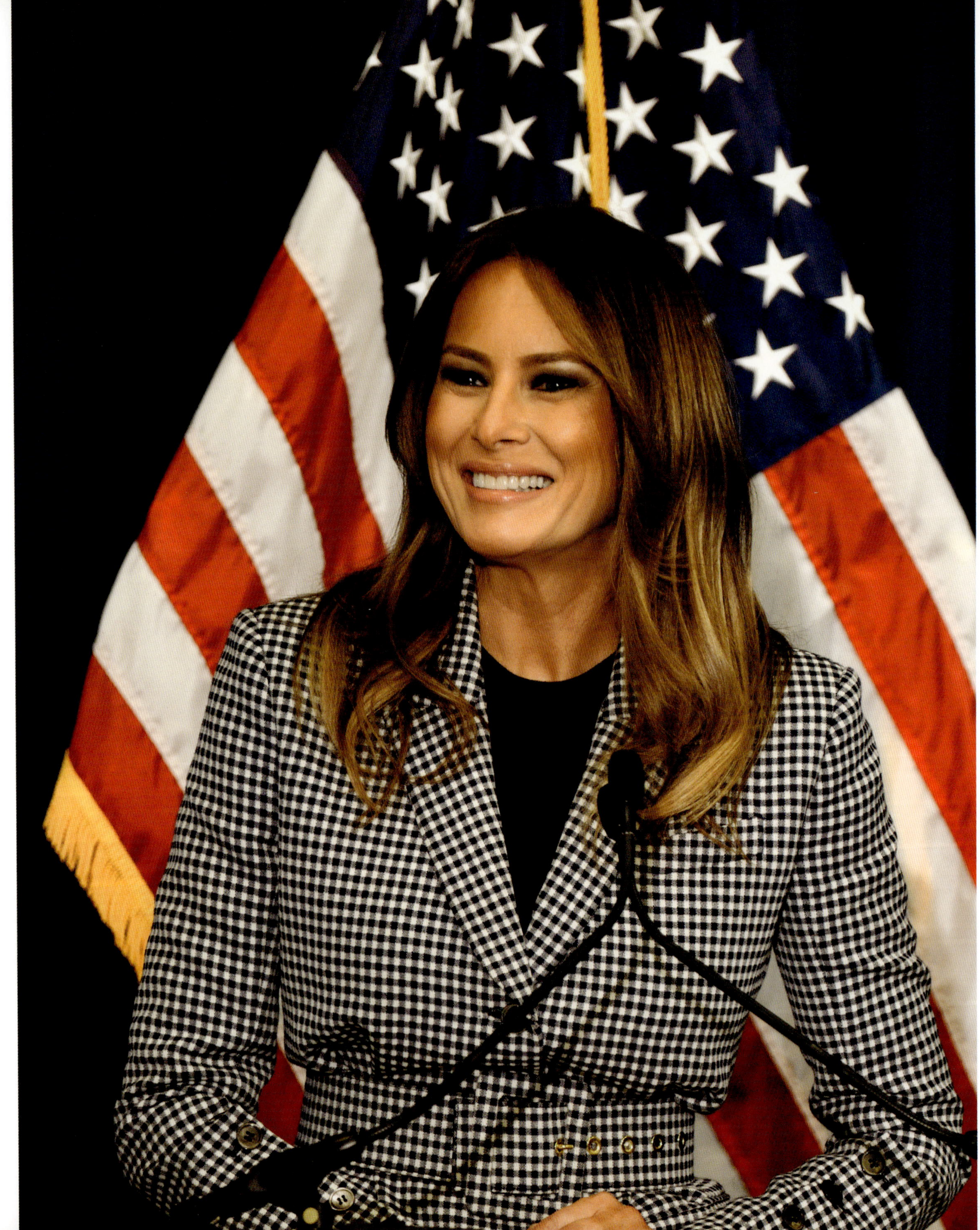

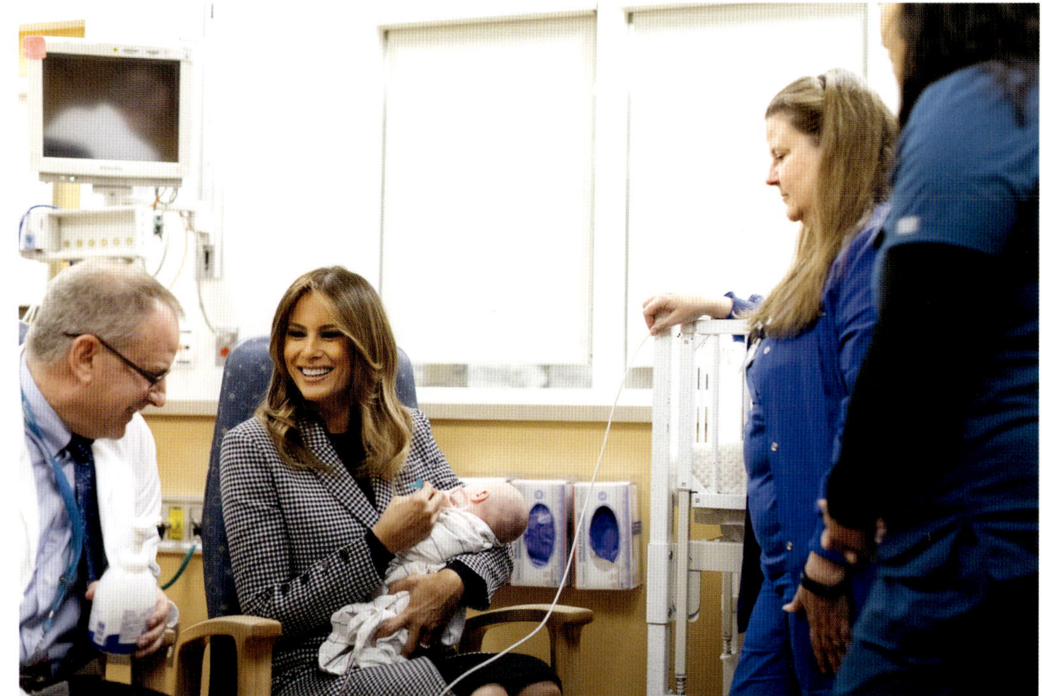

Babies and smiles at Thomas Jefferson University Hospital.[6]

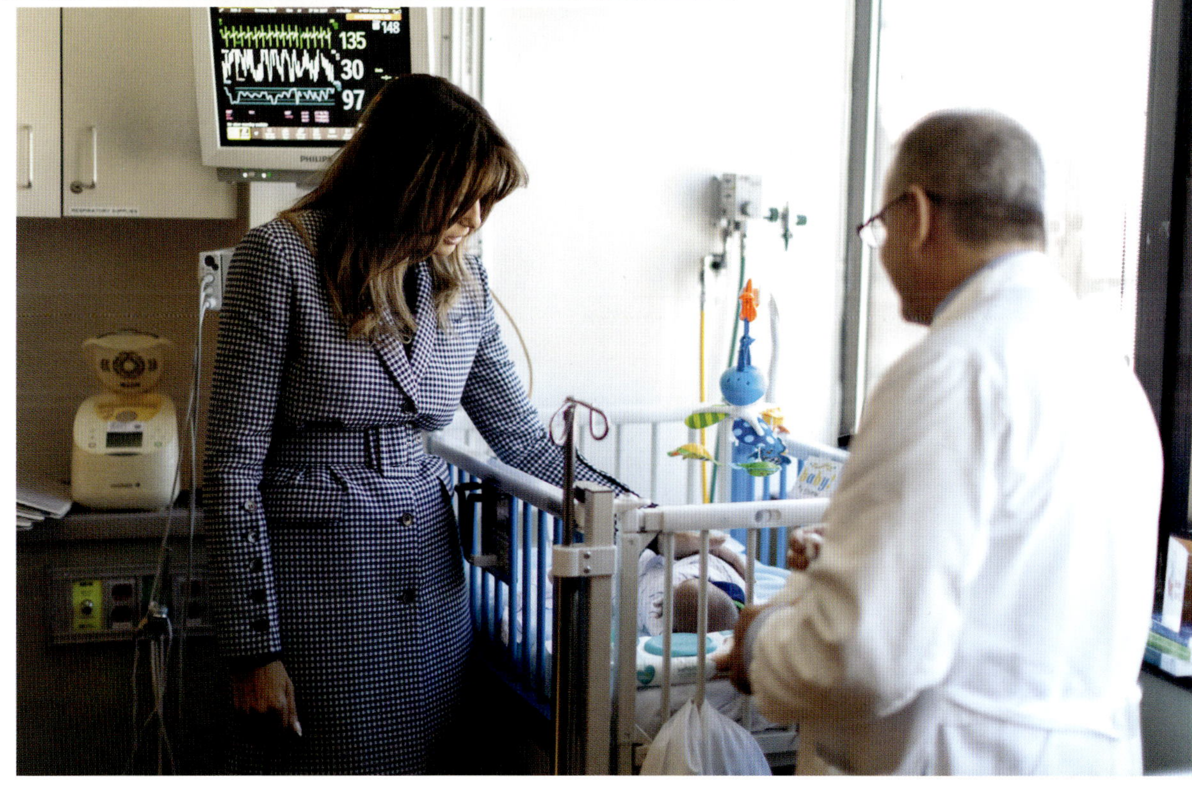

Mrs. Trump visits babies and chats with doctors about Neonatal Abstinence Syndrome.[6]

Left: Melania Trump Speaks at a Neonatal Abstinence Syndrome roundtable discussion. NAS is a group of conditions caused when a baby withdraws from certain drugs they are exposed to in the womb. In most cases the drugs are opioids. Relief from opioid addiction is one of the cornerstones of the First Lady's BE BEST program.[23]

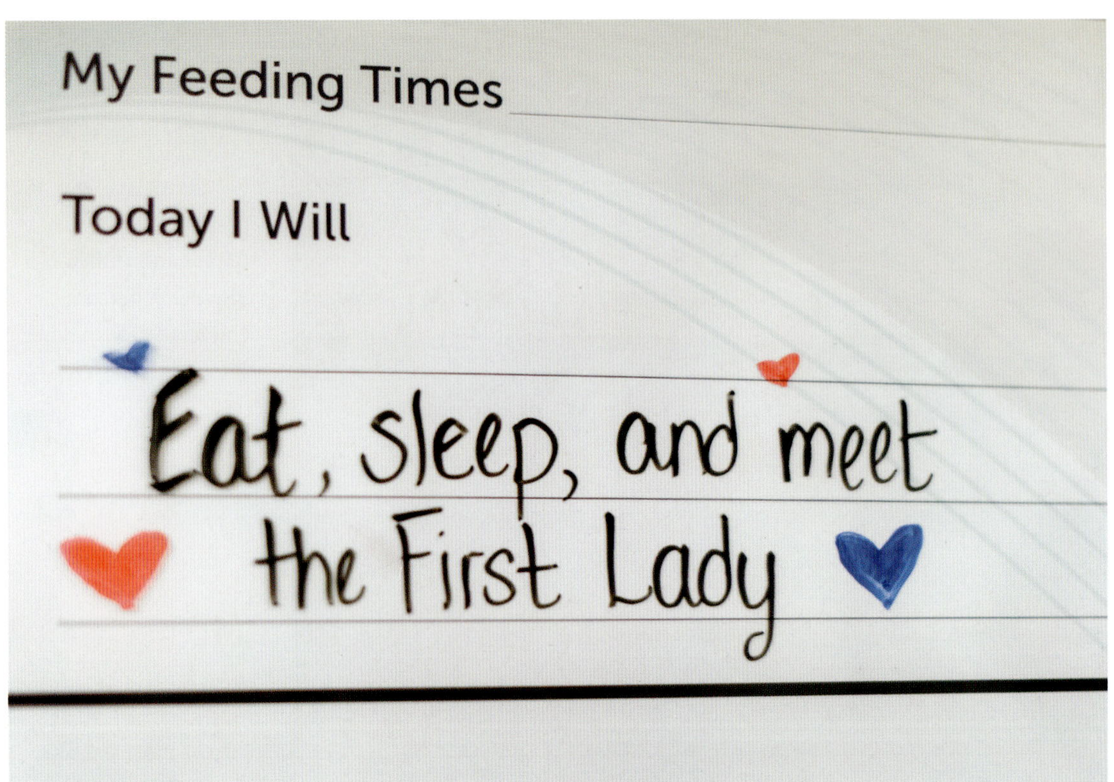

A message for the First Lady.[6]

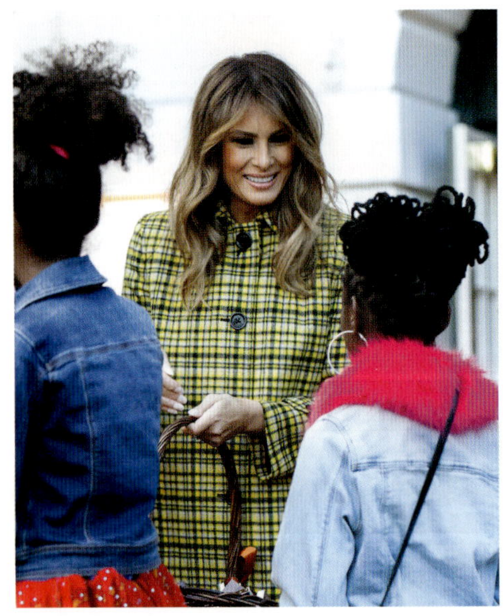

Trick or Treat at the White House.
Handing out candy.[6]

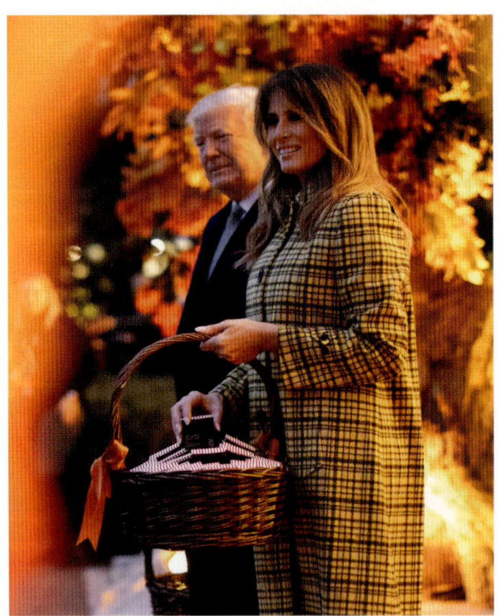

The presidential couple with
their candy baskets.[6]

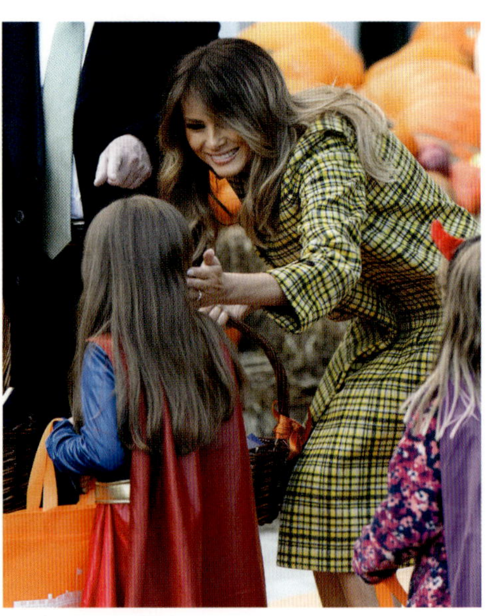

Supergirl gets a treat![6]

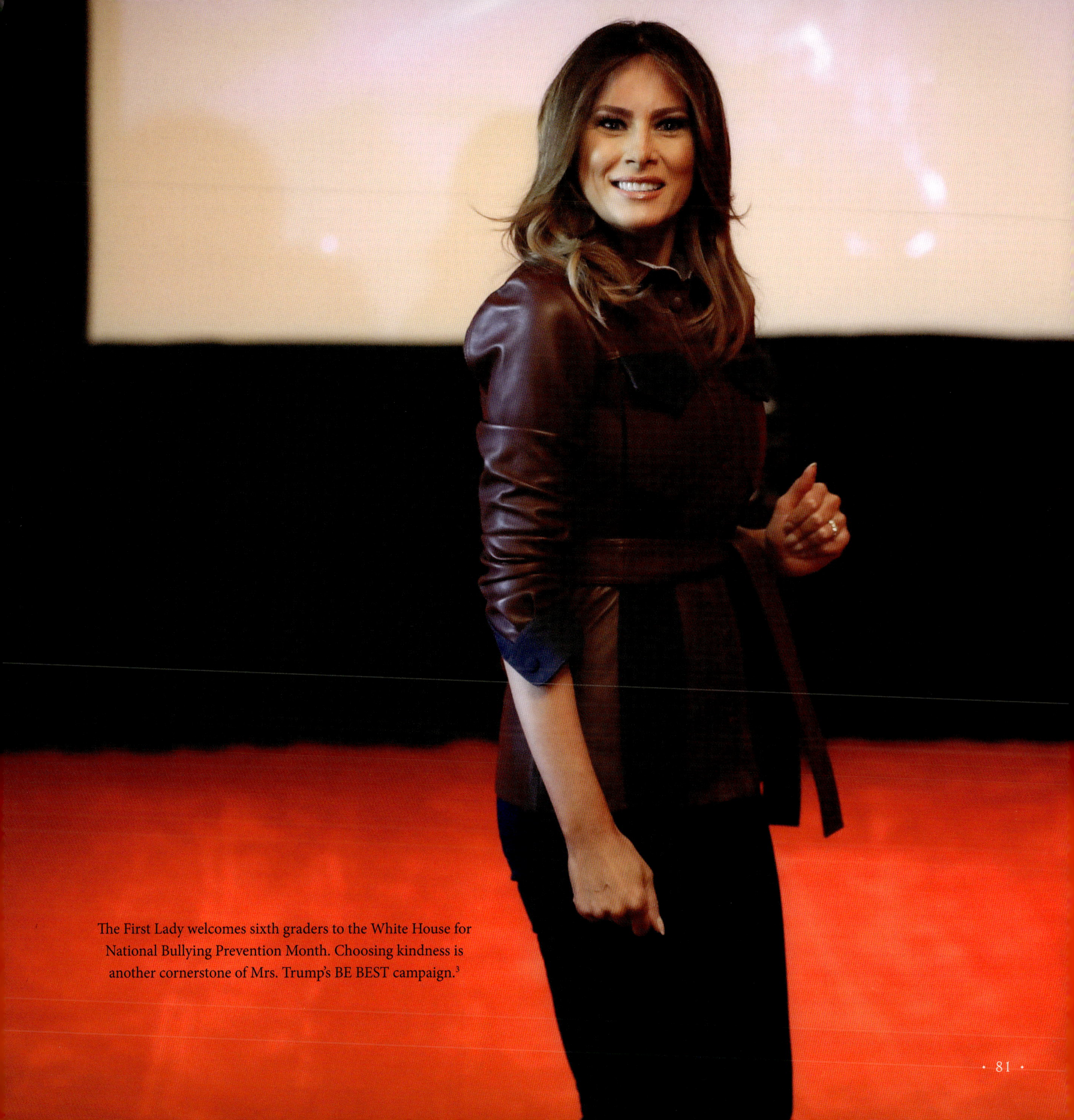

The First Lady welcomes sixth graders to the White House for National Bullying Prevention Month. Choosing kindness is another cornerstone of Mrs. Trump's BE BEST campaign.[3]

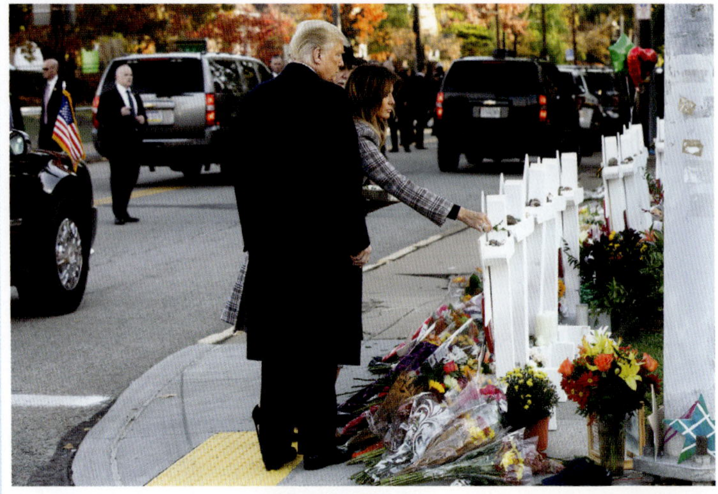

The President and First Lady pay their respects outside the Tree of Life Synagogue in Pittsburg after a mass shooting there in October 2018.[6]

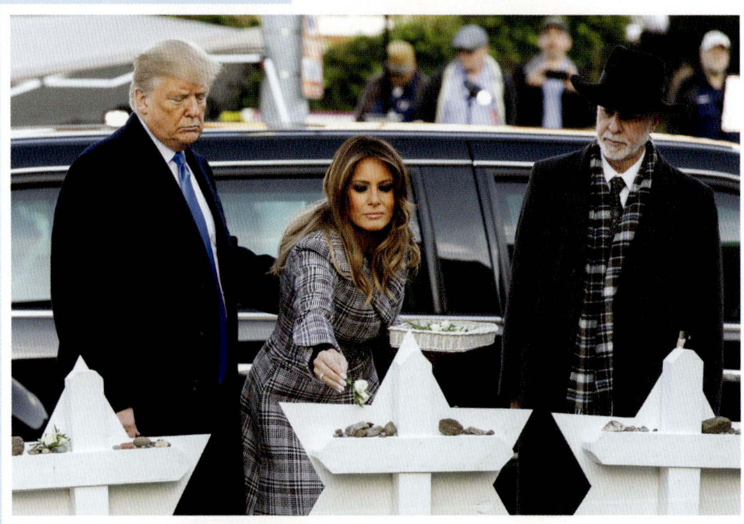

They placed stones and flowers on the memorial of the shooting.[6]

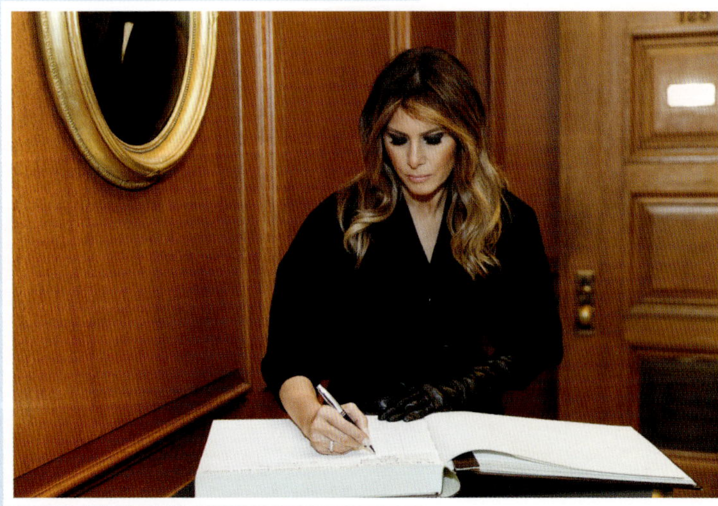

Elegance visits the Supreme Court.[5]

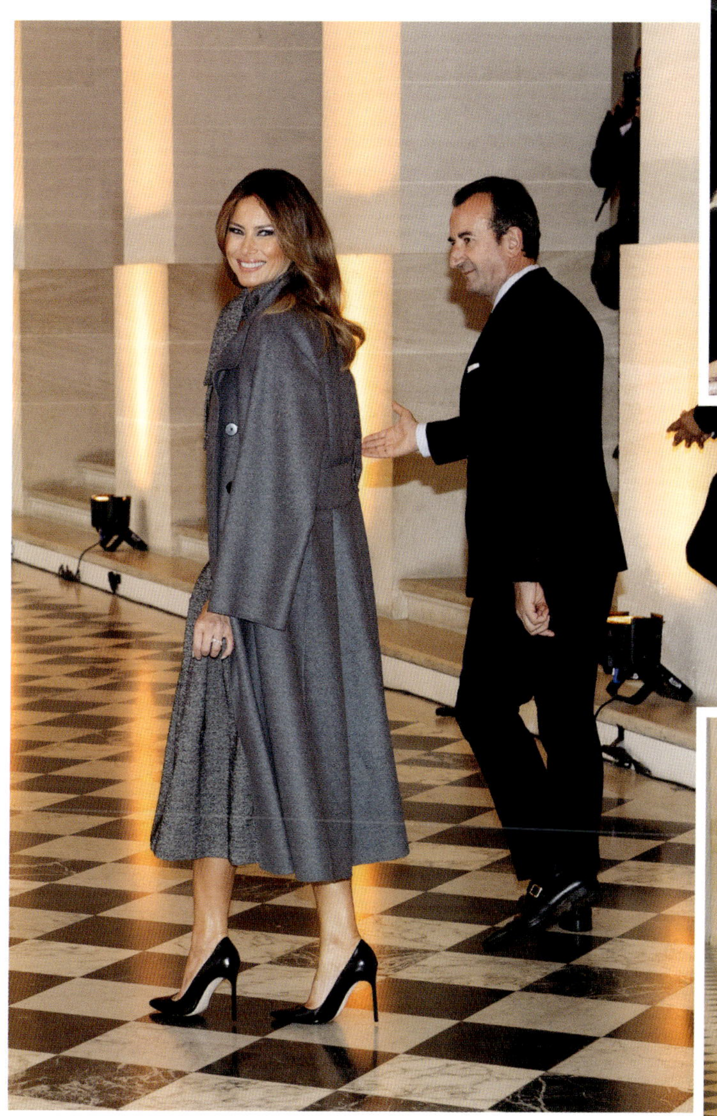

Arrival at the Palace of Versailles. [6]

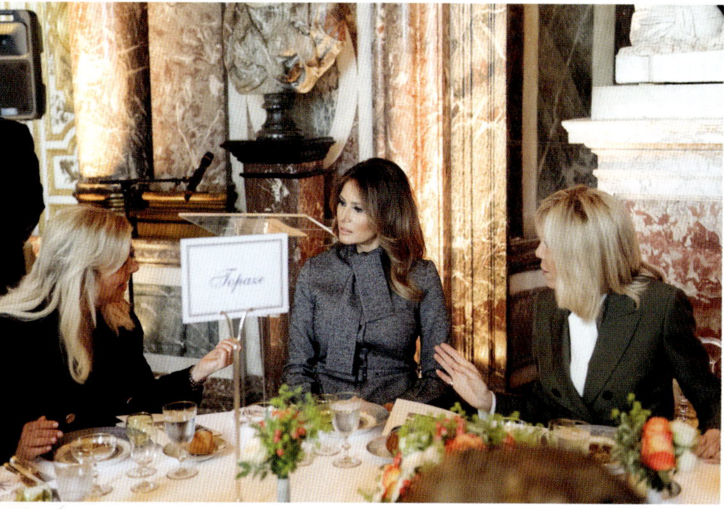

At luncheon with Sara Netanyahu and Brigitte Macron at the Salon de Vénus in the Palace of Versailles in France.[6]

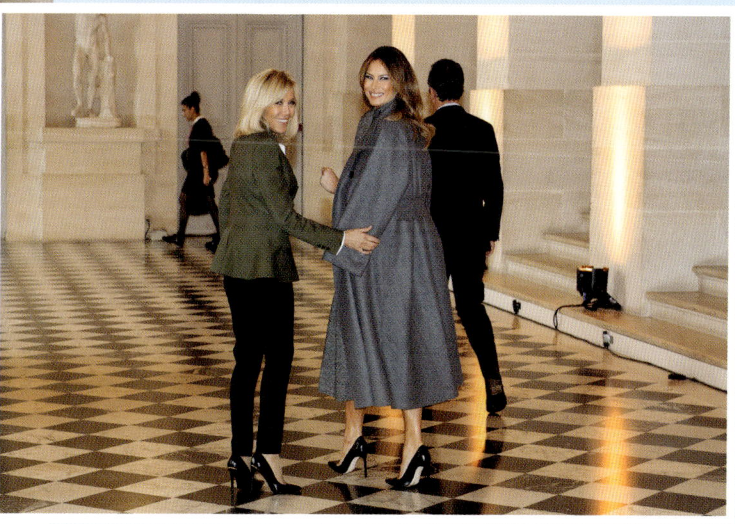

Elegance at Versailles.[6]

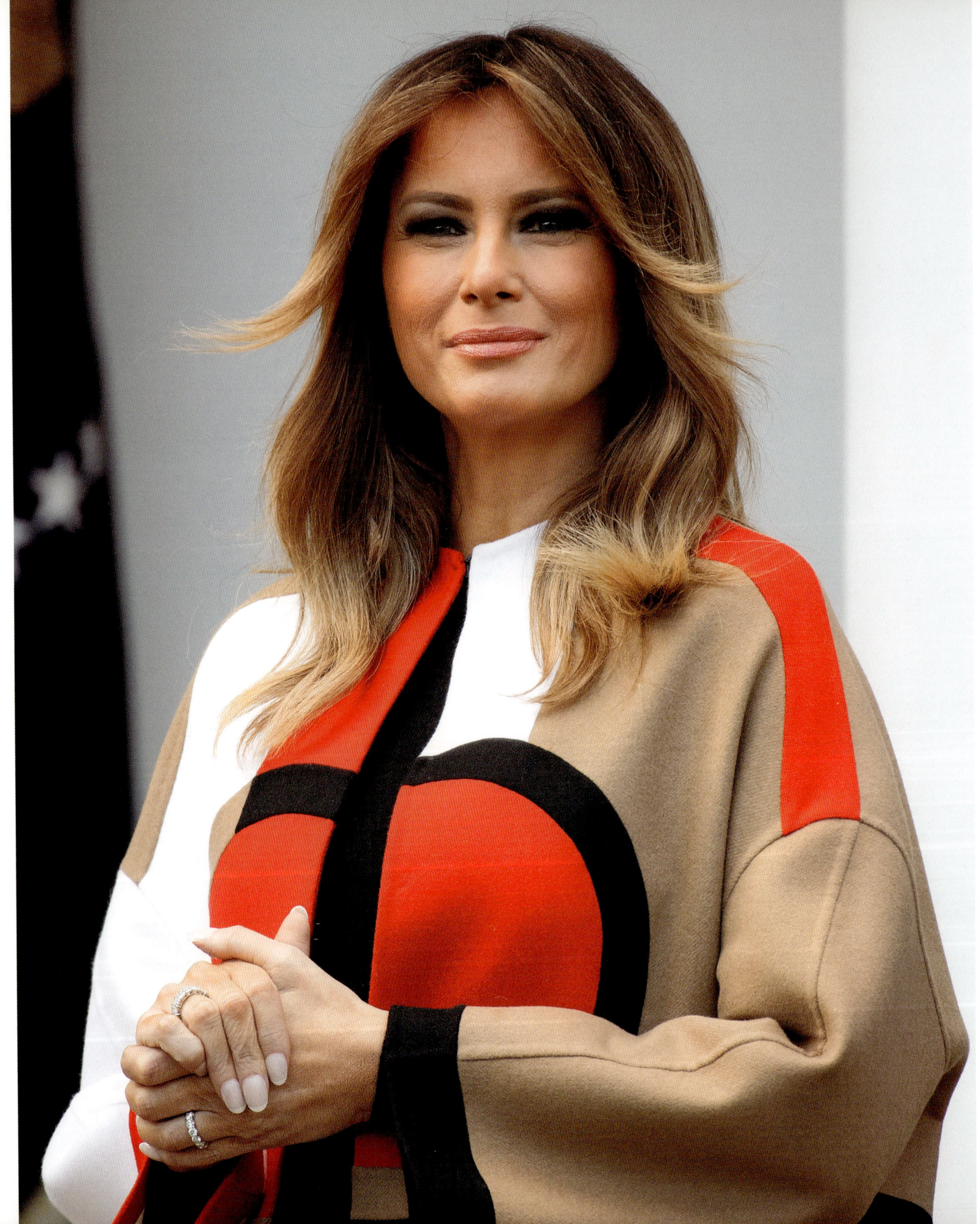

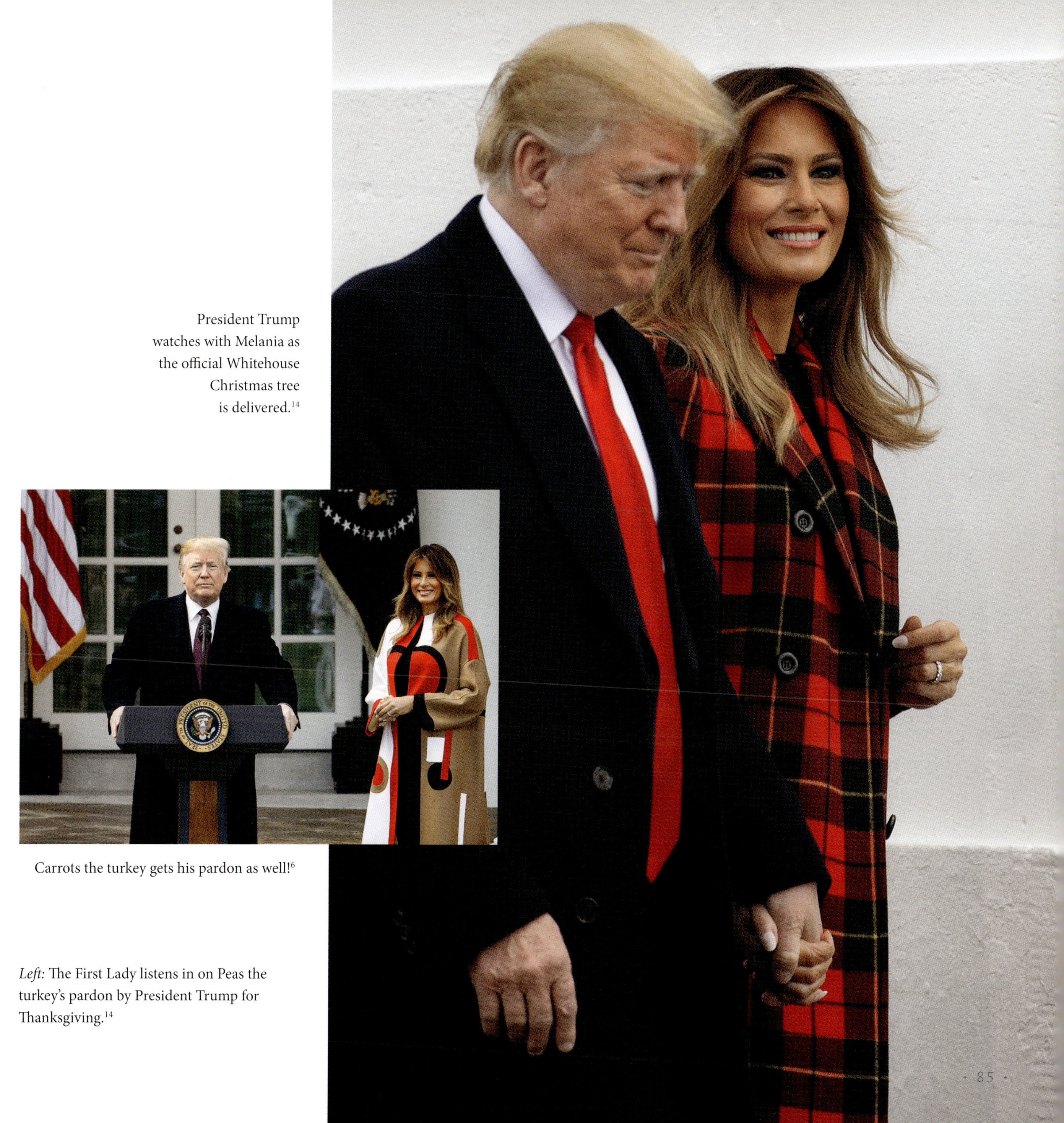

President Trump watches with Melania as the official Whitehouse Christmas tree is delivered.[14]

Carrots the turkey gets his pardon as well![6]

Left: The First Lady listens in on Peas the turkey's pardon by President Trump for Thanksgiving.[14]

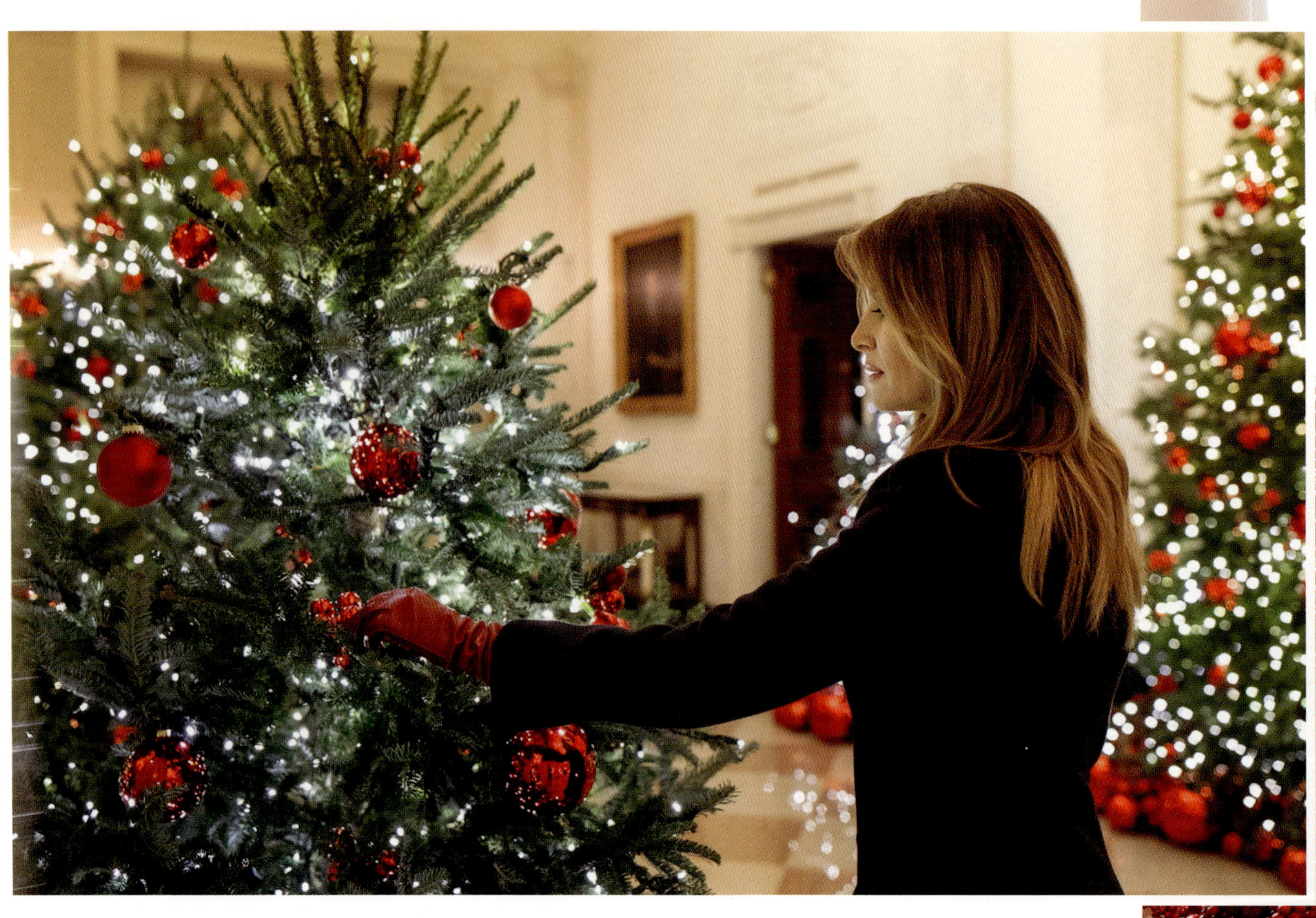

Touching up the White House Christmas decorations.[6]

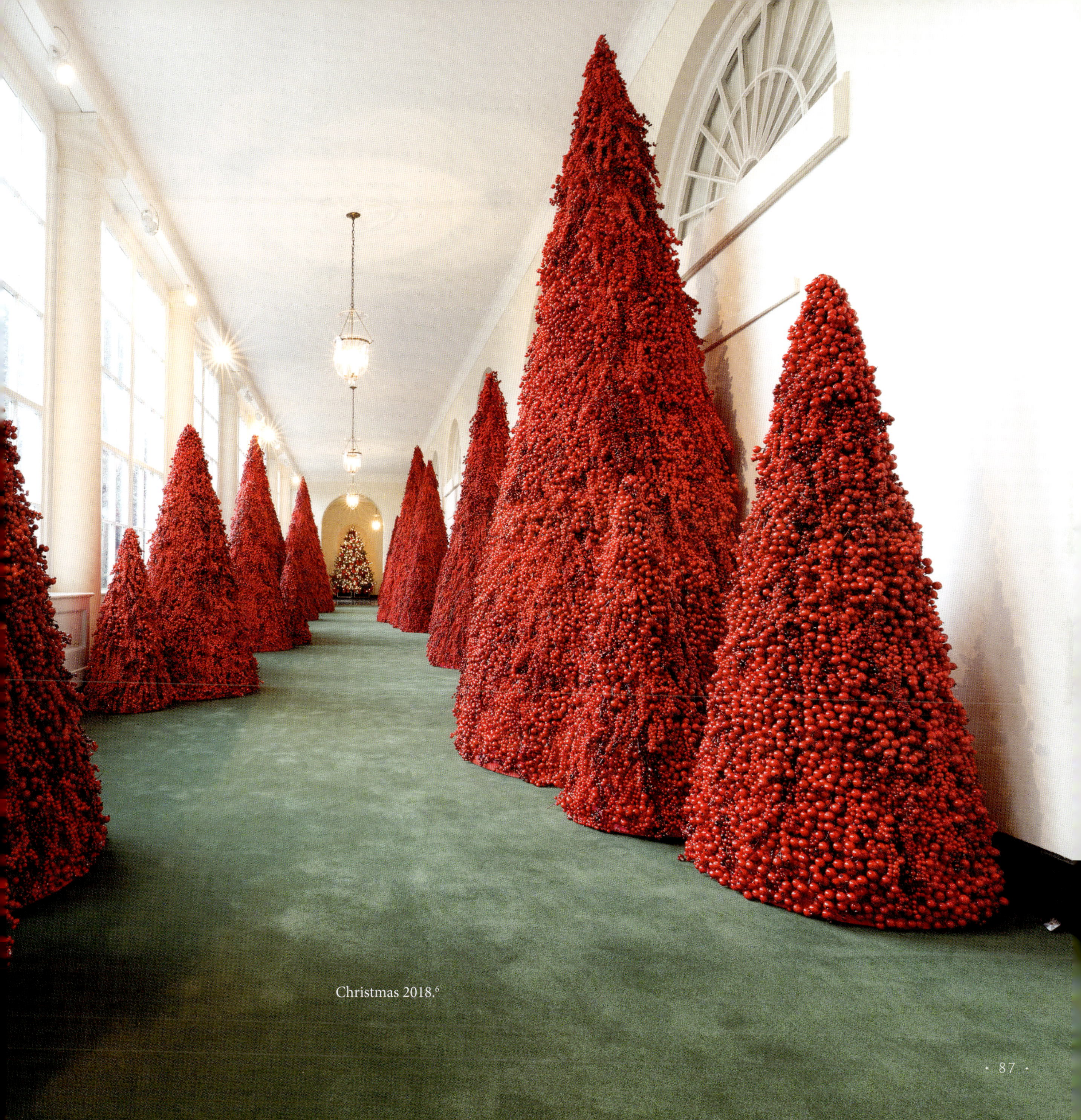

Christmas 2018.[6]

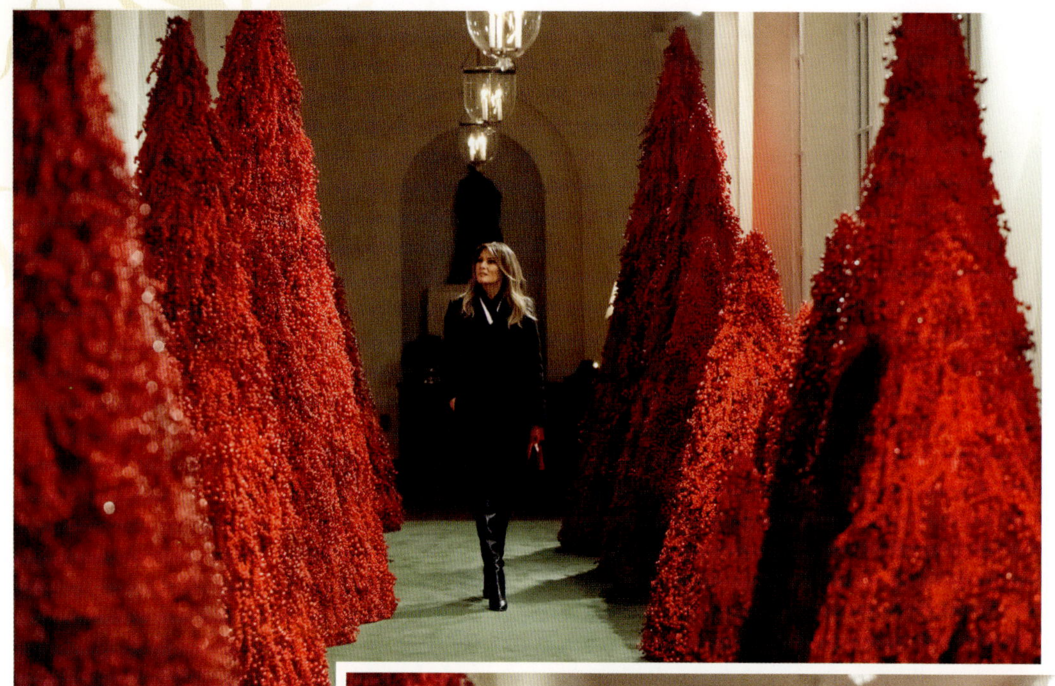

Inspecting the East Colonnade.[6]

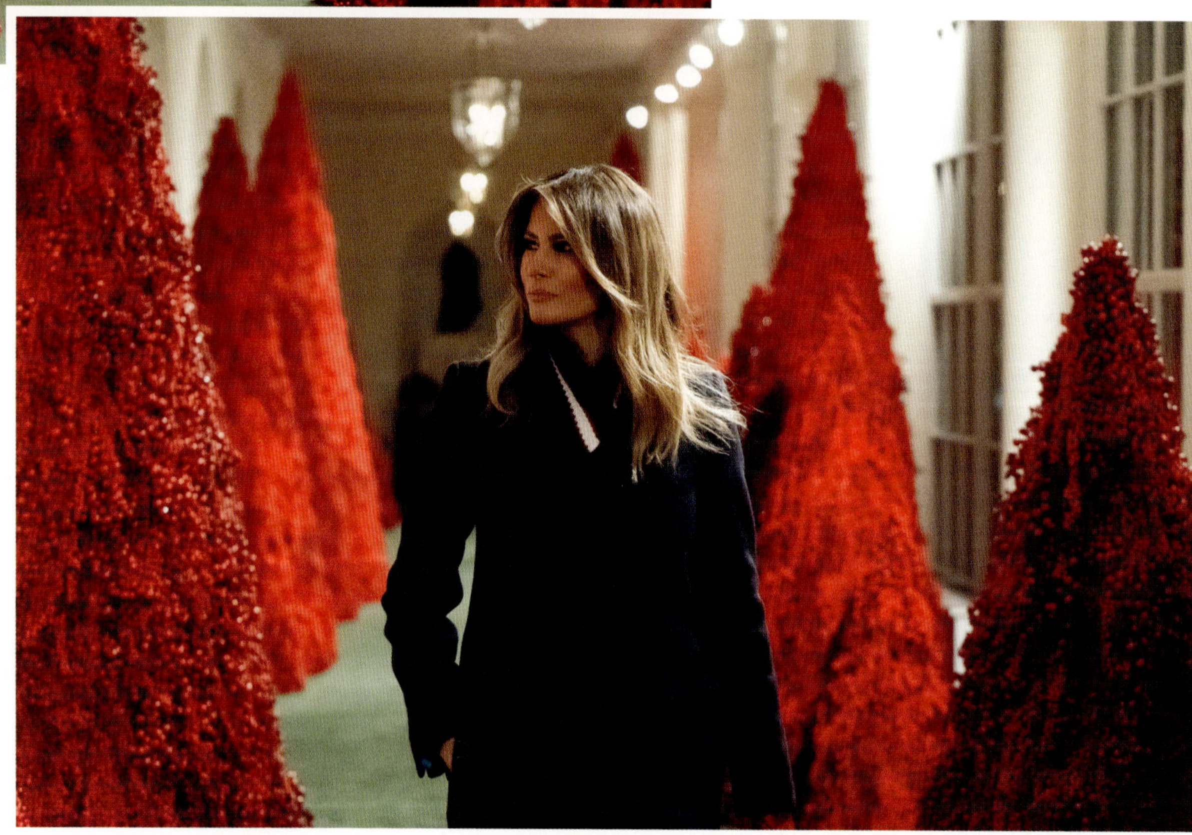

Excellence![6]

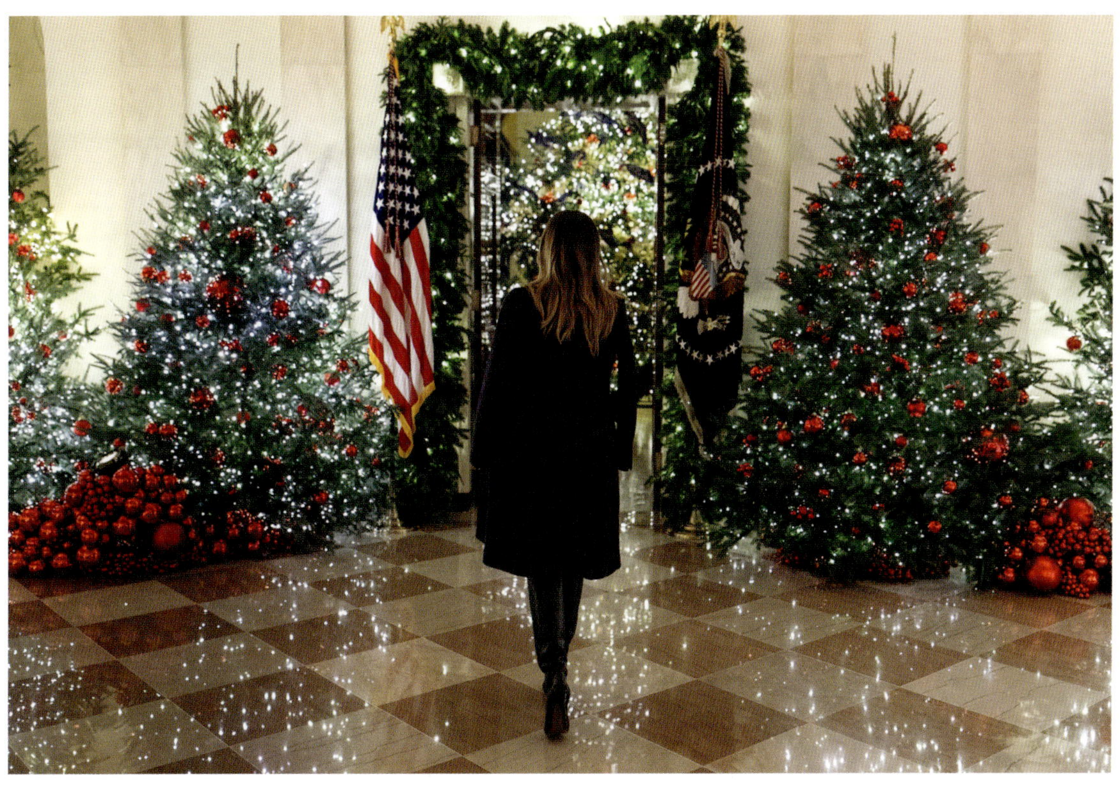

Finishing touches in the Cross Hall of the White House.[6]

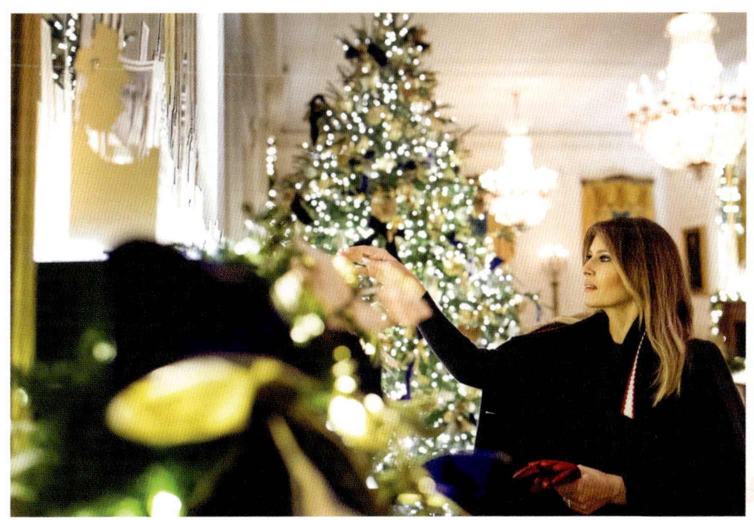

Pure elegance in the lights.[6]

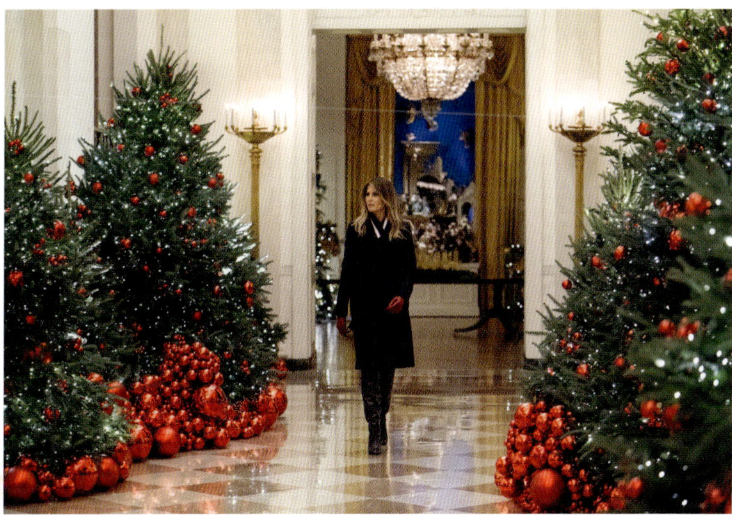

Everything looks fantastic! [6]

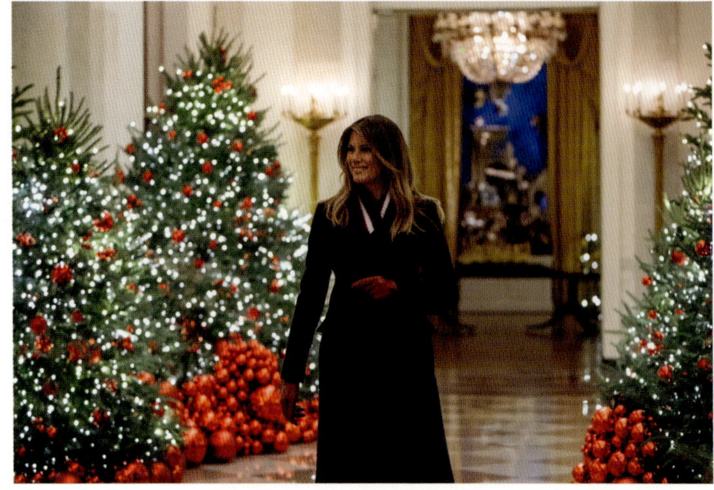

Perfection![6]

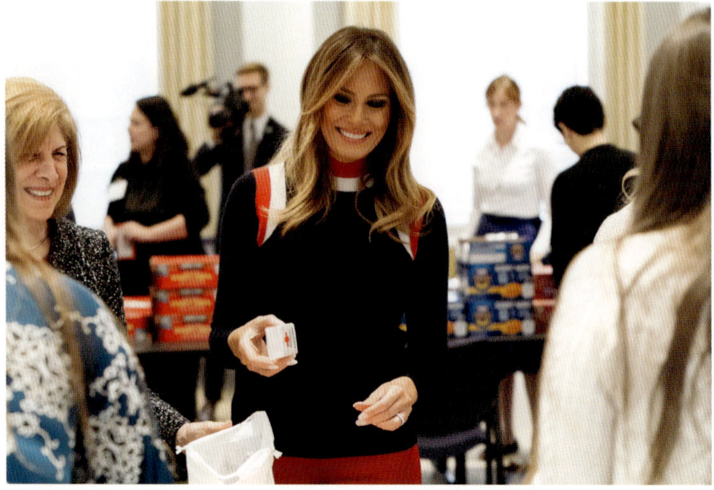

Making Red Cross care packages for overseas military personnel.[6]

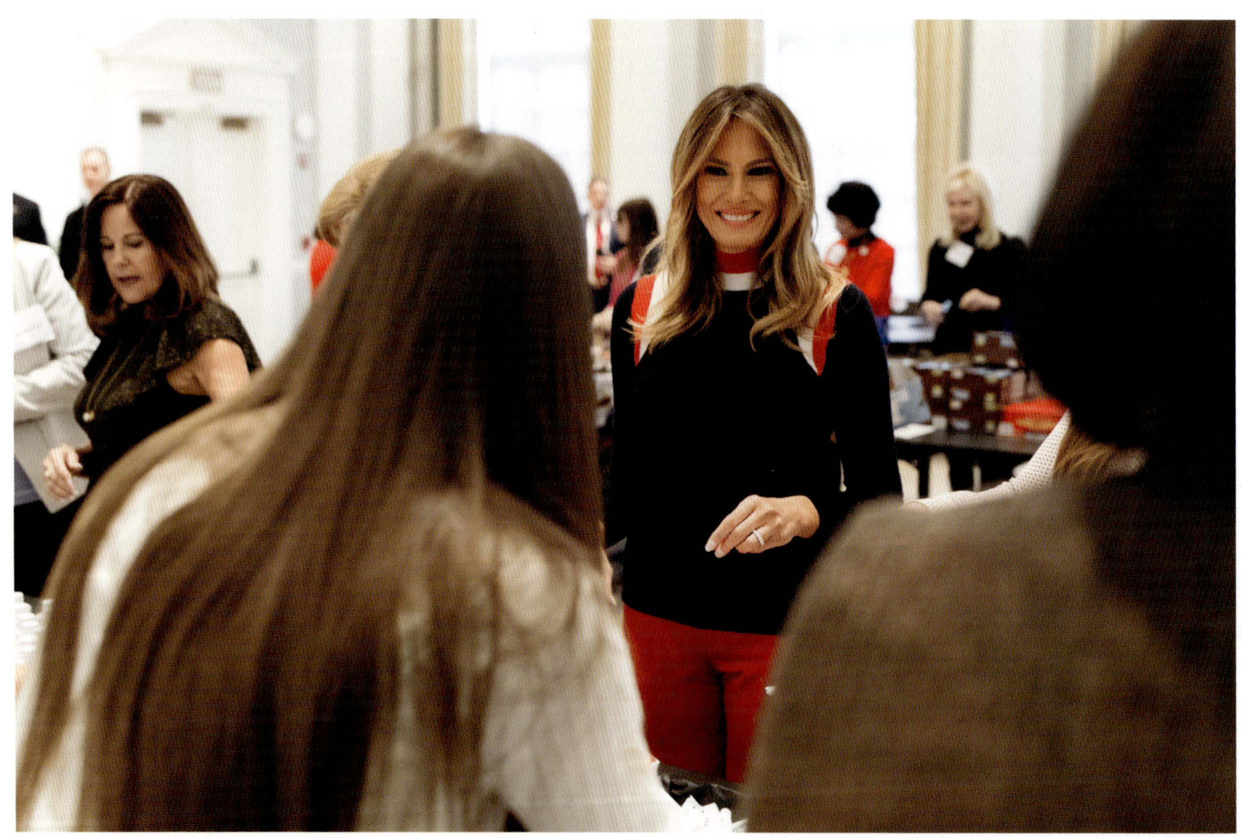

Melania Trump and Mrs. Karen Pence help volunteers assemble military comfort kits for deployed American troops.

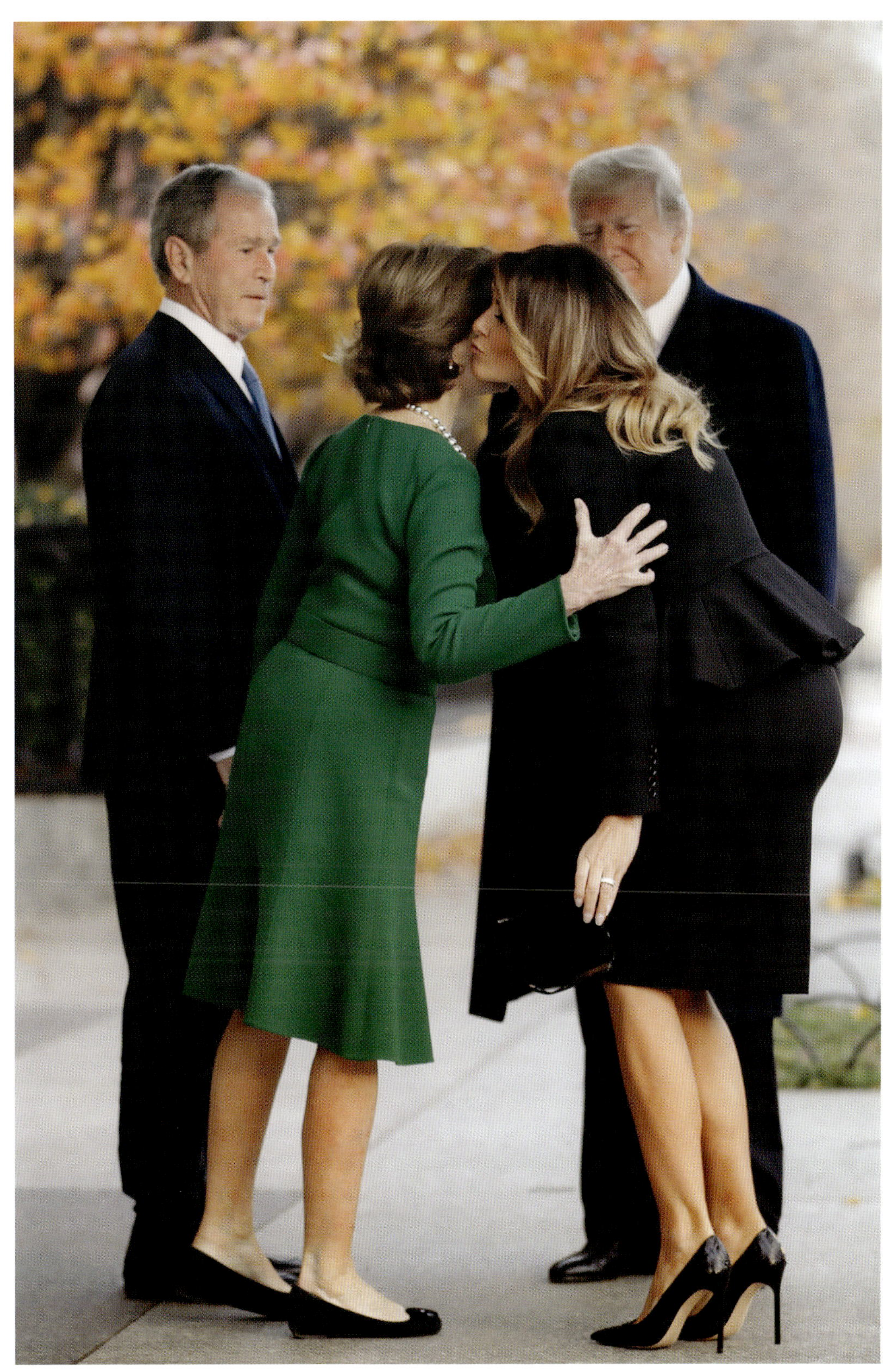

The Trumps pay their condolences to the Bush family prior to George Herbert Walker Bush's funeral.[3]

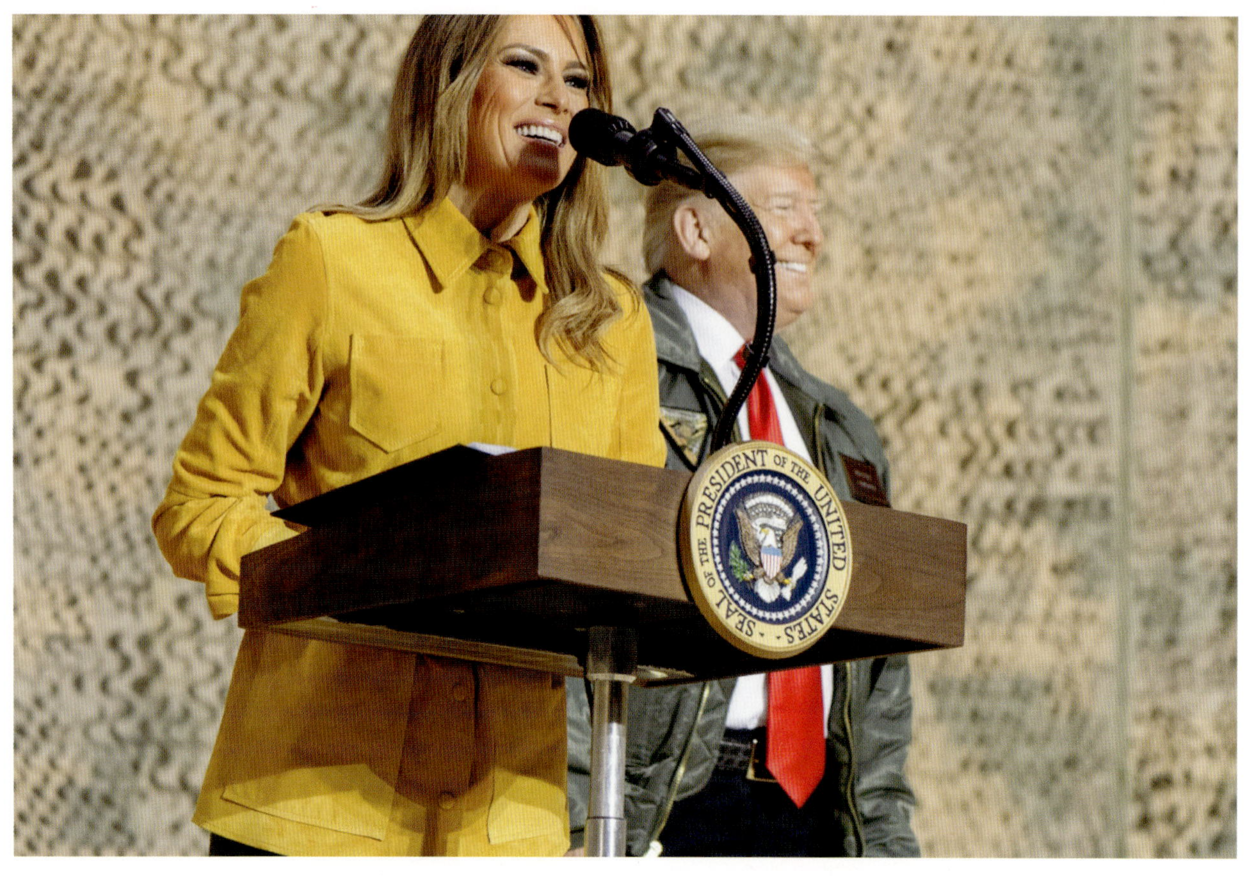

The First Lady speaks to the troops at Al-Asad Airbase in Iraq.[5]

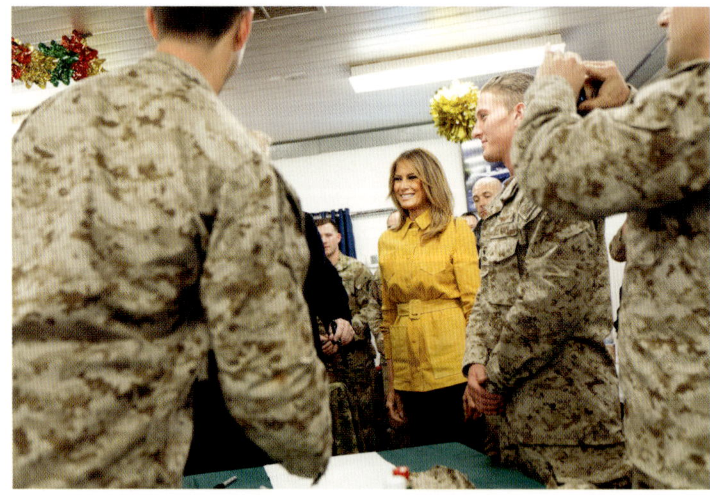

Spending time and shaking hands with military personnel in Iraq.[5]

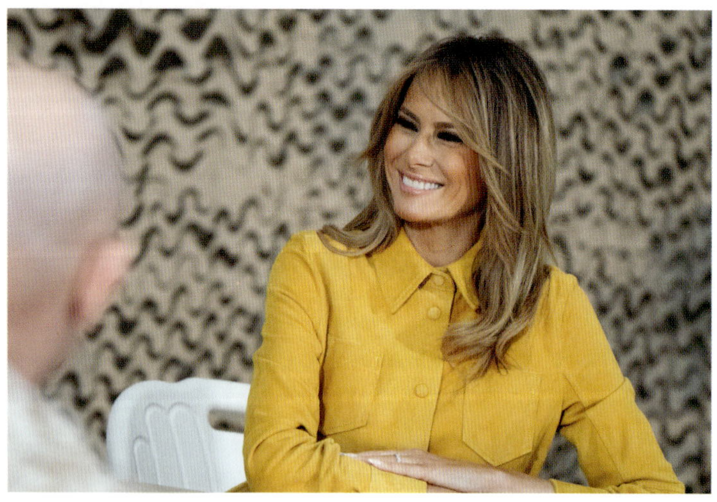

Attending a military briefing with military leaders in Iraq.[5]

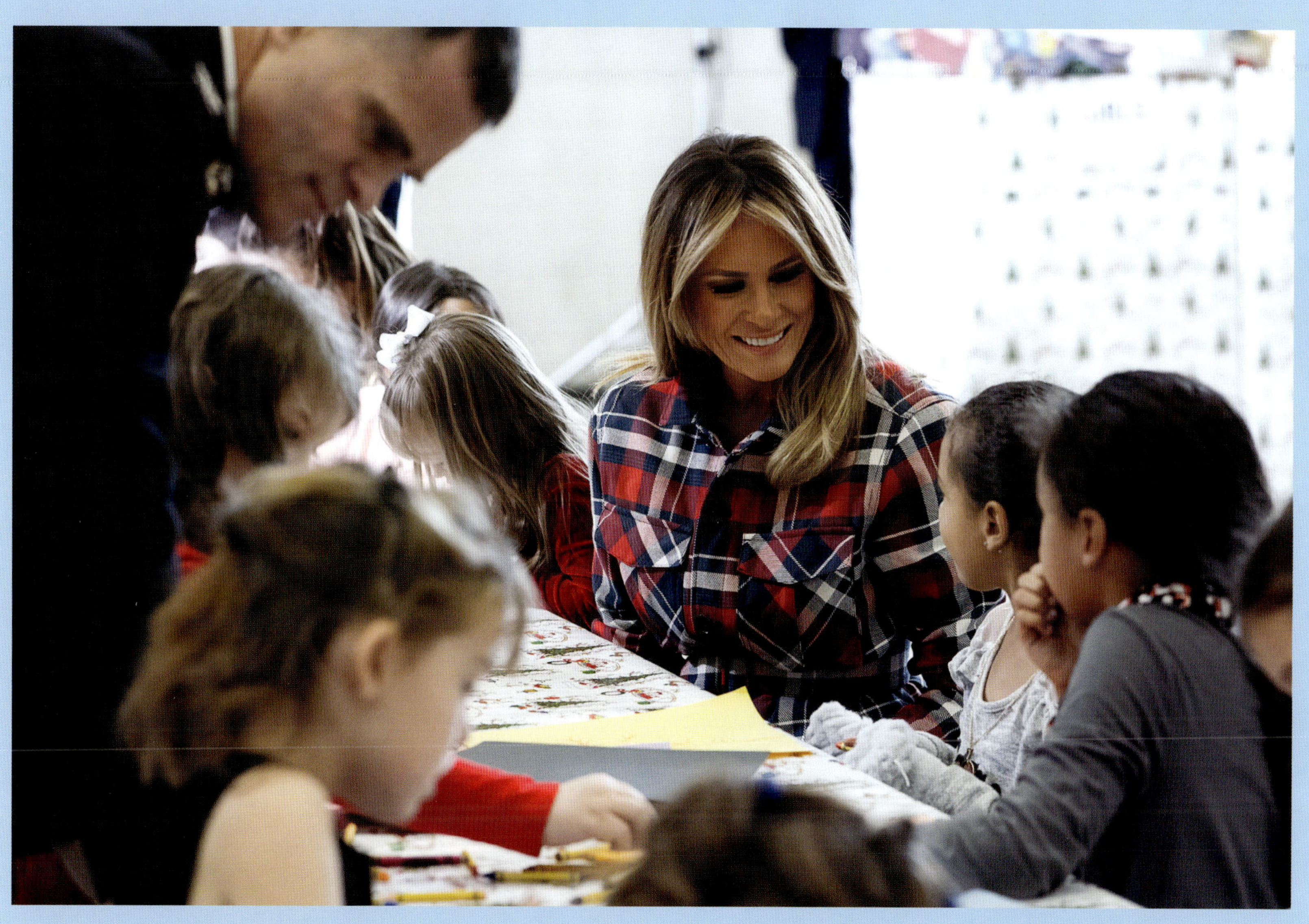

Elegance at Toys for Tots.[6]

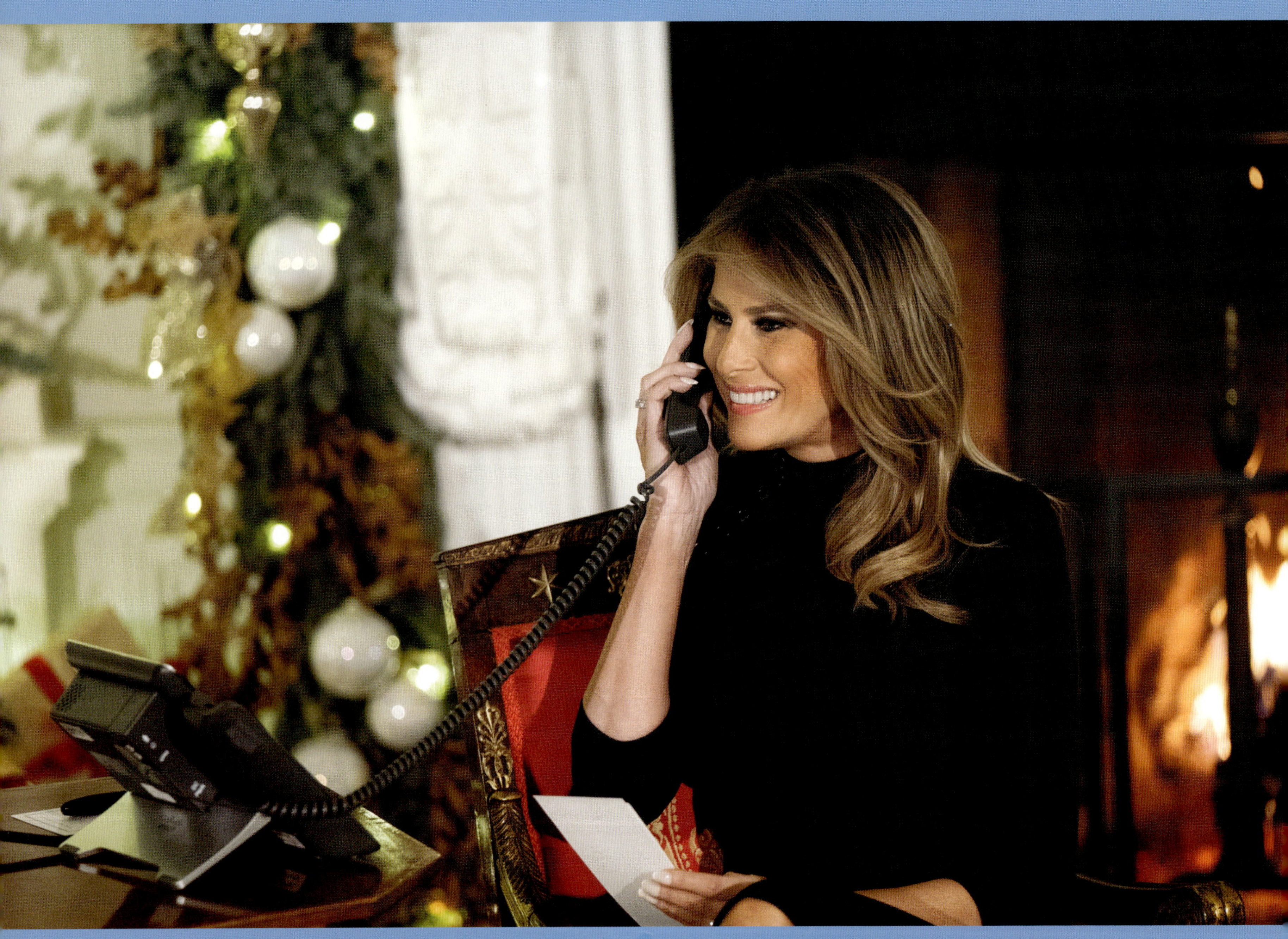

Melania Trump on the phone with NORAD, tracking Santa Claus' location on Christmas Eve. Tracker calls have been a Christmas Eve tradition for sixty years to keep track of Santa's delivery route.[5]

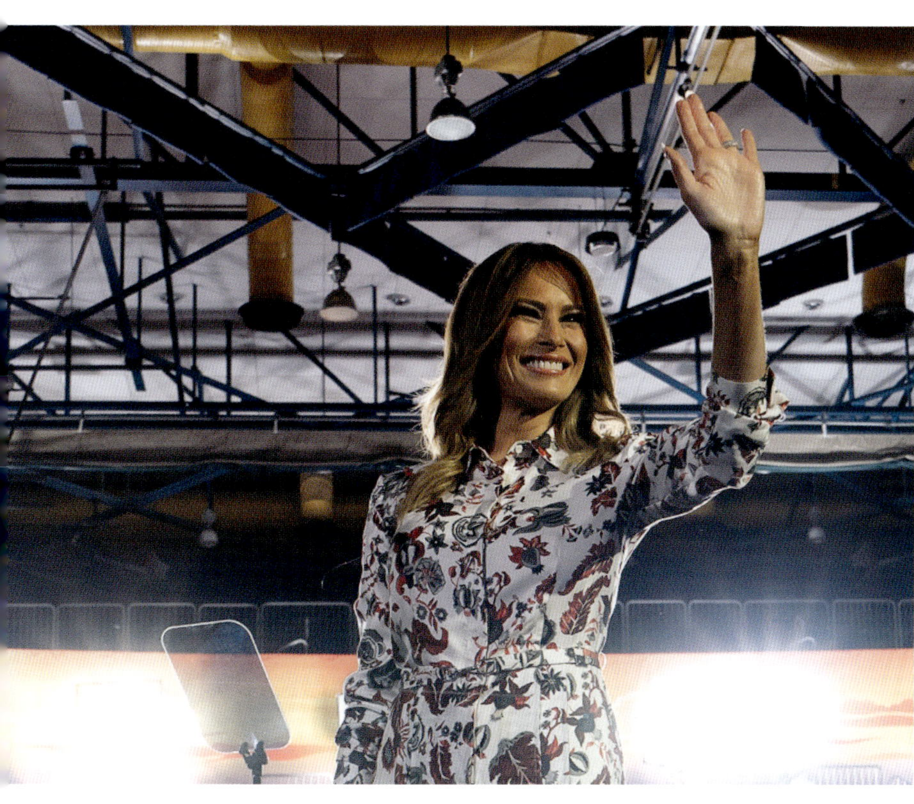

Mrs. Trump waves to members of the U.S. Venezuelan community after remarks by her husband.[6]

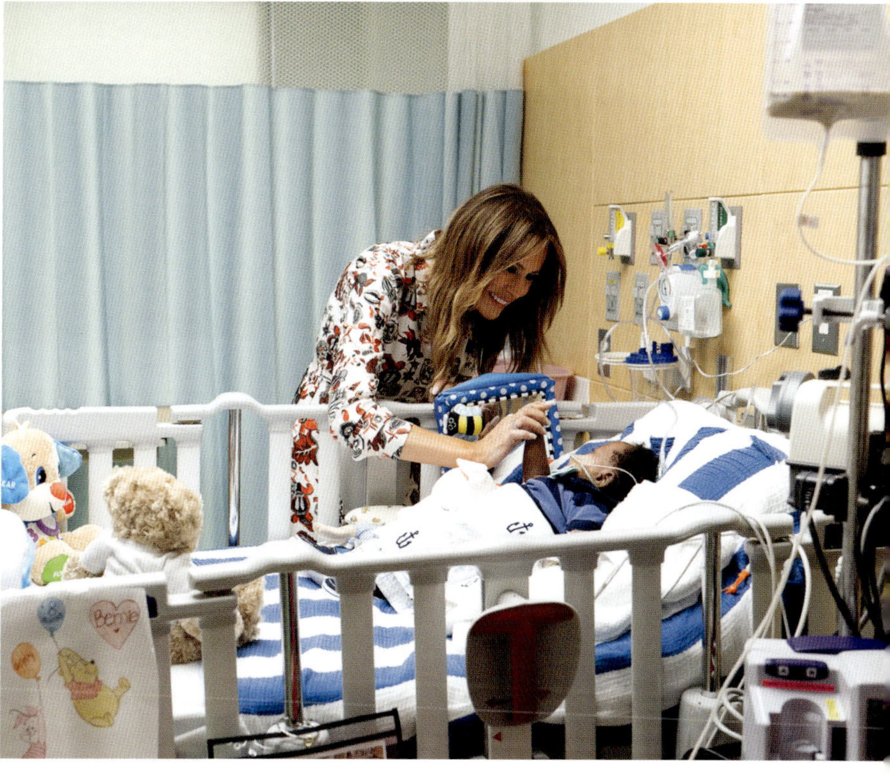

The First Lady is all smiles as she meets eight-month-old Bernard McClain at the Nicklaus Children's Hospital in Miami.[6]

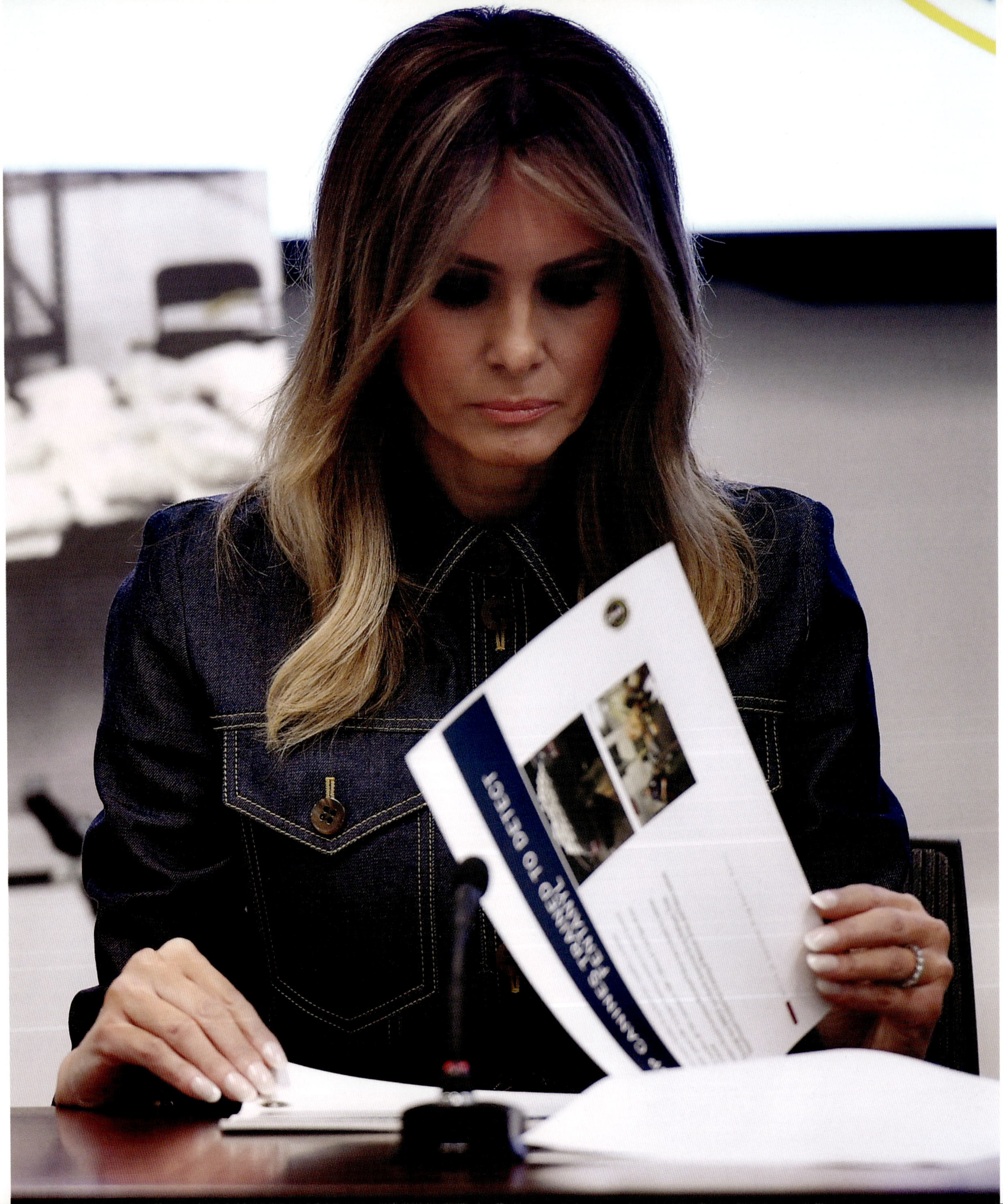

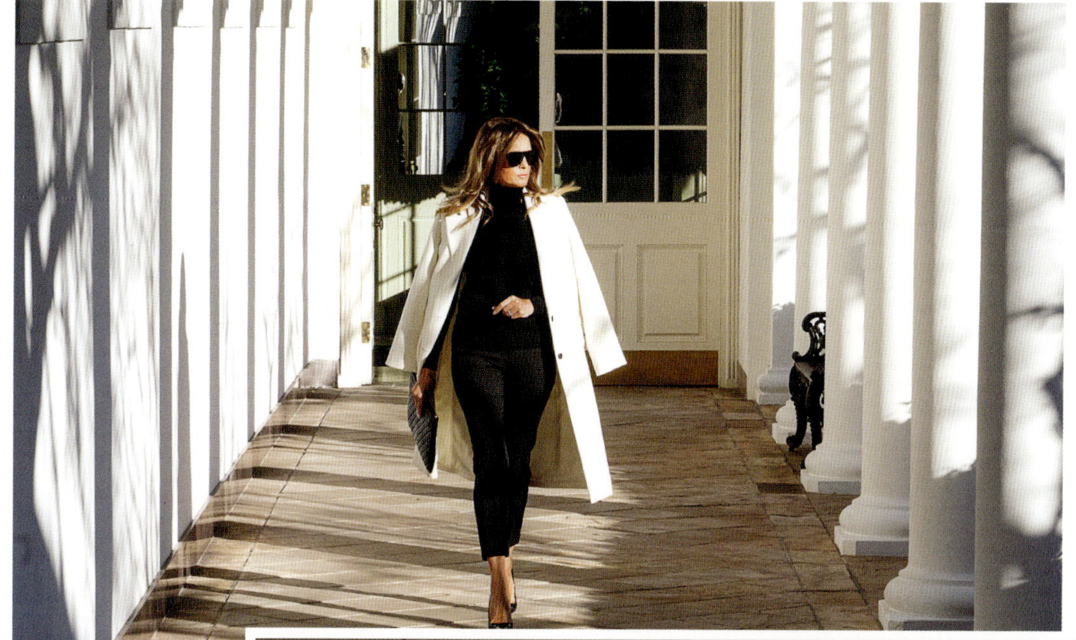

Elegance along the Colonnade.[6]

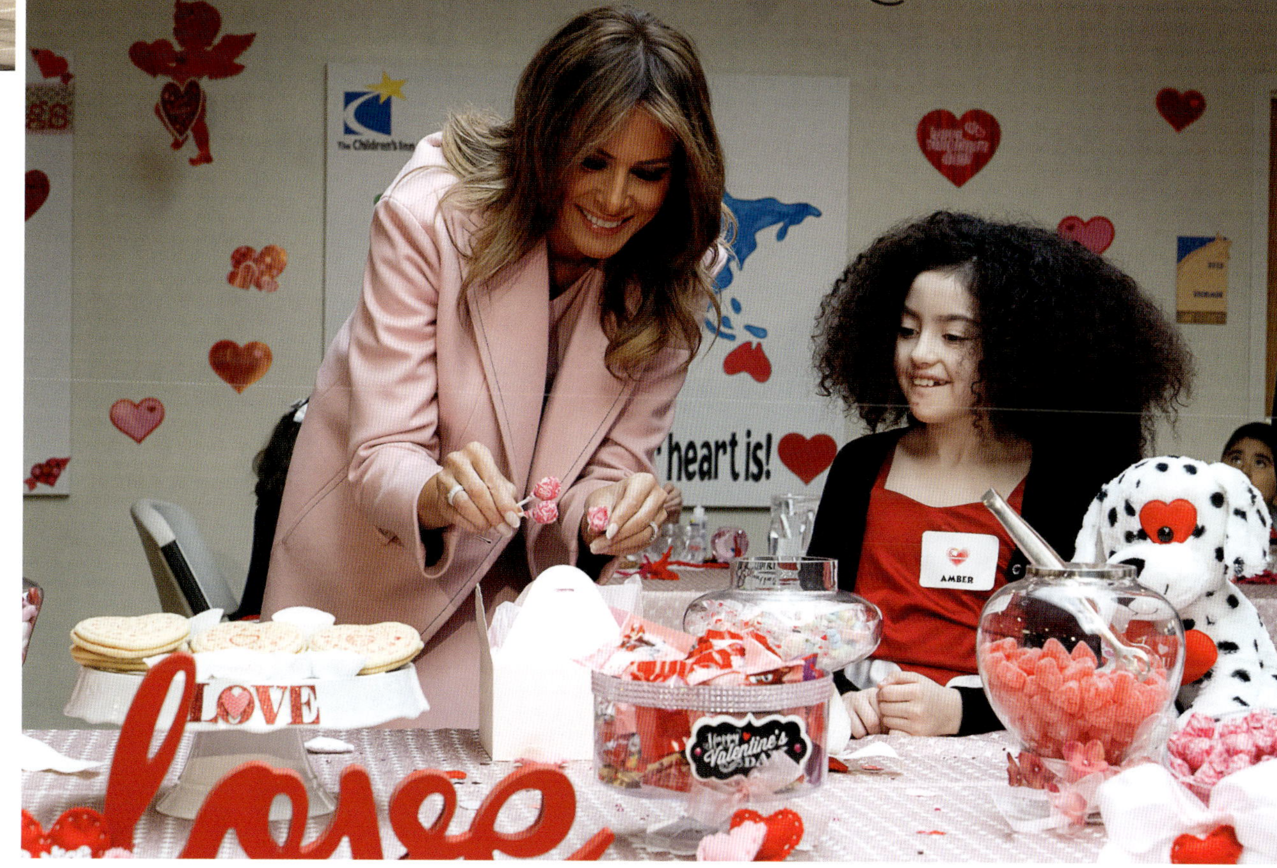

Melania celebrates Valentine's Day with children at the National Institute of Health.[6]

Left: Mrs. Trump taking part in an anti-drug briefing.[12]

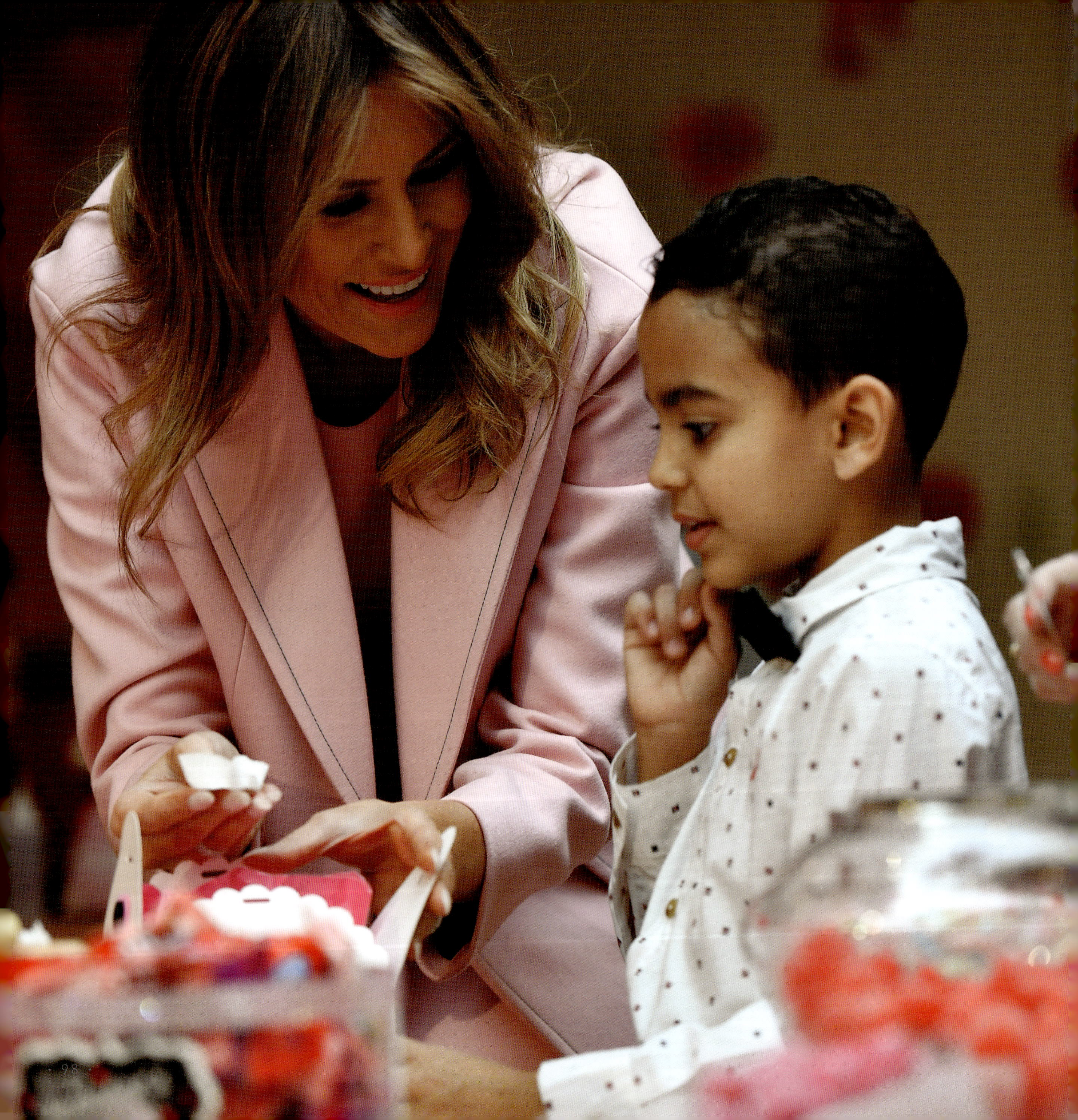

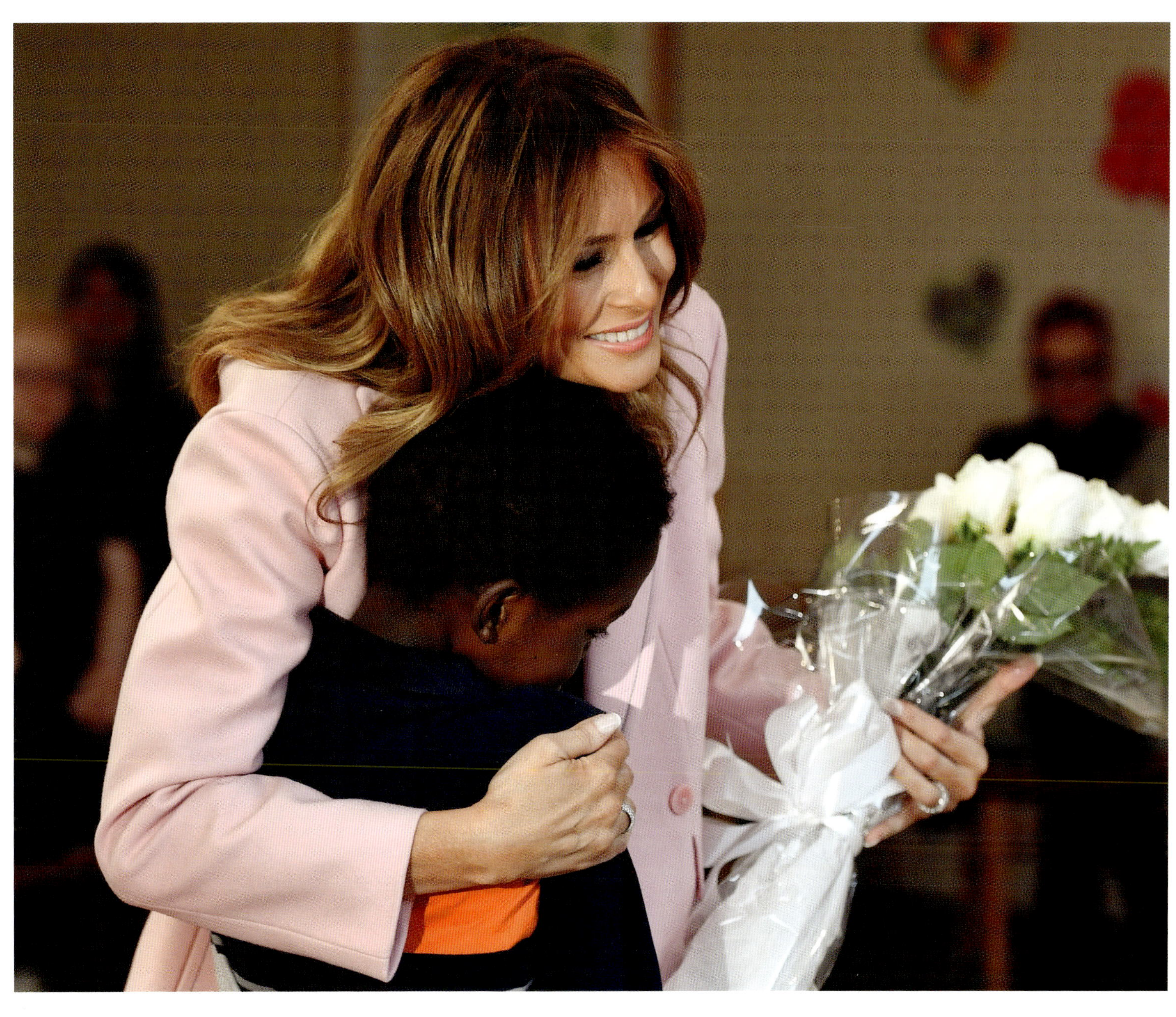

The First Lady gets hugs and flowers from Amani,
a child from Kenya at the Children's Inn at the National Institute of Health in Bethesda, Maryland.[12]

Left: Happy Valentine's Day![12]

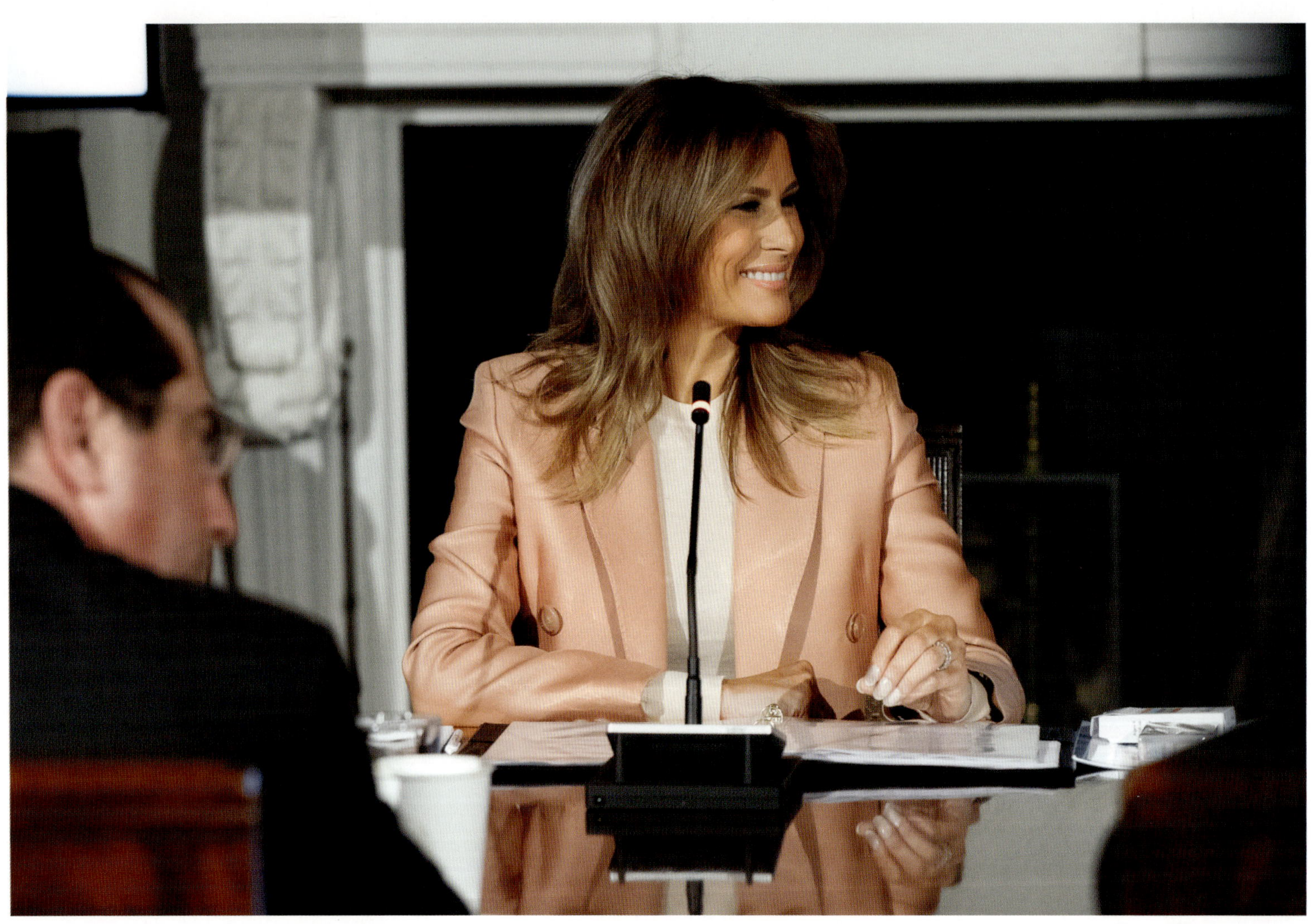

BE BEST interagency meeting focusing on the three pillars of the program: well-being of children, social media safety, and families affected by opioid abuse. Mrs. Trump led the meeting and gave opening remarks.[6]

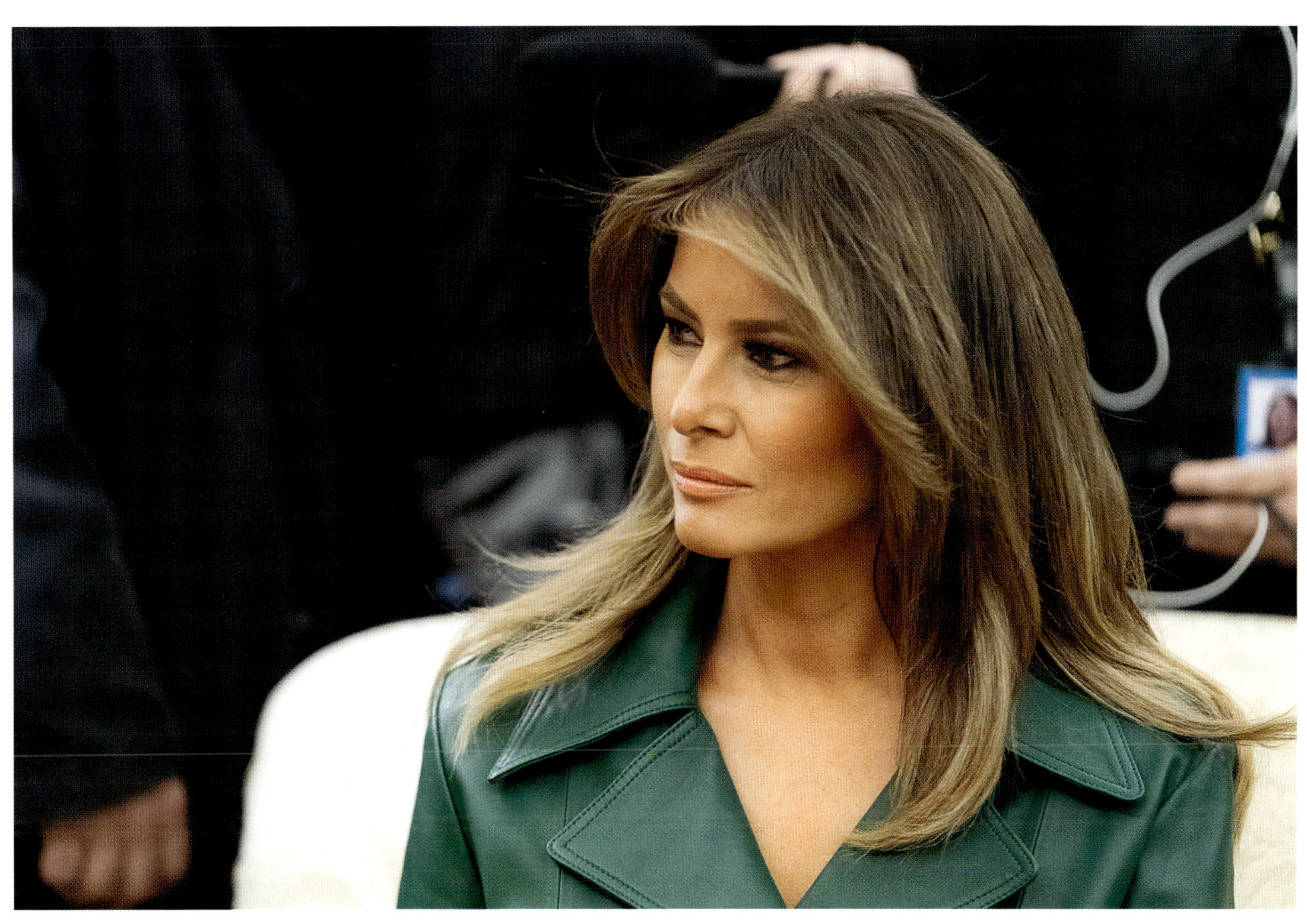

Preparing for a meeting.[6]

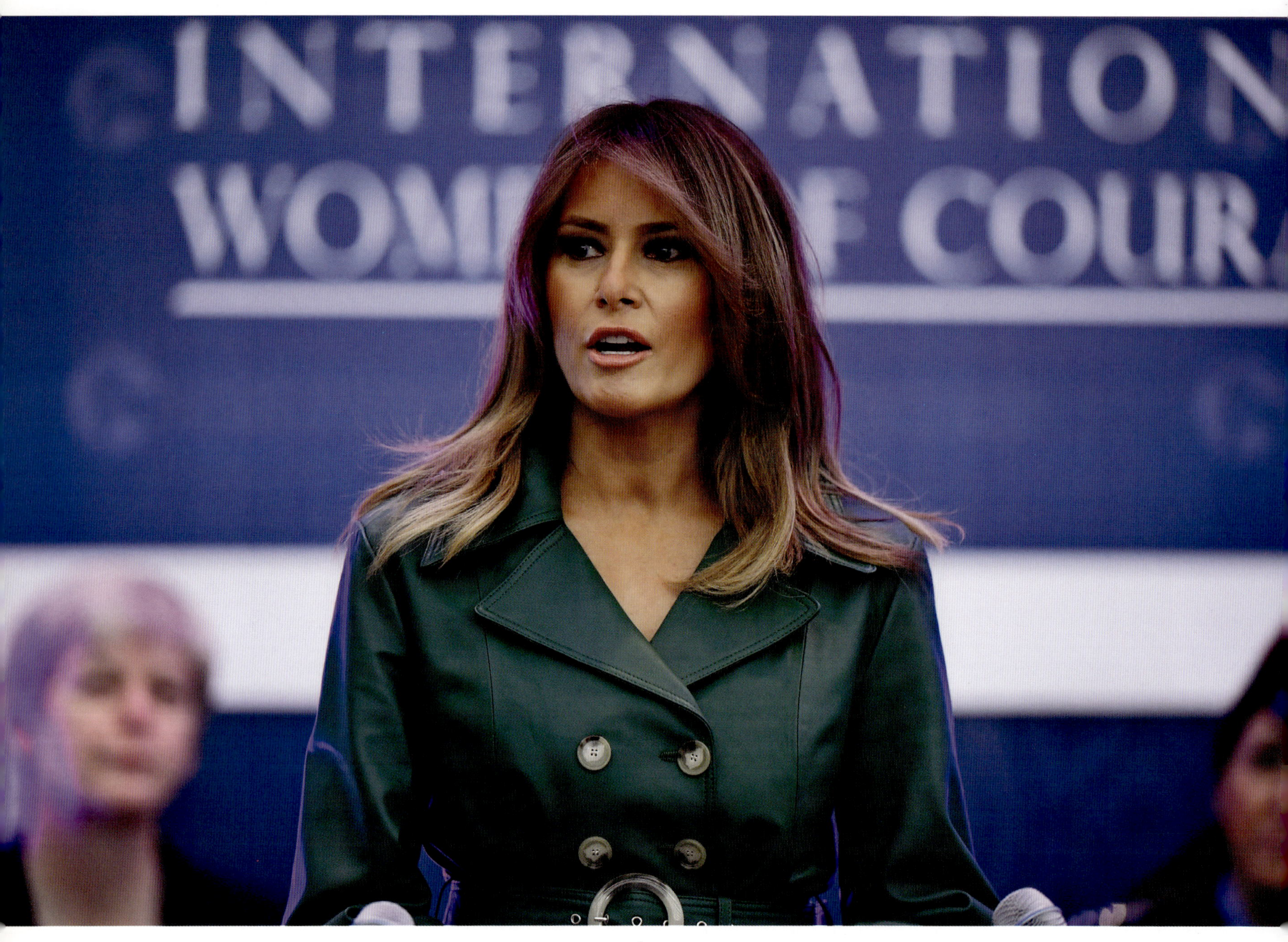

Speaking at the 2019 International Women of Courage awards.[12]

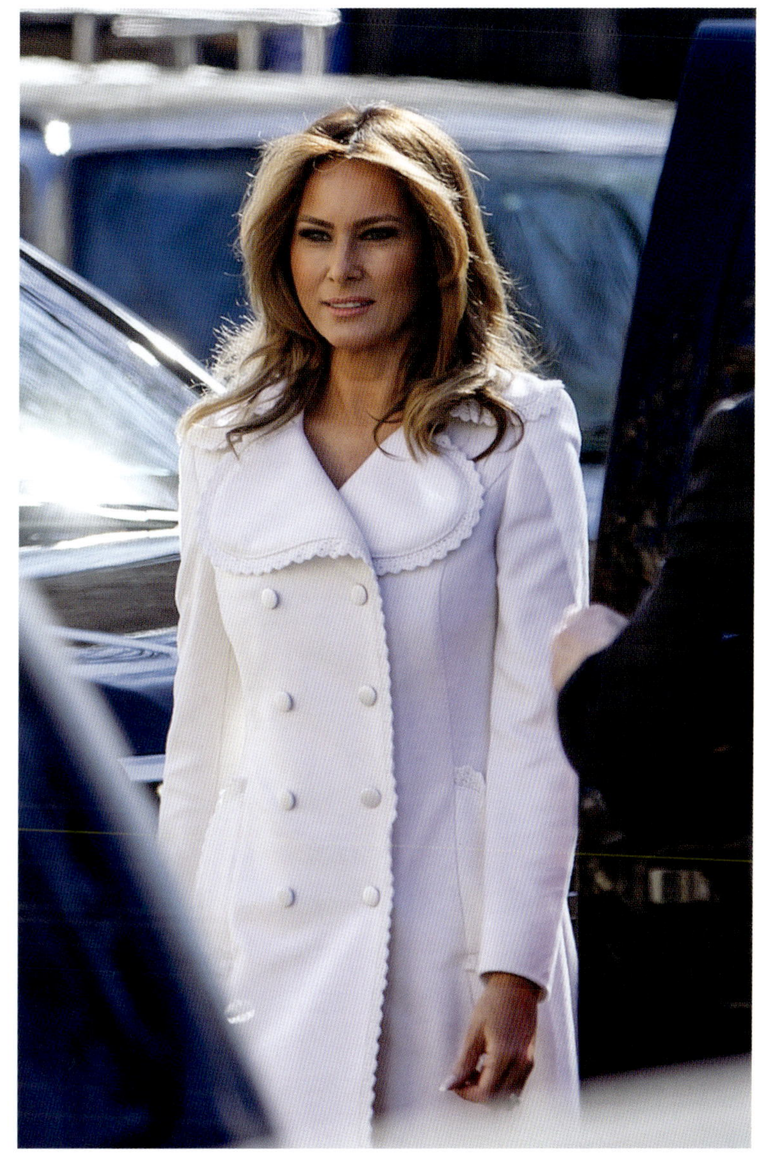

Attending church on St. Patrick's Day at St. John's Episcopal Church.[20]

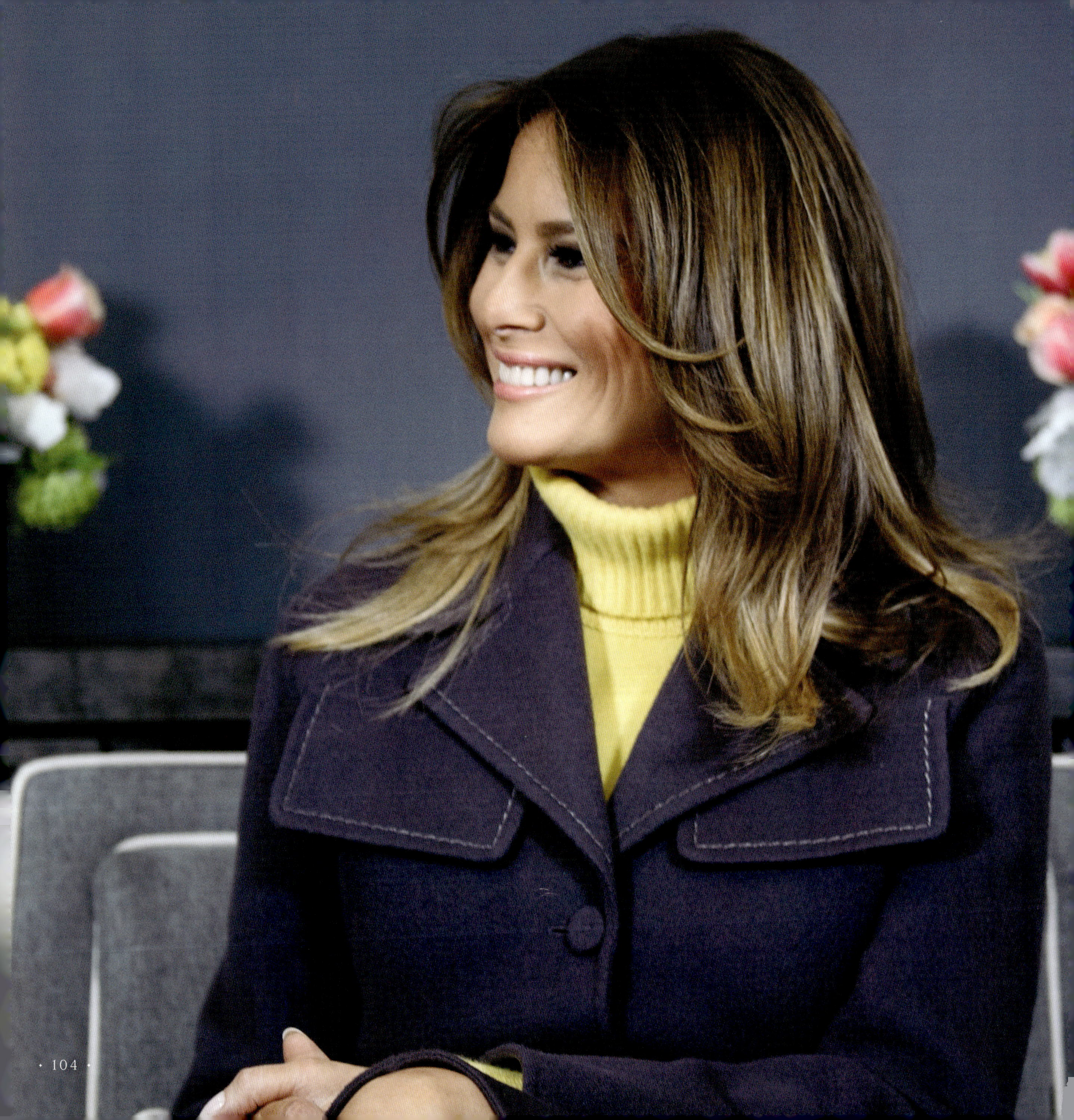

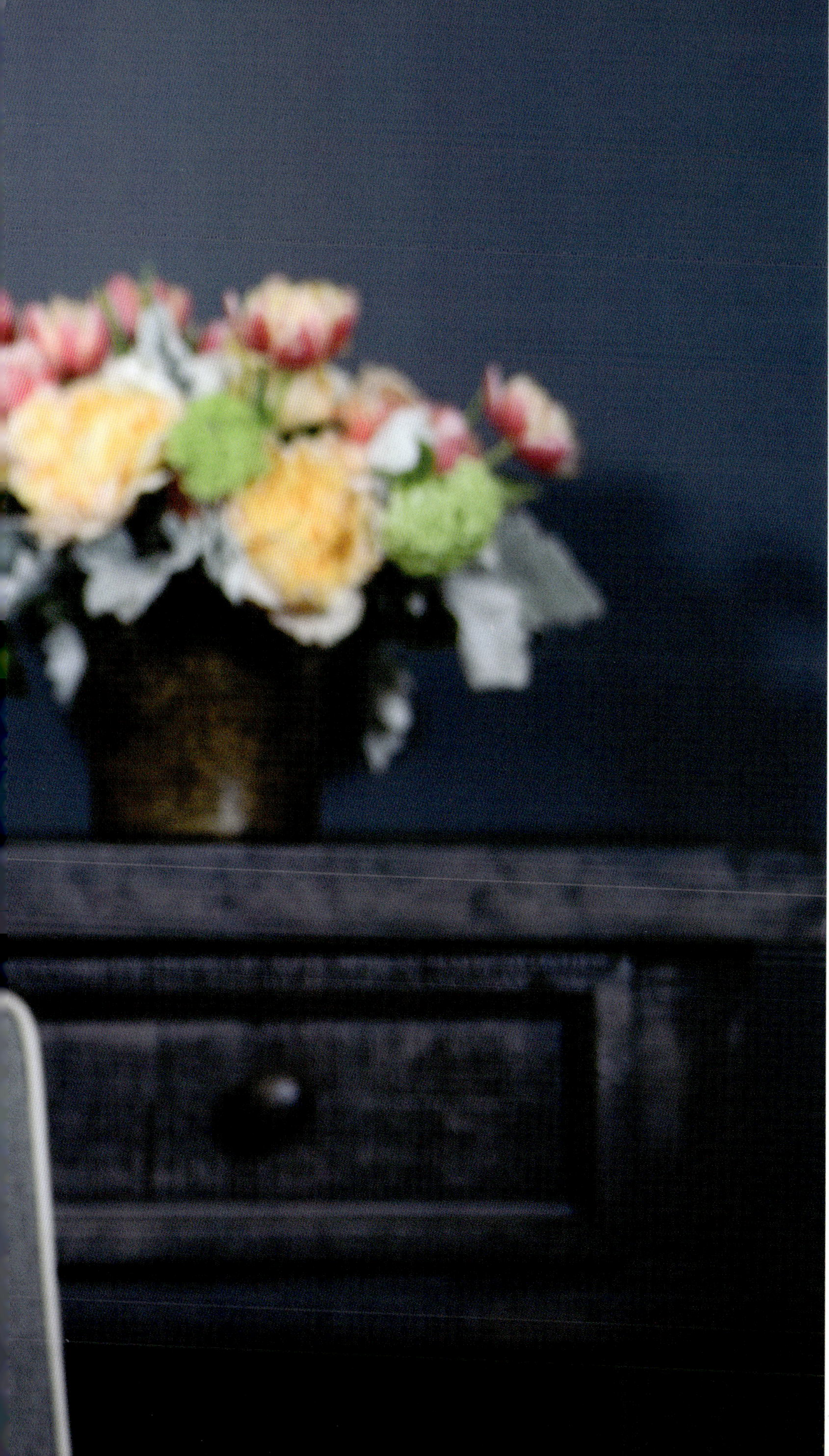

The First Lady on her BE BEST tour.[24]

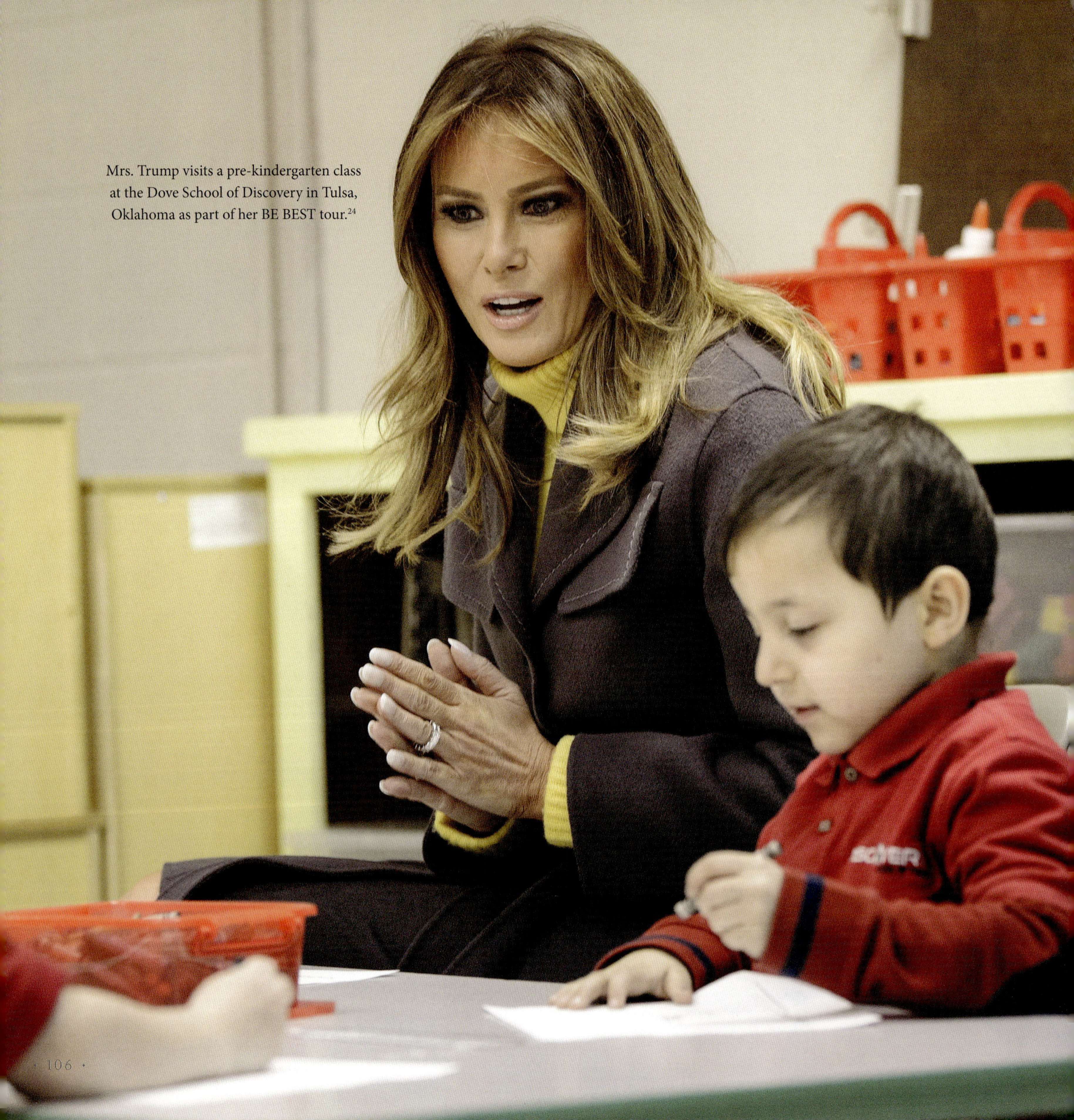

Mrs. Trump visits a pre-kindergarten class at the Dove School of Discovery in Tulsa, Oklahoma as part of her BE BEST tour.[24]

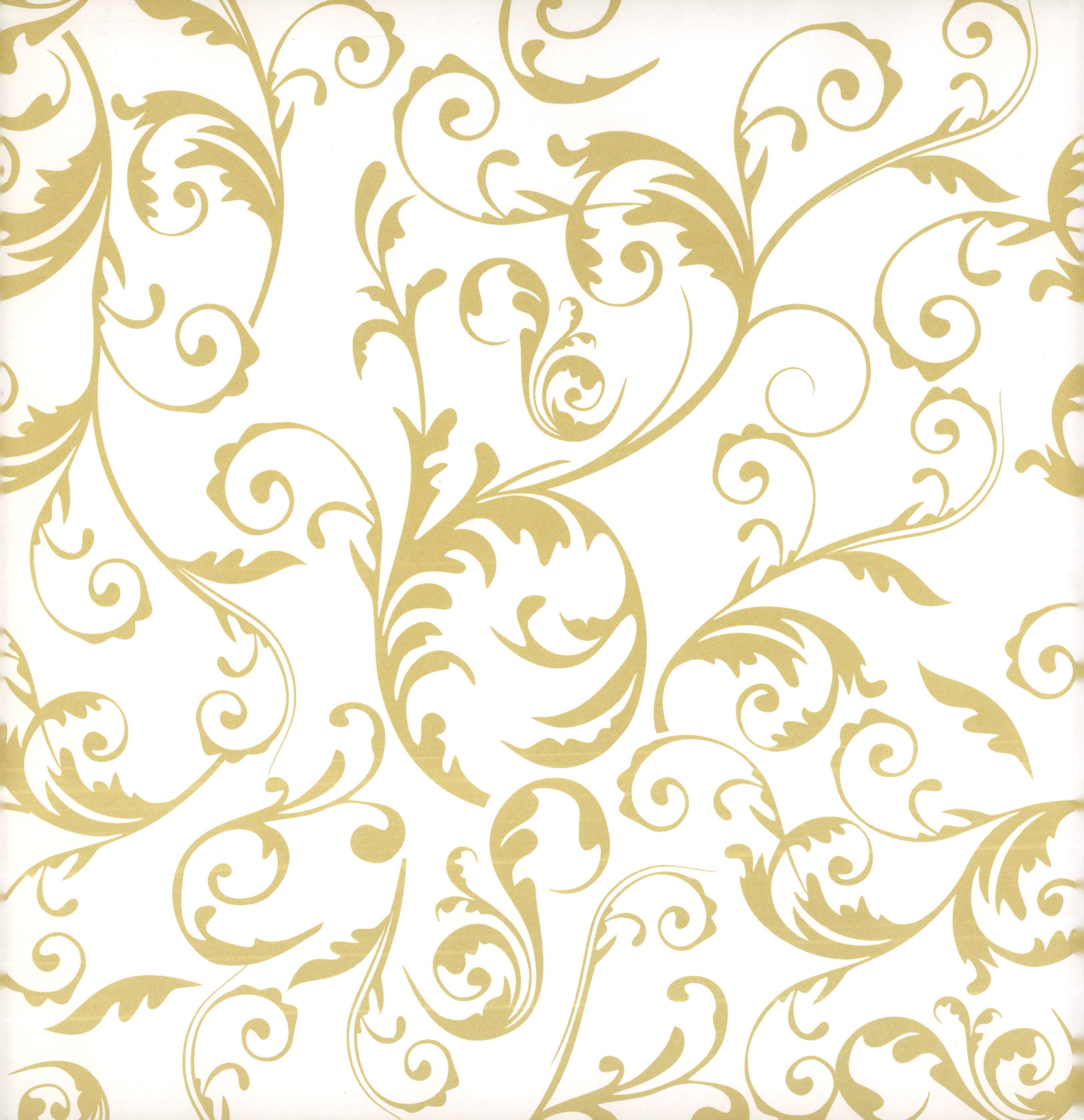